THE LO!

7.

~rials

圓明之台 心形之理
卓矣宮氏 鬱葢是水
惕同喜援 共維熊士
出處驍軼 名聲娧美
乾哉有耻 門人勿訾

心形日流六傳常靜子恭題
八傳常活子書

THE LONE SAMURAI

The Life of Miyamoto Musashi

William Scott Wilson

Shambhala
Boston & London
2013

To
James Craig Brems

Frontispiece: Portrait of Miyamoto Musashi by Ogata Tanko (1812–1868).
Reproduced by permission of the Okayama Prefectural Museum of Art.

Shambhala Publications, Inc.
Horticultural Hall
300 Massachusetts Avenue
Boston, Massachusetts 02115
www.shambhala.com

9 8 7 6 5 4 3 2 1

Printed in the United States of America

⊗This edition is printed on acid-free paper that meets the
American National Standards Institute Z39.48 Standard.
❂This book is printed on 30% postconsumer recycled paper.
For more information please visit www.shambhala.com.

Distributed in the United States by Random House, Inc.,
and in Canada by Random House of Canada Ltd

Library of Congress Cataloging-in-Publication Data

Wilson, William Scott, 1944–
The Lone Samurai: The Life of Miyamoto Musashi / William Scott Wilson.
pages cm
Originally published: 2004.
Includes bibliographical references.
ISBN 978-1-59030-987-2 (pbk.: alk. paper)
1. Miyamoto, Musashi, 1584–1645. 2. Swordsmen—Japan—Biography.
I. Title.
DS872.M53W55 2013
952'.025092—dc23
2012037889

CONTENTS

CHAPTER

FOUR

The Way of Life and Death: Reigan Cave

129

PREFACE

I first became involved in the life and work of Miyamoto Musashi a number of years ago while working on a translation of *The Book of Five Rings*. This was a wonderful opportunity, in part because, from my own perspective, there are few finer ways of getting to know someone than translating what he has written; in part because that short work of Musashi's distills his insights on strategy, Zen Buddhism, and how to live; and in part because, for those who read closely and with a little imagination, the book stands as a record of the sixty-some duels the swordsman fought between the ages of thirteen and twenty-nine. The project turned out to be an intensive course on the very core of what might be called the Musashi myth, and on how that myth came to be.

Soon after this translation was completed, it was suggested that I might write a short volume on Musashi's life and work. This also seemed a great opportunity, providing me with a chance to dig more into the details of Musashi's life and to get a better idea not only of what had motivated him, but also of what has inspired the fascination with which he continues to be regarded. There seemed to be something more to this man's life than a unique sword style and excellent artwork.

As it turned out, the biography took much longer to complete than the translation, and involved far more research. Musashi, as is well known, left us only a few sentences about his own life, but other original sources are legion. These sources ranged from the Kokura Hibun, a monument inscribed with the story of Musashi's life and erected by his adopted son Iori in 1654, to the *Nitenki*, a compilation of stories about Musashi and his disciples published in 1755 through the research of Toyoda Matashiro and his son and grandson; and a Musashi chronology, the *Miyamoto Musashi monogatari nenpyo*, published in 1910. Scattered among these are the records of various clans that were touched by Musashi's presence, such as the *Yoshioka-den*, compilations of warriors' deeds like the *Busho kanjoki* of 1716, and even family records that mentioned Musashi, such as the *Numata keki*. Because of discrepancies in time and place and the personal alliances of the various authors, these sources often had Musashi in different places at the same time, held various and even diametrically opposed opinions on his personality, talents, and accomplishments, and could be quite perplexing in regard to chronology: one, for example, had his father Munisai dying years before Musashi was born.

The following account is the result of sifting through this multitudinous and inconsistent material over and over again, looking for the single, consistent life within. The entire book represents my effort to answer the question, who was Miyamoto Musashi? Or perhaps the question should be framed as, who is Miyamoto Musashi, since the life of this great swordsman/philosopher/artist has never come to a full stop, but instead has been continually rewritten and expanded.

———

Many people have contributed to the preparation of this book, and without their help the project would have been much more difficult, if not impossible, to complete. I offer my profound gratitude to all of them. To Kuramochi Tetsuo and Barry Lancet, my former editors at

Kodansha International, for having suggested and supported the initial project; to Beth Frankl, my editor at Shambhala Publications, and John Golebiewski, her assistant editor, for their efforts and patience in bringing out this beautiful new edition of the work; to Fukuda Chiaki and Kristine Howe, who were able to track down and provide me with so many of the source books I needed; to Kobayashi Shinji, who kept me informed of current "Musashi events" in Japan; to the artists Kate Barnes and Gary Haskins for their insights on Musashi's *suibokuga*, or india ink painting; to John Siscoe for his invaluable advice and support; to my colleague Dave Lowry for his lucid comments on Musashi and for providing materials that would have otherwise been impossible to get; to Scott Maynard for sharing his knowledge of Nippon-to (the Japanese sword); to Robertson Adams for his generous and creative technical support; and to my wife, Emily, who not only read through much of the manuscript, but also patiently watched every Musashi movie with me and always gave me just the right amount of encouragement when the going got rough. As ever, I owe a deep bow of gratitude to my late professors of classical Japanese and Chinese, Richard McKinnon and Hiraga Noburu, whom I still feel helping me along this interesting path.

Map of Japan

SEA OF JAPAN

Sekigahara

KYOTO

Himeji

NAGOYA

OSAKA

Kokura

SHIKOKU

Shimabara

Kumamoto

KYUSHU

H

HOKKAIDO

HONSHU

EDO (TOKYO)
Hakone

Izu Peninsula

PACIFIC OCEAN

KANTO
KANSAI

SITES OF MUSASHI'S MAJOR DUELS AND OTHER EVENTS

1. 1584. Birthplace, according to three different theories:
   1A. Miyamoto-mura, Sanomo-mura, Yoshino-gun, Mimasaka Province (today corresponds to Miyamoto-mura, Ohara-machi, Aida-gun, Okayama Prefecture).
   1B. Miyamoto-mura, Itto-gun, Banshu, Harima Province (Miyamoto, Taishi-machi, Ibo-gun, Hyogo Prefecture).]
   1C. Yoneda-mura, Innami-gun, Banshu, Harima Province (Yoneda-machi [at the border of Takasago and Kakogawa], Hyogo Prefecture).

2. 1596, age 13. Site of Musashi's first match, the duel with Arima Kihei (Hirafuku, Hyogo Prefecture).

3. 1599, age 16. The match with Akiyama (northern part of Hyogo Prefecture).

4. 1600, age 17. The Battle of Sekigahara, where the Tokugawa defeated the Toyotomi (Sekigahara, Gifu Prefecture).

5. 1604, age 21. Three matches with the Yoshioka clan.
   —The match with Yoshioka Seijuro. Yamashiro Province, outside the capital at Rendai Moor (west of Mount Funaoka, Kita-ku, Kyoto).
   —The match with Yoshioka Denshichiro, outside the capital.
   —The match with Yoshioka Matashichiro, outside the capital, at the spreading pine at Ichijoji.

6. 1604, age 21. The match with the priest at the Hozoin (Kofukuji, Nara).

7. 1607, age 24. The match with *kusarigama* expert Shishido (western part of Mie Prefecture).

8. 1608, age 25. The match with Muso Gonnosuke, the master of the five-foot staff. Edo (Tokyo).

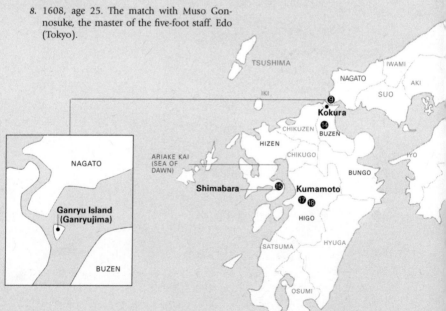

1610, age 27. The match with Hayashi Osedo and Tsujikaze Tenma. Edo (Tokyo).

9. 1612, age 29. The site of Musashi's most famous match, with Sasaki Kojiro at Ganryu Island (Funa Island).

10. 1614–15, age 31–32. Participation in the Winter and Summer campaigns at Osaka Castle.

11. 1621, age 38. The match with Miyake Gunbei (Tatsuno, Hyogo Prefecture).

12. 1622, age 39. Temporary residence at the castle town of Himeji (Hyogo Prefecture).

13. 1628, age 45. Site of the meeting with Yagyu Hyogonosuke. Owari (Nagoya).

14. 1634, age 51. Stays as guest of Ogasawara Tadazane. Kokura (Fukuoka Prefecture).

15. 1637 age, 54. Fighting against the rebels at Shimabara. Shimabara (Nagasaki Prefecture).

16. 1638, age 55. Demonstration of sword style to retainers of Lord Matsudaira Izumo no kami Naomasa (Matsue, Shimane Prefecture).

17. 1640, age 57. Resides as guest of the Hosokawa clan, at the former site of Chiba Castle. Kumamoto (Kumamoto Prefecture).

18. 1644, age 61. The Reigan Cave, outside Kumamoto City, where in his last years of life, Musashi wrote *The Book of Five Rings*.

■ Throughout this volume, Japanese names appear in the traditional order, surname preceding given name.

■ All translations from Japanese and Chinese are by William Scott Wilson, except where otherwise indicated. Quotations from *The Book of Five Rings*, *The Unfettered Mind*, *The Life-Giving Sword*, and *Hagakure* are taken from Wilson's published translations of said works by Shambhala Publications. In some cases, the translations have been slightly modified.

■ MUSASHI-RELATED MANUSCRIPTS: Musashi's name has appeared in a great number of manuscripts written from as early as 1654 to the opening of the twentieth century. Composed by such disparate persons as Musashi's adopted son, Iori, members of opposing swordsmanship schools, village scribes, individual scholars, and even owners of brothels, these sources often give varying dates for important events in Musashi's life, and diverse assessments of his talents and achievements. Writers and scholars have had to sift through these works to determine their own conclusions. Those quoted or made reference to in this book include:

Busho kanjoki	*Mukashi banashi*
Dobo goen	*Musashi kenseki kensho ehon*
Ganryu hidensho	*Musashi koden*
Ganryu kendo hidensho	*Musashi yuko gamei*
Gekijo yoroku	*Nitenki*
Gekken sodan	*Numata keki*
Harima no kagami	*Sayo gunshi*
Hiratake keito	*Sekisui zatsuwa*
Honcho bugei shoden	*Suihyo shokan roku*
Kaijo monogatari	*Tanji hokin hikki*
Kokura Hibun (a monument)	*Watanabe koan taiwaki*
Kuro sawa	*Yoshioka-den*
Miyamoto Musashi monogatari nenpyo	

THE LONE SAMURAI

PROLOGUE

In the first decade of the seventeenth century, a master of swordsmanship by the name of Sasaki Kojiro made his way down to the southern island of Kyushu and, with the permission of the Hosokawa lords of that area, established a *dojo* in the port city of Kokura. Kojiro had trained constantly in his art from his youth, and over the years had developed a swift and subtle style that seemed to allow no defense. The better swordsmen he had fought might, just before their defeat, have been dimly aware of how Kojiro's sword seemed to first arc down and then suddenly turn upward like a swallow in graceful and acrobatic flight. Kojiro became a popular teacher, attracting a number of Hosokawa samurai who admired both his technique and the fact that he had never been defeated. In addition, Kojiro's lineage as a martial artist was impeccable.

And there was something else: the sword Kojiro used in his bouts was nearly his equal in fame. His weapon of choice was an unusually long sword that he carried on his back made by a famed Bizen swordsmith around the year 1334. Many of the long blades surviving from that troubled time in Japanese history had been shortened to the standards of later periods, but this one had been suffered to retain the distinctive shape and size typical of that era. Because of the superb talents

1

of the swordsmith and the quality of the steel he had used, the sword was a thing of fascinating beauty and the cutting edge, despite having been put to practical use many times, had never even been chipped. Kojiro was proud of this weapon and had named it the Drying Pole, perhaps because it was so long that it almost resembled the long bamboo poles used for drying laundry. It was partly because of that length that opponents were often unable to approach its owner and deliver a blow with their own shorter blades.

It was not uncommon, during these times, for bouts to be arranged between serious swordsmen who wished to prove their abilities, whether to the local lords, prospective students, or simply to themselves. Such a match had been arranged for Kojiro, to take place on 13 April 1612 on Funa Island, a small island surrounded by the swift waters of the Kanmon Straits, not far from Kokura. His opponent, a man known as Miyamoto Musashi, was known to be undefeated as well, but no one knew much about his style or his lineage, and he had a reputation for being unkempt and even unpredictable. Conflicting stories circulated about the man's prowess and courage. Nevertheless, Kojiro looked forward to the bout, as it could only enhance his reputation at Kokura and possibly bring him closer to an official position with the famous Hosokawa clan.

———

On the appointed day, Kojiro was rowed over to Funa Island from Kokura, arriving well ahead of the scheduled time. His opponent was late, but because the man's point of departure was from a far northeasterly section of Shimonoseki and because of the rapid and changing currents in the straits, this was perhaps not unusual. Considering Kojiro's possession of the unique sword and the method with which he used it, he likely wondered, as he waited, what kind of sword his opponent would carry. This Musashi was supposedly something of an itinerant and without many possessions, but what would that mean in terms of the weapon he used? No one in Kojiro's entourage had had any idea, but considering the mystique surrounding the Drying Pole, its provenance, and the technique of its owner, no one cared much either. Still, Kojiro must have wondered, since he knew that the soul of a swordsman was bound up in the weapon he carried at his side.

After a long wait and some loss of patience on Kojiro's part, Musashi's boat finally came into view. As it approached the island and his opponent stepped out into the shallows, Kojiro squinted into the glare from the bright waters to appraise the man and the blade he had brought. As his eyes focused on the four-foot wooden sword Musashi had just carved from an oar, Kojiro's first thought could only have been, "Who is this?"

———

Kojiro might well have been indignant. The sword was considered the soul of the warrior and, just as opposing combatants would proudly declare their personal lineage before a fight, they also took great pride in carrying weapons that had distinguished histories. Kojiro was a traditionalist in this sense, and his indignation at being challenged with a carved oar can be understood.

Kojiro personified the ideal of swordsmen of his day: his lineage was impeccable and his teachers well known; through disciplined training, he had created his own seemingly flawless style; he had won the approval of the highly respected Hosokawa clan and been allowed to establish a school in Kokura; and he appeared to be on his way to becoming the official sword instructor to that clan. Above all, Kojiro respected the sword and technique—both of which were part of the mythology of Japan: in myth, the very islands of the country were created by ocean water dripping from a blade, and techniques and styles were taught by gods and demons. Through his success in all the traditional aspects of the culture of the sword, Kojiro was an inspiration to his many devoted disciples and the numerous swordsmen all over Japan who had heard of his rise to fame.

Musashi was a swordsman of an entirely different stripe. Seeming to have appeared out of nowhere, he claimed no teacher, no school, no lineage. Like the poets Saigyo and Basho, the painter Fugai, and the sculptor Enku, he was a perpetual peripatetic—never entering into a long-term contract of service with a local lord, or even marrying or settling down. As he roamed the length and breadth of Japan, Musashi trained himself in the powers of observation and intuition—which he valued far above technique—to an extraordinary degree, and the results of this discipline were manifested in both his swordsmanship and his art. Perhaps due to his preference for independence and freedom, he established no school of the martial arts and was never associated with a professional atelier. He was outstandingly talented and highly cultured, but there was something rough and eccentric at the core of his character throughout his life. He died surrounded by his few disciples, but he was fundamentally a loner. Astonishingly, he rarely used a real sword.

Musashi was above all a free spirit, and this was reflected in his avoidance of service to a single *daimyo*, even though he was on excellent terms with a number of highly respected clans. It was also reflected in his transcendence of the warrior's ancient idealization of the sword and technique. While he respected the sword, he was not fixated on its use, and would happily take up anything at hand when confronted by an opponent. He encouraged his disciples not to have preferences or to rely on anything, including the sword, the very "soul of the samurai."

Like Kojiro standing at the shore, we find ourselves wondering who this Miyamoto Musashi was. Although he had little or no formal training, Musashi established himself as Japan's most famous swordsman during his youth and went on to become known as one of the country's most respected painters. He used a wooden sword in nearly all the sixty-some bouts that made him famous and wrote a book on swordsmanship that is now read worldwide, three hundred and fifty years after his death. Eschewing position and family, he had little need for the comfort and security that most of us require.

What Musashi established with the sixty-one years of his life was a legend and an ideal for the Japanese people for which there is no equivalent in Western culture. His life has been the inspiration for countless stories, dramas, novels, movies, and television series; one of the two largest battleships built by Japan during the Pacific War was named for him.[1] There are figures of speech in modern Japanese that refer to someone with a "Musashi-like" character—and it is likely that Musashi's name is as well, if not better, known than many of the most important figures in Japanese history and culture. All this despite the fact that Musashi never intentionally set out to change that history or affect that culture. How could this be?

The Way of the Sword:
Banshu to Ganryu Island

FIRST STRIKE

One morning in 1596, just outside the village of Hirafuku in the province of Banshu, Arima Kihei, a swordsman of the Shinto-ryu, sat waiting for a formal apology. This was to be delivered by a thirteen-year-old boy, Miyamoto Bennosuke, the local *gaki daisho*,[1] or "commander-in-chief" of every ruffian in the area, and the chief instigator of every outrage in Hirafuku.

Kihei had arrived in the area a few days earlier, put up a simple bamboo fence, and erected a placard announcing in large gold letters that he would accept a match with anyone willing to enter a contest of skill with him. Why he chose to come to such an out-of-the-way place as Hirafuku is uncertain. He may have heard that a master of the sword and the *jitte*, a certain Hirata Munisai, lived not too far away, and hoped to attract his attention.

He was, however, to be disappointed. It was a young Bennosuke, rather than the seasoned Munisai or any other wandering swordsman, who noticed the placard. On his way home at the time from a calligraphy lesson, Bennosuke took out his brush and ink, smeared over the gold letters of Kihei's sign and, in a fit of bravado, wrote, "Miyamoto Bennosuke, residing at the Shoren-in, will give you a match tomorrow."

When Kihei returned to the spot and saw this bit of vandalism, he responded by sending a disciple to the Shoren-in, where the youngster Bennosuke lived with his uncle, the priest Dorinbo. As Kihei's disciple informed the priest that his master wished to accept the challenge from this Bennosuke, the priest turned ashen and explained that Bennosuke was only thirteen and that his challenge was just an adolescent prank. When informed of this, Kihei magnanimously sent a message to Dorinbo that he understood, but would need a formal apology from the boy in order to clear his honor. The priest readily accepted these terms.

So the following morning Kihei sat waiting for the priest and the boy to set the matter right. A number of villagers who had heard of the incident also gathered, probably to witness and enjoy the humiliation of this wayward child who was always causing so much trouble.

But as Dorinbo and Bennosuke approached, people noticed that the latter was carrying a six-foot staff. Then, to everyone's surprise, just at the moment the apology was to be made, instead of bowing in humility, Bennosuke charged. Kihei was not expecting this and may have been caught off guard, but he was a practiced swordsman. Dodging the blow, he unsheathed his sword and took a stance. Surely the onlookers must have thought that the brash young challenger had no chance at all. But after a few exchanges, Bennosuke suddenly threw down his staff and grappled with Kihei. He then picked the swordsman up bodily and threw him down headfirst. Recovering his staff, he beat Kihei to death and returned home.

Long before writing *The Book of Five Rings*, Bennosuke would become known as Miyamoto Musashi.

In that book he refers to this match quite simply: "From long ago in my youth, I set my mind on the martial arts, and had my first match when I was thirteen. My opponent was a martial artist of the Shinto-ryu, Arima Kihei, whom I defeated."

But another record, the *Tanji hokin hikki*, provides insight into Bennosuke's mental attitude at the time of the match: "At this point [Bennosuke] thought, 'I was unbeaten by the enemy because I gave no thought to my life. I simply walked in and struck.' "

This attitude would inform his psychology for the rest of his life and become one of the main undercurrents of *The Book of Five Rings*.

His "enemy," Arima Kihei, was most likely one of the many *shugyosha* of that period; a sword practitioner who perfected his skills and enhanced his reputation by wandering through the provinces of Japan engaging in combat—often mortal—with other swordsmen. A *shugyosha* took disciples or established his own style or school, but also always hoped to be noticed by the local lord, who might offer him an official position as sword instructor to his clan. The life of the *shugyosha* was by no means an easy one. It involved a long list of rigorous ascetic practices: in his travels, the *shugyosha* was exposed to cold and hot weather, often sleeping in the mountains and fields with little shelter from the wind and rain; he bore hunger without carrying money or rations for his travels; he walked through the most inaccessible places and was always in danger of losing either his reputation or his life in a chance match along the way.[2]

Of the unfortunate Kihei himself, almost nothing is known, but he may not have been the most exemplary of *shugyosha*. One account, the *Sayo gunshi*, published in Hyogo Prefecture in 1926, relates: "There was a certain Arima Kihei who gambled and acted outrageously. Although an accomplished swordsman of the Shinto-ryu, in town he was despised as though he were a snake or scorpion."[3]

His style, the Shinto-ryu, was that of the legendary Tsukahara Bokuden, a master swordsman of a generation earlier; but the word "Shinto-ryu" may indicate any number of styles or substyles. There were, and still are, the Katori Shinto-ryu, the Kashima Shinto-ryu, and

Bokuden's style as well. All of these came from the eastern provinces at that time and were offshoots of one basic tradition. (Interestingly, there was also an Arima Shinto-ryu created by a certain Arima Yamato no kami, and it may be that Kihei was either a member of that family or a disciple of the school.)

Nothing else is clear: only that Kihei was killed by the thirteen-year-old Bennosuke (it should be noted in Kihei's defense that, according to some accounts, Bennosuke had the stature of a young man three or four years older).

For his part, Bennosuke coolly returned to the Shoren-in to continue his studies in calligraphy, Confucianism, and Buddhism under the loose—and perhaps, after this turn of events, timid—direction of his uncle Dorinbo. He also studied some painting, probably on his own; when he departed the temple for good, he left a painting of the Zen patriarch, Daruma, presaging his emergence some thirty-five years later as one of Japan's finest india ink painters. But, for the three years following the match, he lived now at the Shoren-in near Hirafuku,[4] and now with his sister, Ogin, in the village of Miyamoto, close to the provincial border in Sakushu. Finally, in the early spring of 1599, he deeded all of his family's possessions—weapons, furniture, and family tree—to his sister's husband, Yoemon, and walked out of Miyamoto and up into the hills with one of his friends. At Kama Slope, having been presented with Bennosuke's staff as a keepsake, his friend turned back to Miyamoto and obscurity. Bennosuke—who from this point became known as Miyamoto Musashi—walked out of obscurity and on to become Japan's most famous and singular swordsman.

ORIGINS

There is nothing particularly remarkable about the low mountains and hills between the villages of Hirafuku and Miyamoto. In the late

1500s, the area contained scattered farming villages dotted with houses and fields and, in Miyamoto, a river of no very great size. Yet while the landscape was generally one of peace and tranquility, if a traveler climbed the Kama Slope, as Musashi did on his departure, he would come out onto a pass in the middle of the mountains. This was the highway between Harima (Banshu) and Mimasaka (Sakushu), which during the ensuing Edo period (1603–1868) was part of the road used for the *sankin kotai*, the journey to Edo (Tokyo) taken by the *daimyo* every two years. The road itself was an ancient one, probably used as a trail first by the bear and deer that had inhabited the forests, later by hunters, and finally by merchants transporting wares from the western seaboard to the capital. No doubt it would have been a thing of wonder to a small boy of great curiosity and imagination, growing up in one of these otherwise remote country villages. It was the road out.

Harima, however, did have a colorful history. The Akamatsu clan had settled there early in the twelfth century, eventually building Shira-hata Castle and establishing itself as the local *daimyo* family. The Akamatsu were descended from a Minamoto Morofusa, who in turn came from the Genji line of the Emperor Murakami, and thus the clan could consider themselves distant relatives of the imperial family. The Akamatsu did well in the area for three hundred years, but came to their end in 1441 when the head of the clan, Mitsusuke, made the great tactical error of assassinating the Ashikaga shogun, Yoshinori. Although the shogunate itself was not very strong at the time, other *daimyo* led by Hosokawa Mochiyuki took this opportunity to destroy Mitsusuke and his clan's castle.

The Bessho, a junior line of the Akamatsu, survived this disaster and prospered enough to built several castles in Harima. One of these castles, commanded by a Bessho Shigeharu, was attacked and fell in 1578; Shigeharu escaped by the skin of his teeth to the village of Hirafuku, where he changed his name to Tasumi, literally "one living in the fields." It was Shigeharu's daughter, Yoshiko, who gave birth to Musashi in 1584, thus linking him to the Akamatsu, to the Minamoto or Genji, and, anciently, to the imperial line.

Musashi's father was Hirata Munisai, a landed samurai with the status of senior vassal to the Shinmen clan, whose last name he was eventually given permission to use as his own. The Shinmen family was a pillar of the warrior community in Mimasaka and its progenitor was Tokudaiji Sanetaka, the twenty-eighth-generation descendant of the famous Fujiwara Kamatari. Involved in the attempted restoration of Emperor Godaigo between 1334 and 1338, Sanetaka was exiled to Awai-no-cho in Mimasaka. His son, Tokuchiyo, went to Kyoto and asked for absolution (*shamen*; 赦免) of the family's crimes. This was granted, and the clan was given the status of warrior and changed its name to Shinmen (新免), or "newly absolved." Tokuchiyo, now called Shinmen Norishige, married the daughter of Akamatsu Sadanori, the governor of Mimasaka; his son Naganori also married into the Akamatsu clan.

Finally, Munisai's father married into the Shinmen clan and Munisai's first wife, Omasa, was the daughter of Shinmen Munesada, the fourth-generation Shinmen. It is in light of this genealogy that Musashi sometimes stated his full name to be Shinmen Musashi Fujiwara Genshin.

Munisai thus became a minor power in the area and was invested with a small fief; his house in Miyamoto was an old-style mansion, surrounded by a good bit of land enclosed by walls of stone and no doubt including a fine *dojo*. It was here that Musashi played as a young child, climbing the trees and roaming the low mountains.[5] His older sister, Ogin, married into the nearby Hirao family, and in the garden of that house today stands a zelkova tree that is said to be the second generation of one from which the young Musashi took a branch to make into the first of his many wooden swords.

An instructor to the Shinmen clan, Munisai was a master of several of the martial arts including the Two-Sword Style, the use of the *jitte, jujitsu,* and the proper use of armor.[6] He was known in particular as a skilled practitioner of the Tori-ryu of swordsmanship, a style he would use to good effect against Yoshioka Kenpo in Kyoto. Munisai also taught *jujitsu* to Takenouchi Hisamori, who stayed as a guest at the Hirata house when Musashi was about four years old and who would later establish the Takenouchi-ryu of that art. Thus, Musashi was raised in a household that placed a great emphasis on the martial arts and he most likely began receiving some instruction from his father at an early age. Certainly weapons of all kinds were constantly around him and he must have often sat enthralled at the conversations of the talented men who came and went, gathering around the stern Munisai for instruction and edification.

But Musashi's childhood was not a happy one. Not long after he was born, Munisai divorced his second wife, Yoshiko, who was Musashi's mother, and she moved back to her home in Harima. Munisai then married yet again, and Musashi seems not to have gotten along well with his new stepmother. In addition, there were hurtful rumors that his real mother was not Yoshiko at all, but in fact was Omasa, Munisai's first wife—a claim that the village of Miyamoto (now Miyamoto, Ohara-machi, Aida-gun, Okayama Prefecture) officially makes to this day. When he was about eight years old, Musashi's relationship with his father began to deteriorate to the point where the young boy began making the difficult trip over the mountains to visit Yoshiko and her family, eventually dividing his time between Harima and Mimasaka. It was at about this time that his formal education was placed in the hands of his uncle, the priest Dorinbo.

One day, the situation with his father came to a head. The following story is found in the *Tanji hokin hikki*:

> Bennosuke watched his father's martial arts from the time he was
> quite young. As he got older, he gradually started to voice criti-
> cal remarks. Munisai began to think that this child was not very

likeable, despite the fact that he was his own son. One day, while Munisai was carving a toothpick, his son approached and began criticizing his *jitte* technique. Angered, Munisai took the dagger he was using to carve the toothpick, and threw it at his son as though it were a *shuriken*. Bennosuke dodged the weapon and it lodged in the pillar behind him. Munisai became all the angrier, took out his short sword and used it too as a *shuriken*. Bennosuke dodged this as well and fled outside. After this, he never returned to the house but, rather, lived with a priest related to his mother in Banshu. Thus he abandoned his hometown.

Musashi now considered Hirafuku to be his real home, and it may be for this reason that he declares in *The Book of Five Rings*, "I am a warrior born in Harima." But local records in Miyamoto copied as far back as 1689 clearly state that Musashi—officially, at least—lived in that village until 1596, and so would have retained a strong sense of its rhythms and environment. One of his favorite haunts would have been, just as it is to village children in Japan today, the local shrine, with its wide spaces and old trees. In ancient times, the Aramaki, or Sanomo shrine, had once stood at the top of the mountain to the rear of the village—hence the village's name: Miyamoto, "at the foot of the shrine." The shrine was later moved to the base of the mountain, close to the northern side of the Miyamoto River. Here the young Musashi would have watched the Shinto priests as they beat a huge drum throughout the day; at night he would have drifted off to sleep to the same sound: that of two drumsticks, constantly in motion, swirling like swords in expert hands.

FINDING HIS STRENGTH

When Musashi climbed the Kama Slope at age sixteen, he embarked on the homeless, ascetic life of a *shugyosha*, a life that he would continue in one form or another until his final years. His belongings were few: the clothes on his back, perhaps a small sewing kit, a bamboo canteen, at the most a very small amount of pocket money, an ink stick and writing brush, and, of course, his sword.[7] As he walked over the stony mountain paths, he wore a pair of straw sandals that would quite often need repairing or replacing. If he was lucky, he might find a straw hat for his head. There was unlikely to be anywhere to stop for food when he was hungry, or a pleasant place to lie down when he was tired. For those who believed in folktales, the dark mountains were filled with foxes and *tanuki* (a sort of badger), both experts at bewitching the unsuspecting. For those who did not believe such tales, there was still the very real danger of bandits.

In the spring of 1599, Musashi walked through the mountains and into the neighboring province of Tajima. Here he had a match with a swordsman by the name of Akiyama, whom he defeated. Nothing is known of where the match took place or of Akiyama's lineage, and, in *The Book of Five Rings*, this opponent is simply described as "strong." But the memory of this fight must have been an intense one for the sixteen-year-old Musashi. Of all of his more than sixty matches to come, he seems to have remembered this one perhaps most clearly as he reviewed his life some forty years later, alone in the Reigan Cave.

As Musashi walked on alone, large groups of warriors were beginning to gather slowly around Sekigahara, a large plain to the north and east of Tajima. In October of the following year, a battle would be fought there that would settle both Japan's course for the next three-and-a-half centuries and the direction of Musashi's life.

For several decades, two men had been directing the reunification of a Japan badly splintered by the ineffectual Ashikaga shogunate. Oda Nobunaga (1534–82) had emerged from a small fief in the middle of nowhere to nearly succeed in unifying the country with his ruthless and creative military genius, and had been stopped only when he was assassinated by one of his own generals, Akechi Mitsuhide. Toyotomi

THE WAY OF THE SWORD

Hideyoshi (1536–98), another of Nobunaga's generals, quickly squelched the rebellion and had brought the country to the verge of total unification and control when he too passed away, possibly from a brain tumor. Before he died, Hideyoshi appointed a board of five *tairo*, or chief ministers, to govern the country until his son Hideyori reached majority, hoping that in this way the Toyotomi clan would continue to rule the country. Now, one of those *tairo*, Tokugawa Ieyasu (1542–1616), was bringing those hopes to naught.

Due to a complicated balance of ever-shifting loyalties, Japan in the year 1600 was essentially divided into two camps: those generals and *daimyo* who favored the more-or-less incumbent Toyotomi clan (largely from Kansai and western Japan), considered the Western forces; and those who were betting on the increasing strength of the forces of Ieyasu (mainly from Kanto and the eastern part of the country), the Eastern forces. There were several battles in different locations, but the main battle took place at Sekigahara on the misty morning of 21 October 1600. It is uncertain how many troops eventually engaged in the fighting, but the initial balance was approximately even, at about eighty thousand men on each side. By the time the battle was over, sometime during the Hour of the Sheep (from one to three P.M.), the Tokugawa armies had routed the Toyotomi, helped in part by the perfidy of some of the generals on the losing side. The casualties were in the tens of thousands. Many of the defeated who had not been killed in the battle itself were hunted down in the rain and mud and slaughtered in the days and weeks to follow. Some, however, were able to escape to fight another day. Musashi, although still only in his teens, was one of these.

The Battle of Sekigahara was a *shugyosha*'s dream. Along with the life of ascetic self-discipline he put himself through, he would welcome the chance to join in a battle—this was referred to as "borrowing the battlefield"—to prove his mettle. For an unemployed warrior, fighting in battle gave him a chance to be noticed for his skills and, if he excelled, to be taken on as a martial arts instructor under the patronage of the lord whose forces he had joined. Thus he might become a samurai in the true meaning of the word, "one who serves."

So Musashi now traveled on toward Sekigahara, eventually joining up with the forces of the Shinmen clan. This clan was under the command of Ukita Hideie, who had been one of Toyotomi Hideyoshi's favorites; he had been chosen to be one of the five *tairo* by the dying Hideyoshi and was a mainstay of the Western forces. Hideie's father, Naoie, had conquered Bizen, Mimasaka, and Bitchu and established Okayama Castle a generation earlier, and the Ukita was considered one of the most powerful clans in the area. With his mother's connection to the Shinmen, it is not surprising that Musashi would have cast his lot with that clan, but it may also be that Hideyoshi's dreamlike rise to power from peasant status inspired Musashi to join that great man's side. Musashi had been six years old when Hideyoshi had destroyed the powerful Hojo clan, and seven when Hideyoshi conquered the great city of Odawara. Two years later, Hideyoshi had begun his invasion of Korea. These stories were the talk of the nation, and the young Musashi would have listened to them as any child would, dreaming of what he would do when he grew up.

All sources indicate that Musashi fought with extraordinary valor at Sekigahara, despite his youth. One typical account, from the *Musashi yuko gamei*, states: "Musashi's achievements stood out from the crowd, and were known by the soldiers in all camps."

According to the Kokura Hibun monument erected in 1654: "Musashi's valor and great fame could not be overstated, even if the oceans had mouths or the valleys had tongues."

If we look to Musashi's own comments about the battle, however, we will be disappointed, for he alludes to it only once, in a note to Hosokawa Tadatoshi written decades later, and then only in the broadest terms: "I have participated in over six battles since my youth."[8]

In the end, the Western forces lost the battle. Ukita Hideie was condemned to death by Ieyasu, but his sentence was commuted to permanent exile on an island off the Izu Peninsula. He eventually shaved his head and became a monk, living to the great old age of ninety. Other commanders were not so lucky: many lost their fiefs and their families and, of course, many lost their lives. The battle had been one of the most definitive in Japan's history, marking its course for the next two hundred and fifty years. And much as it defined the Yagyu clan, who had fought for the Tokugawa, as permanent members of the establishment, it would also define Musashi—who had fought on the losing side—as an outsider for the rest of his life. The Tokugawa hegemony was now evident everywhere and marked the future of the battle's participants well beyond the grave. Even the composers of the Kokura Hibun, erected in faraway Kyushu nine years after Musashi's death, needed to be circumspect in their language. They did not, for example, mention on which side he had fought, and they even felt compelled to describe the actions of the Western forces as an "insurrection of the Taiko Toyotomi's favorite retainer, Ishida Jibunosuke."

After the battle, seventeen-year-old Musashi was once again on his own. He had lost his gamble at war and had nearly lost his life. But he had gained the pride of having served the Shinmen, the Ukita, and even the late hero Hideyoshi. He had also gained experience in a protracted battle. He would think about this experience for the rest of his life and record many of these thoughts in his final statements in *The Book of Five Rings*.

It is interesting to note that Musashi's father, Munisai, also participated in these conflicts, but in Kyushu and for the Eastern forces.[9] For unknown reasons, he had previously resigned from the Shinmen clan and gone to Nakatsu in Buzen to serve Kuroda Yoshitaka (Josui), receiving an annual stipend of two hundred *koku*.[10] As part of Ieyasu's forces in the southwest, the Kuroda attacked Tomiki Castle in Bungo, and

Munisai would have seen action there. It was in Kyushu that Munisai met the important Hosokawa vassal, Nagaoka Sado no kami Okinaga, and became his instructor in the martial arts. This relationship would play a critical role in Musashi's career.

Like most of the survivors on the losing side of the Battle of Sekigahara, Musashi spent a number of years after the war keeping a low profile, doing his best to keep body and soul together. He spent some time secluded in the mountains, but also did a lot of traveling, no doubt meeting other *shugyosha* on the road and testing his skills. What would soon become apparent, however, was that his self-discipline and training during this time must have been rigorous and intense. In 1604, at age twenty-one, he would walk into Kyoto and bring to ruin one of the most respected schools of swordsmanship of that time.

Kyoto and Matches with the Masters

The Yoshioka clan had been well-known residents of Kyoto for generations. The earliest Yoshioka Kenpo, whose personal name was Naomoto, was a master of black and tea-colored dyed goods in the Shijo area of the capital. It was in the constant rolling back and forth of the dyeing implements that he was enlightened one day to the special style of sword handling for which his school would become famous. The name "Kenpo," which became the hereditary title of the head of the family, connotes a man who adheres to righteousness, and his dyeing methods and prices were said to be just and proper.

It was this Naomoto who attracted the attention of the twelfth Ashikaga shogun, Yoshiharu, with his great feats in battle, and who thus became the first Yoshioka instructor to that house. The second generation was his younger brother, Naomitsu, who also took the name Kenpo and became a martial arts instructor to the Ashikaga clan. It was Naomitsu who was instructor to the "Swordsman Shogun"

Yoshiteru, who also employed Tsukahara Bokuden and Kamiizumi Ise no kami Nobutsuna, founder of the Shinkage-ryu. And it was Naomitsu who opened the Heihosho, or Place of the Martial Arts, in the Imadegawa section of Kyoto. Naomitsu's son, Naokata, became the third generation and instructor to the fifteenth and final Ashikaga shogun, Yoshiaki.

Finally, there were Naokata's sons, Seijuro and Denshichiro. The family annals, the *Yoshioka-den*, remarks of them:

> Here, then, the Yoshioka brothers. They gained fame in the style of the martial arts, and were unprecedented in past or present in the mysteries of the arts. The elder brother, Seijuro, and his younger brother, Denshichiro, were the so-called Kenpo Brothers. It was from the time of the Kenpo Brothers that the art was daily renewed, becoming more prosperous day by day and transcending the art of former generations.

Seijuro, in particular, was considered to be an excellent swordsman. He had become the fourth-generation head of the Yoshioka clan, but the Ashikaga shogunate was now defunct and the clan enjoyed no special standing. One of his methods of training was to go out late at night to a forest on the outskirts of Kyoto and, as a spiritual discipline, exercise the practice of "fixing the vision" (*shikan*; 止観). This was originally a practice of Esoteric Buddhism in which, in contrast to the Zen practice of filling the mind with Emptiness, the practitioner was to concentrate on a single object of worship and, so, sweep away any other extemporaneous thoughts. Seijuro was said to have reached such a level of concentration that, when he focused his thought on a single bird on a treetop in the forest, hundreds of birds would fly up to the treetops at once. It was this Seijuro, the almost transcendentally skilled scion of the respected Yoshioka clan of

Kyoto, that the twenty-one-year-old self-taught Musashi challenged to a duel.

Musashi's decision to challenge Seijuro was not random. By defeating Seijuro, he would not only show the whole world what he could do but also demonstrate a thing or two to his father, Munisai, who was still teaching martial arts in Kyushu.

A generation earlier, Munisai's talent had come to the attention of the Ashikaga shogun, who had called him to Kyoto for a "comparison of techniques" with the shogun's own instructor, Yoshioka Naokata. The Kokura Hibun gives this brief description: "With a limit of three matches, Yoshioka had the advantage once and Shinmen won twice. At this point Shinmen Munisai was awarded the designation of a martial artist 'with no equal under the sun.' "

One can imagine that Seijuro would have been quick to accept this challenge, regardless of the fact that Musashi seemed to have no experience, no status, and probably little skill. With this fight, Seijiro planned to ensure that the residual spot on his family's name would be eradicated forever.

The place for the match was to be outside the capital, at the moor adjacent to the Rendaiji temple. Seijuro was armed with a real sword, while Musashi carried the weapon that would become one of his trademarks— the *bokuto*, or wooden sword. The Kokura Hibun describes the fight:

> Musashi and Seijuro fought with the power of dragon and tiger at the Rendaiji Moor[11] outside of Kyoto, but with one blow from Musashi's wooden sword, Seijuro collapsed and fell unconscious. This match had been promised beforehand to conclude with a single blow, so Seijuro barely escaped with his life. His disciples carried him away on a plank and nursed him back to health. He eventually abandoned the martial arts and became a Buddhist priest.

The unproven youth from the countryside had beaten the head of the Yoshioka family so thoroughly that the humiliated man withdrew from his famous clan's profession and took the tonsure.

No doubt Musashi beat Seijuro with unexpected skill, but he had also used psychology in arriving late enough that the proud man, anxious to clear away this small embarrassment from his family's name, became agitated with anger and expectation. Musashi had broken Seijuro's famed concentration before the fight ever began, and so secured his victory beforehand. No birds flew up to the treetops at this match.

The Yoshioka, however, were duty-bound to regain the family honor. Hadn't Seijuro's defeat been a simple fluke? Could the respected Yoshioka school, for generations instructors to the shogunate in the capital, lose its reputation—and thus its future—to a nameless, uncouth *ronin* from a farming village? To let the debacle end at this juncture would be unimaginable. And so a second match was arranged, this time pitting Musashi against Seijuro's younger brother, Denshichiro.

Denshichiro had a reputation as a very strong man and was, after all, one of the Kenpo Brothers. He carried a wooden sword over five feet long and sharpened at the end, a weapon that would have required considerable strength to handle at all, let alone with any skill. The bout was to be held at a location outside the capital, and a time was set. It would be astonishingly short. Musashi, having studied the Yoshioka character and gauged Denshichiro's temperament, showed up late once more, with the desired effect. When Denshichiro made an aggressive and angry attack, Musashi dodged the blow, wrested the sword from his opponent, and stabbed him through. According to a number of records, "Denshichiro fell where he had stood, and died."

The match was over in a matter of seconds, and the astonished disciples who had come to watch their teacher make quick work of the upstart Musashi could do nothing but carry Denshichiro's lifeless body back to Kyoto. The fourth generation of the Yoshioka Kenpo had come to a devastating end.

It is not difficult to guess what happened next. Stories of revenge, or *adauchi*, have always occupied an important place in Japanese history, which is not surprising given the crucial role that honor plays in traditional Japanese culture. Whether the damage to one's honor was egregious or subtle, the wounded party was expected to take revenge. And in a society where news spread like ripples from a stone thrown into a still pond, there was no escape: the dishonored party was absolutely bound to action. Not to act would mean perpetual disgrace.

This was the situation in which the remnants of the Yoshioka clan, their disciples and students, found themselves: they had an inescapable obligation to act, regardless of how tragic the consequences might be.

And so yet another match was arranged with Musashi, this time against Seijuro's son, Matashichiro, now considered the fifth-generation Kenpo. But the match was only a ruse—a fact that seems to have been known to everyone, including Musashi. Matashichiro was just a symbol of the clan's honor. The real plan was for battle.

The place was again to be on the outskirts of Kyoto, at the famous spreading pine at the Ichijoji temple.[12] To make sure that there was no chance of suffering another defeat, the Yoshioka brought more than a hundred men, armed with everything from swords and spears to bows and arrows.

Meanwhile, Musashi's reputation had skyrocketed, and he had taken on some very eager students himself. Just before the match, a number of these students learned of the Yoshioka family's plans, warned their teacher, and offered to accompany him to the bout. Musashi, however, knew that involving students in an *adauchi* would be considered the same as enrolling them in a battle, something strictly prohibited by the authorities. The Yoshioka clan was essentially finished and so perhaps had no other recourse. But Musashi had his life ahead of him, and had somehow gained a confidence and an inner strength far beyond that of ordinary men. His students were forbidden to walk with him into the trap set by the Yoshioka.

Earlier in the year, when he fought Seijuro and Denshichiro, Musashi had put his opponents at a psychological disadvantage by causing the men to wait and thus lose their mental equilibrium. This time he reversed his strategy and started off early. On his way, he passed by a shrine to Hachiman, the god of war, and stopped for a moment to pray for victory. But as he walked up to the altar and was about to shake the gong's cord to get the god's attention, he suddenly realized that, in ordinary times, he had never put faith in the gods and buddhas. To do so now would be wrong. Chagrined, he released the cord and backed away. Why would the gods listen to him now, when he had never relied on them before? In truth, was he to rely on the gods or on himself? Dripping with sweat from embarrassment, he bowed to the shrine in thanks for the revelation and hurried on.

This incident made a deep impression on Musashi—and when writing *The Book of Five Rings* nearly forty years later, he made it clear that the principles of swordsmanship must be understood as though the student himself had discovered them. This was a major departure from other sword styles of Musashi's time. Of the great number of styles that arose in about the mid-sixteenth century, many of their progenitors let it be known that they had learned those styles not on their own, but through divine revelation. Tsukahara Bokuden of the Shinto-ryu, for example, received a "divine decree" at Kashima Shrine; and Ito Ittosai, the founder of the Itto-ryu, had his style revealed to him after seven days and seven nights of seclusion at the Grand Shrine at Mishima. The list goes on: the eyes of Okuyama Kyugasai of the Shinkage-ryu were opened by the gracious deity of Mikawa Okuyama; Jion of the Nen-ryu was enlightened to the secrets of his styles at Kurama Temple in Kyoto; Hayashizaki Jinsuke, founder of *iai-do*, discovered his new Way at Dewa Tateoka Hayashizaki Shrine; and Fukui Hei'emon had the principles of the Shindo Munen-ryu revealed to him by the Izuna Gongen in Shinshu.

Musashi bowed in veneration to the gods and even worshipped the Buddhist bodhisattvas, but the ever-practical swordsman had little patience with revelations or secrecy. These, he felt, were nothing more than impediments to self-reliance. As he lay dying years later, he wrote in "The Way of Walking Alone," his last testament for his disciples, that one should "Respect the gods and buddhas, but do not rely on them."

Musashi walked on and studied the topography on the way: the fork in the road that passed by the northern stretch of the Shirakawa River, the rice fields with narrow paths running between them, and even Mount Ichijoji and Mount Uryu at the back of the road. By dawn he was waiting to face the Yoshioka at the Spreading Pine.

Presently, Matashichiro and his accompanying "troops" arrived at the pine, carrying lamps and muttering that their opponent would probably be late again. Suddenly, Musashi jumped out from behind the pine and yelled, "Did I keep you waiting?"

Once again, his psychological tactic worked flawlessly. The Yoshioka were thrown into confusion, and, not yet able to see well in the half-light of dawn, each no doubt had the grim fear that Musashi might be just behind him. For his part, Musashi dashed straight into the crowd of men as they fumbled for their swords, found the cowering Matashichiro,[13] and cut him through the middle. The shocked students slashed about, thrust their spears, and shot off arrows in total disarray. Taking advantage of the general panic, Musashi herded the frightened men together like so many cattle, cutting them down one after another before he finally withdrew along the route he had planned earlier.

It was a complete rout. The Yoshioka men who had somehow escaped with their lives now fled back to the capital, their disgrace so complete that no chance of recovery was possible. The last of the Yoshioka line had been cut down in the first moments of battle, and a single swordsman had put to naught a sword style that had been celebrated for generations. Although an arrow had pierced his sleeve, Musashi himself had received not a single wound.

Nothing remains of the Yoshioka style today, so it is difficult to know what it actually entailed. The *Musashi koden* states: "As for their martial art, either they had studied from Gion Toji, a man who had understood the mysteries of swordsmanship, and were continuing his line; or they were the descendants of the Eight Schools of Kyoto in the line of Kiichi Hogen."

Both Gion Toji and Kiichi Hogen are legendary figures without clear historical origins, but the "Eight Schools of Kyoto" represent the Western style of swordsmanship and are often compared to the "Seven Schools of Kashima," representing the Eastern tradition. In traditional accounts, at least, Hogen lived in the twelfth century at the Ichijo Canal in Kyoto and was a master of the esoteric study of the yin/yang. He is said to have taught the martial arts to the famous twelfth-century general and strategist Minamoto no Yoshitsune, but he imparted the truly secret skills of the sword only to the "Eight Priests of Kurama," and it was with these that the Eight Schools began. Hogen was famous for his strategy, part of which is contained in his enigmatic saying:

> If the opponent comes, then greet him; if he goes, then send him off. To five add five and make ten; to two add eight and make ten. By this, you create harmony. Judge the situation, know the heart; the great is beyond ten feet square, the small enters the tiniest atom. The action may be fierce, but when facing what is in front of you, do not move the mind.

According to a book circulated among the adherents of Hogen's style during the Edo period, their swordsmanship was for the most part that of the Chujo-ryu. The *tachi* they used was short, and the distinctive feature of their martial technique was to press in close on the opponent's chest. We will encounter this style again in connection with Musashi's famous bout on a small island far to the southwest.

The famous school of the Yoshioka was closed, never to reopen. The remaining members of the clan went back to, or perhaps had never really left, their craft of dyed goods; and for some generations after these events, their store remained open in Kyoto's Nishinotoin district, where they had once proudly traded upon their skill at a much different art.[14]

The dream of the first Yoshioka, Naomoto, had floated like a bubble along the Kamo River through the city of Kyoto, only to disappear with the flash of a new morning's light.

At this point people were no doubt beginning to wonder and talk about the quality of that light.

But one who we can be sure was not interested in talking about that subject was Musashi himself. Musashi's laconic style is well known: even about his famous fights with the Yoshioka he wrote nothing specific, but noted in *The Book of Five Rings* that "I went to the capital and met with many famous martial artists; and although I fought a number of matches, I was never unable to take the victory."

Sharpening His Tools

In the Earth chapter of *The Book of Five Rings*, Musashi compares the warrior to a carpenter, noting that "the carpenter skillfully prepares all the different kinds of tools, learns the best way of using each one, takes out his carpenter's square, works correctly according to the plans, does his work unfailingly, and makes his way through the world."

As we have seen, his father, Munisai, was an expert at the sword, the *jitte*, the proper use of armor, and even *jujitsu*. Thus, as was mentioned, Musashi must have been exposed at an early age to a great variety of weapons. Not long after his defeat of the Yoshioka clan, he turned his attention to other forms of the martial arts, and his steps toward the ancient capital of Nara.

The Buddhist monks at Nara had long been known for their prowess with military weapons and their willingness to use them in times of conflict. One of their favorite weapons was the spear, and the temple most closely associated with the spear was the Hozoin, a subtemple of the famous Kofukuji.

The first generation of the Hozoin style of spear technique was Kakuzenbo Hoin In'ei. Born in 1512 during the violent years of the Ashikaga shogunate, he first studied the spear under the martial artist Daizen Taibu Shigetada. Once In'ei was visited by the famous swordsman Kamiizumi Ise no kami, who soundly defeated him. Kamiizumi had already defeated In'ei's friend, Yagyu Muneyoshi (Sekishusai), and so the two friends now became Kamiizumi's disciples. In'ei became an expert with both the sword and the spear under Kamiizumi, but his specialty was the forked spear, which he would develop to great deadliness.

In'ei was from the famous Nakamikado clan, and was of the same generation as the famous generals Takeda Shingen and Uesugi Kenshin. This was a period of intense interest in the martial arts—and In'ei, although a priest, was at the vanguard of his times. Eventually banished from the Hozoin temple for his love of weaponry, he took the opportunity to wander the provinces and visit more than forty martial artists before he was allowed to return to the temple. One of those martial artists was the above-mentioned Daizen, from whose lessons In'ei developed his own *kamayari*, or sickle-spear, technique.

Priest-soldiers had traditionally used the halberd, which they considered a holy weapon for the protection of Buddhism, as opposed to the straight spear, the weapon of common soldiers. The innovative In'ei, however, found that fixing a sicklelike blade to the spear increased its efficiency. This was the *kamayari*. The secret poem that expressed the virtue of the weapon goes:

> Thrust, and it's a spear;
>> Hurl, and it's a halberd;
> Pull, and it's a sickle.
>> In any and all events,
>> You should not miss.

This weapon was far more efficient than the regular spear or halberd. It was used not only for thrusting, but for sweeping, cutting, dragging, and striking. Because of this innovation, In'ei's fame spread to the surrounding areas and he attracted many disciples.

By the time In'ei turned eighty-three in 1603, he had come to the realization that Buddhist priests should have nothing to do with instruments of violence and death. He closed the *dojo* that had once employed over forty teachers and forbade his successor, Kakuzenbo Inshun, to teach the martial arts. He died four years later, at age eighty-seven.

But the Hozoin spear tradition did not die with In'ei for, a few years after his death, it was reestablished by Inshun, who had become abbot of that temple. Born in 1589, Inshun was five years Musashi's junior and was rumored to have been In'ei's son. He continued studying spear technique from a Nichiren priest at the neighboring Ozoin temple who had also studied under In'ei.

It was this priest from the Ozoin—known to us only by the name of his temple—that Musashi met in a match not long after the fight at Ichijoji temple. The priest was armed with a *kamayari*, while Musashi stood his ground with a short wooden sword. Despite his apparent disadvantage, Musashi beat the man in both of two matches, showing no concern about being in a compound surrounded by warrior priests who very much wanted their man to win. For his part, the monk felt no rancor but, on the contrary, was so impressed that he had Musashi stay for a sumptuous meal. The two became so engaged in talk about the martial arts that the sun had risen before they became aware of the time. Then Musashi thanked his opponent-host and went on his way.[15]

After Musashi left Nara and the Hozoin, he disappeared from the written records for about three years. But there is little doubt that during that time he continued to live the life of a *shugyosha*, meeting other such men and wandering the country. Musashi, like other *shugyosha*, learned firsthand on his travels about nature, topography, local customs, and the character of men—especially of other swordsmen. He also no doubt learned about the characteristics and features of local castles, the production of local goods, and the cultures of the various provinces. This was exactly the sort of information that was valued by the feudal lords, who were happy to hire *shugyosha* with expertise in such matters. In turn, this was the outcome that most wandering swordsmen sought: a position as trusted servant of a prosperous master and a stipend worthy of his talents. Musashi, however, turned neither his knowledge nor his talent into practical security. His sights were set much higher.

In 1607, Musashi was passing through the province of Iga when he met a man known only by his family name, Shishido, who was a master of the sickle and chain, the *kusarigama*. This Shishido lived in a relatively isolated part of the mountains in Iga, where he farmed and ran an informal local smithy, making his own weapons. The sickle was originally a farming instrument, but according to the chronicles of the Genpei wars, it was used as a weapon called the *naikama*, or *nagikama*, as early as the twelfth century. The *naikama* was a sickle attached to a long handle and was used to cut the opponent's feet and ankles with a sort of mowing motion. According to tradition, when used as a weapon in China, it was attached to a nine- or ten-foot chain. The chain was attached to either the upper or lower section of the sickle's handle, which was a little over one-and-a-half feet long. The chain was then used to immobilize the opponent's body or weapon, while the counterweight at the end was used to wound or kill him. The sickle was employed to finish him off.

The match between Musashi and Shishido took place in an open field, and once again Musashi had to fight while being watched closely by a number of his opponent's disciples. After successfully arresting Musashi's sword with the chain, Shishido moved slowly in to finish him off with the sickle, when Musashi suddenly unsheathed his *wakizashi* and, throwing it like a *shuriken*, fatally pierced the man's chest. At this point, Shishido's shocked disciples all drew their swords and slashed out at their leader's assailant. Musashi, however, chased after them and they scattered, running "off in the four directions."

Musashi was an expert at throwing blades. The Kokura Hibun states:

> He either let fly with a real sword or threw a wooden one. But there was no way for either a fleeing or running person to avoid it. Its force was exactly like unleashing the strength of a bow made of stone: one hundred releases, one hundred hits. It cannot be thought that even Yang Yu-chi [a famous archer of the Spring and Autumn Period in China] had mysterious skill like this.

He also taught this skill to his disciples. According to the *Watanabe koan taiwa*, published about twenty-five years after Musashi's death, Takemura Yoemon, who was either Musashi's adopted child or his disciple, was no less expert with the *shuriken* than was Musashi himself. Yoemon, it notes, "could float a peach in the river and then pierce it to its core with a sixteen-inch knife."

————

Tokugawa Ieyasu had politically unified Japan by December 1602. The following year, the imperial court awarded him the ancient title, Sei-I

Tai-Shogun, or Great General Who Conquers the Western Barbarians, which gave tacit court approval to his assertion of ultimate authority. By February of the following year, he began rebuilding the castle at Edo (Tokyo), which was to be the new capital. By June he had declared that every *daimyo*, from fiefs around the country, would be required to leave members of his immediate family in Edo year-round, to ensure his "good intentions" toward the Tokugawa government; in other words, family members of all *daimyo* were effectively to be held hostage in the capital to prevent rebellions from starting in the countryside. To make sure that these hostages could live in dignity commensurate with the status of their clans, mansions were built, quarters for samurai were established, and roads were constructed. With the labor, materials, and supporting businesses involved in the reconstruction, Edo was quite suddenly transformed from a backwater town to the new center of politics, business, and, if not high culture, at least cultural activity. Money and power had come to town.

Swordsmen had also arrived in great numbers. Yagyu Munenori had become sword instructor to Ieyasu's son Hidetada as early as 1601, and had now established his line of the Yagyu-ryu in the new capital. The Toda-ryu was there as well, and the Itto-ryu under Ono Tadaaki, who was also an instructor to the shogunate family. Edo had become a magnet for those *shugyosha* who hoped either to be noticed by a visiting *daimyo* or to meet other martial artists and sharpen their skills.

Musashi was in Edo by 1608 and, preceded by the reputation he had gained at Kyoto, met a number of talented men. To survive, he started his own small school and took on such students as Hatano Jirozaemon, who later had a number of disciples of his own. Another disciple was Ishikawa Sakyo, a retainer of Honda Masakatsu. Sakyo is said to have been skillful enough to combine the Unmoving Sword and the Diamond Sword techniques, and this synthesis was eventually added to the Musashi style. It is easy to imagine that Musashi's *dojo* was a busy place, despite the fact that he was only twenty-five years old.

One day early on, a man by the name of Muso Gonnosuke walked into Musashi's *dojo* accompanied by eight disciples and requested a match. Gonnosuke was a big man—well over six feet tall—who had learned the deepest secrets of the Shindo-ryu and was invested with the secrets of the Kashima-ryu's One Sword technique. After further study in Hitachi under a Sakurai Yoshikatsu, he had toured the northern provinces wearing a *haori* that bore a large crest of a crimson sun on a white background. On his shoulders was embroidered in gold characters: "Greatest Martial Artist in the Realm, Founder of the Hinomoto-ryu, Muso Gonnosuke."

It should be noted here that, while Gonnosuke may have had a flair for style, his dress and braggadocio were no more unusual for *shugyosha* than Arima Kihei's self-promoting, gold-lettered placard. Flamboyantly dressed swordsmen were not rare during this time. Their clothes were a means of gaining attention, and carried two messages: "I'm a skillful swordsman ready to be hired by an appreciative lord," and "Anyone, at any time, is welcome to test his skills against mine." Clothes on occasion either made or unmade the man, depending on the relative skill of the swordsman who happened to notice him.

Musashi, on the other hand, did not conform to this style, and in fact did not comply with many of the sartorial rules of his day. He was an independent, and in large part a nonconformist. He dressed and bathed as he pleased. At any rate, Gonnosuke walked into Musashi's *dojo* and requested a match, and one of his disciples produced a four-foot wooden sword from a brocade bag. Musashi, who at the time was carving a small willow bow, quickly accepted the challenge and took up a piece of firewood as his only weapon. Gonnosuke attacked without further ado, and Musashi sent him tumbling with a single blow.

Gonnosuke was humiliated and left without a word,[16] but he was a man of great determination and skill, and this would not be the end of the matter. Dismissing his disciples and retreating to Mount Homan in Chikuzen to pray and meditate over this defeat, he was answered one night in a dream with the words: "Know the reflection of the moon in the water with a log."

Gonnosuke understood this "log" to be the five-foot staff, or *jo*, and the moon in the water to mean the center of his opponent's chest. Soon thereafter he was employed by the Kuroda clan in the Fukuoka fief of Chikuzen for the *jo* technique he then originated. Much later, he returned to challenge his nemesis again, with the match this time resulting in the only draw of Musashi's career. The technique that Gonnosuke created is called the Shindo Muso-ryu, and it is practiced to this day.

————

Musashi stayed on in Edo for another two years or so, continuing to teach students and take on opponents. His matches in 1610 with two of these opponents, Osedo Hayashi, a Yagyu stylist, and Tsujikaze Tenma, known more for his strength than his swordsmanship, are described in the *Nitenki*:

> When Musashi was residing in Edo, Osedo Hayashi, a samurai in the Yagyu clan, went with a certain Tsujikaze, a strong martial artist, to ask for bouts with the swordsman. Musashi gave his consent, and immediately stood and faced them. Osedo advanced and was about to strike, but Musashi took the initiative and struck first. Osedo collapsed where he stood.
>
> Next, Tsujikaze attacked, but for some reason fell backwards, hit his back on a waterjar at the edge of the veranda and died.[17] Generally speaking, this Tsujikaze was a man of great strength. He was able, for example, to run alongside a galloping horse, and to bring it to a halt by wrapping his arms around its neck.

By 1612 the situation in Edo had become tedious for Musashi. He was essentially barred from comparing skills with the best swordsmen of the day, such as Yagyu Munenori, because of Munenori's connection with the Tokugawa and because of the precarious political status Musashi had after having fought for the Toyotomi. To make matters worse, the tension between these two clans was escalating day by day. The Toyotomi were ensconced in their castle at Osaka and still had the backing of a number of *daimyo* and *ronin*. So early in the year, Musashi traveled on foot to the Fujiwara area of Shimousa Province, ostensibly for the opening of new land. This was probably a ruse, because he did not stay there long, nor had he likely decided, at age twenty-nine, to give up the sword and begin a career in agriculture.

Musashi clearly had something else in mind—and by February or March, he had already started on the long trip to the southwestern island of Kyushu.

Demon of the Western Provinces

Musashi's mark for an appropriate match was Sasaki Kojiro, a swordsman popularly known as the Demon of the Western Provinces. Kojiro had arrived in the port city of Kokura in Buzen some two years earlier and, as his nickname implies, had attained great fame. Certainly he had caught everyone's eye with his striking appearance—he wore a crimson *haori* with his long sword, known as the Drying Pole, slung across his back—but his skill too was astonishing and he had thus far defeated every opponent he had faced.

Hosokawa Tadatoshi, who six years later would become the lord of Kokura, had been enamored of the martial arts from his youth and was himself a skilled practitioner of the sword. Thus, when news of Kojiro's presence in Kokura reached him, he happily interviewed the man and soon hired him as an instructor to the Hosokawa clan. Although Kojiro was not actually taken on as a retainer to the clan, he received a substantial fee and was able to open his own *dojo* in the castle town, eventually gaining a great number of disciples.

Ganryu Sasaki Kojiro was born in Jokyoji Village at Ichijogatani in Echizen. Ichijogatani was the home of the prosperous and cultured Asakura clan, who had been the lords of Echizen over the course of five generations spanning more than a hundred years. Their instructor of the martial arts was one Toda Seigen, the main heir to the Chujo-ryu. It, like the Shinto-ryu and the Kage-ryu, was a fundamental style of the Japanese martial arts and had been established as far back as the Kamakura period (1185–1333) by Chujo Hyogonosuke. Seigen himself was an extraordinarily accomplished practitioner who continued to perfect his martial art after he retired from teaching in his old age due to an eye disease. Secluding himself at his home in Jokyoji Village, he was commonly known as "the blind swordsman." His ideal had been a technique called the "No-Sword" (muto), exemplified by the phrase, "If shortness [of the sword] is taken to an extreme, it becomes nothingness" (Tan kiwamareba mu); as his art advanced, his short sword became shorter and shorter still.

Seigen had met Kojiro when the latter was quite young, and had recognized in him the makings of a great swordsman. For the purposes of his own research, he hired the teenaged Kojiro as a sparring partner. In their daily matches, Seigen wielded a short tachi about one-and-a-half feet long, while requiring Kojiro to oppose him with a much longer blade. With this intense training, Seigen developed a style he hoped would eventually lead to the abandonment of the sword as a weapon altogether; but for his part, Kojiro eventually gained great ability with the long sword and became one of Seigen's top disciples. The moment of truth came when Kojiro was able to defeat Seigen's younger brother, Jibuzaemon, in a match; at which point Kojiro went out on his own. He wandered the provinces of Japan as a shugyosha, eventually arriving in Kokura and establishing himself under Tadatoshi's patronage.

Musashi came to Kokura from Kyoto in April 1612, visiting the mansion of Nagaoka Sado no kami Okinaga, a chief retainer of the Kokura fief and, it will be recalled, a former student of Musashi's father, Munisai. Musashi was now twenty-nine years old. After a short while, he made his wishes known to his host in a formal request, which records note as follows: "It would seem as though a Ganryu Sasaki Kojiro is now residing in this area, and I have heard that his technique is excellent. My request is for permission for us to have a 'comparison of techniques.' I make this in reference to your relationship with my father, Munisai."

Okinaga, whether out of deference to his old teacher or his impression of the intense Musashi, was quick to comply. Putting Musashi up at his own mansion, he contacted his lord, Tadaoki, and made the petition his own. Martial arts enthusiast that he was, Tadaoki had no doubt heard of Musashi's bouts with the Yoshioka in Kyoto, and must have been quite curious about this man. But he was also acting out of respect for Sado, a trusted and respected retainer, when he gave his permission for a match to be held the following day, April 13.

The place was to be a small, lonely island between Kokura and Nagato Shimonoseki, a little less than two-and-a-half miles from either shore. Known in ancient times as Anato no Shima, it was in Musashi's time called Mukaijima ("the island over there") by people in Buzen on the Kyushu side, and Funa Island ("boat island") by those in Shimonoseki on the Honshu side, because of its boatlike appearance from that shore. The match was set to begin during the first half of the Hour of the Dragon (seven to nine A.M.). A decree was posted throughout the castle town and the surrounding area stating that absolutely no favoritism was to be shown either man and that spectators were strictly forbidden to travel to the island.

Okinaga quickly informed Musashi of the decision and offered to escort him to the island the next day in his own boat. Overjoyed, Musashi thanked Okinaga for his efforts in arranging the match that he had so greatly anticipated.

That night, however, Musashi disappeared. A search was made through the castle town, but he was nowhere to be found. Word spread quickly, as did rumors that Musashi, when confronted with the prospect of a bout with the Demon of the Western Provinces, had turned tail and run.

Okinaga, as might be imagined, was chagrined. He had his own prestige on the line in this matter, having taken up Musashi's petition and encouraged Lord Tadaoki to agree to the match. If Musashi had now truly fled, it would be a source of embarrassment not only for him, but worse, for Tadaoki as well. Upon some reflection, however, Okinaga realized that if Musashi really were a coward, he would not have waited until the night before the match to escape. He also reasoned that, as Musashi had come to Kokura from Shimonoseki, he may well have gone back to that city to spend the night away from the inevitable distractions in Kokura, and would probably go to the island from there.

A courier was sent and, sure enough, Musashi was found staying in Shimonoseki at the residence of a wholesaler, Kobayashi Tarozaemon. The courier explained the situation in Kokura, and Musashi responded with a letter that demonstrated both his respect for Okinaga and his circumspection.

> I have heard that, concerning tomorrow's match, you would send me in Your Excellency's boat, and I am heavily honored by your solicitude. However, at this time, Kojiro and I are hostile opponents; and if Kojiro is sent by Lord Tadaoki's boat and I am sent by Your Excellency's boat, I wonder if this would not place you in opposition with your lord.
>
> Please let me be of no concern to you in this affair. I considered speaking to you about this right away, but thinking that you would not agree, purposefully did not make any mention of it. I must strongly refuse Your Excellency's boat. Tomorrow morning I will cross over to Mukaijima from this place. Please do not

be the least bit concerned, and be convinced that I will come in good time.

April 12
Miyamoto Musashi
—*To Lord Sado*—

Musashi was clearly concerned that any sign of favoritism toward him on Okinaga's part might result in some friction between lord and retainer, and he was determined to prevent this. His actions had predictably resulted in doubt about his courage and sincerity, but Musashi seems to have been concerned only for Okinaga's relationship with the Hosokawa. It was important to him that this relationship would continue smoothly for his sponsor long after the following day's bout had ended.

Nevertheless, when the sun came up the next morning, Musashi was still sound asleep. The master of the house, Tarozaemon, woke him up and informed him that the Hour of the Dragon had already arrived. At this point, a courier came from Kokura, informing Musashi that Kojiro's boat had already left and made the crossing. Musashi responded that he would be there soon, but then got up, washed his hands and face, and ate a leisurely breakfast. Requesting an oar from Tarozaemon, he sat and carved a large wooden sword until another courier arrived urging him to make the crossing immediately.

Musashi then dressed himself in a silk-lined garment, folded a towel over his sash, put a wadded cotton garment over the silk one, boarded the boat and left. At the helm was Tarozaemon's servant. Musashi sat in the middle of the boat twisting a paper string, with which he then tied back his sleeves. Finally, putting the wadded cotton garment over his head and shoulders, he lay down.

On the island, Kojiro and the verifying officers waited with impatience and consternation. In the boat, Musashi was apparently asleep.

In the end, Musashi arrived at Mukaijima after the Hour of the Serpent (nine to eleven A.M.). He had Tarozaemon's servant stop the boat on a small, narrow sandspit projecting from the island, and removed the wadded cotton garment. Placing his sword in the boat and his short sword in his sash, he pulled his sleeves up high and got out of the boat, barefooted, into the shallow water. Holding his wooden sword in a lowered position, he took several steps in the little waves and walked up the beach. As he walked, he took the hand towel from his sash, folded it into the length of a *hachimaki*, and tied it around his head with the knot in the middle of his forehead.

In contrast to Musashi, Kojiro was dressed colorfully in a sleeveless scarlet *haori* and dyed leather knickers. On his feet were new straw sandals, and in his hand was a sword over three feet long, reputedly fashioned by one of the great swordsmiths of Bizen.

Kojiro felt insulted at having been made to wait. Seeing Musashi approaching in the distance, he rushed to the water's edge. He angrily informed his opponent that he himself had been on the island at the appointed time and demanded to know whether Musashi had come late out of fear. Musashi silently ignored him and simply advanced. In a rage, Kojiro unsheathed his sword and dramatically threw the scabbard into the water. Musashi stood in the shallows, smiled, and uttered his now-famous words, "You've lost, Kojiro. Would the winner throw away his scabbard?"

Inflamed, Kojiro moved quickly toward Musashi and swung his sword straight forward, aiming for the middle of the forehead. At the same instant, Musashi struck with his wooden sword in the same way, hitting Kojiro directly on the head. Kojiro fell where he stood. The tip of his sword had cut through the knot of Musashi's *hachimaki*, and the hand towel had fluttered to the ground, but Musashi's wooden sword had made a direct hit. Musashi lowered his sword and stood motionless for a moment, then quickly raised it to strike again. Kojiro was lying flat on the ground—but, at that moment, he wielded his sword to the side in a mowing motion, aiming for Musashi's thigh. Musashi leapt back, and received a three-inch cut in the lining of his *hakama*, probably less than an inch away from his femoral artery.

Musashi's wooden sword now came down, splitting Kojiro's ribs, and Kojiro, blood flowing from his mouth and nose, lost consciousness. Musashi crouched down and put his hand above Kojiro's mouth and nose, checking for signs of life. There were none. He turned to the verifying officials, bowed briefly, then stood up and walked briskly to the beach. Jumping deftly into the boat, he helped the helmsman pole away from the island, and could soon be seen only dimly in the offing.

It was noontime, and in the spring sea between Kokura and Shimonoseki, the bright sun reflected off the wavelets and a breeze began to rise. Musashi had fought the greatest fight of his life, one that is still discussed with great animation nearly four hundred years later.

Musashi's approach to the fight with Kojiro seems to have involved a two-tiered strategy. The first tier involved psychology, the same weapon he had used against the Kenpo Brothers. By making the opponent wait, he disturbed his equilibrium: anger and consternation thwarted the necessary concentration. Kojiro had had to wait in the bright morning sun, eventually, no doubt, clenching his fists in frustration. By the time Musashi arrived, refreshed and fully focused, his opponent was completely distracted by his hurt pride and impatience. The second tier was Musashi's knowledge that Kojiro had a preference for long swords and would likely rely on the advantage of that length. It was a long sword that he had used to defeat Toda Seigen's brother Jibuzaemon and every opponent since. Musashi therefore fashioned his oar into a wooden sword just a bit longer than Kojiro's weapon, to take that advantage from Kojiro and make it his own. According to the Kokura Hibun:

> Ganryu said, "I would like to settle the match with real swords."
> Musashi replied, "You handle a naked blade and show me every

mystery it has. I will raise my wooden sword and manifest its secrets." Thus the promise was made as hard as lacquer.

Musashi's "secret" may have been as little as one inch. At any rate, many years later, in the Wind chapter of *The Book of Five Rings*, he would warn his students against depending on the length of a weapon:

> There are other styles that prefer a long sword. From the standpoint of my own martial art, this can be seen as a weak style. The reason is this: not knowing how to defeat others in any situation, they put virtue in the length of their sword and think they can win by the distance from their opponent.
>
> Those who prefer long swords will have their explanation, but it is only their own individual quibbling. It is unreasonable when seen from the True Way in this world.

But Kojiro was just as famous for his lethal *tsubame-gaeshi* ("swallow return") style. Seigen himself seems to have initiated this style, but it was Kojiro who developed it further, or at least made it famous. The technique itself is not well understood today, but it seems to have been based on an instantaneous return of the blade after the first strike, and it was probably modeled after or compared to the swallow showing its white underside when suddenly reversing its course in midflight. The *Ganryu hidensho* describes it this way:

> The sword is held straight ahead, as though to strike the opponent on the forehead. Advancing straight ahead, you keep your eye on the tip of your opponent's nose. Then, striking all the way to the ground, you immediately bend down to a crouch, bring your sword up over your shoulder, and thereby defeat your opponent.

In other words, the first strike is a feint, and it is the return strike that is the actual attack. Essentially, this is a *kaeshiwaza*, or "returning technique."

Kojiro, nevertheless, did not use his famous technique against Musashi, unless the final strike at Musashi's thigh might be considered the "return." Instead, he went straight for his opponent in a *jodan* position, his long sword held high over his head. What happened? Was Kojiro too rattled to use the technique that had always brought him success? Was there a fear factor? Certainly he, too, was aware that Musashi had single-handedly dismantled the Yoshioka, but that was a decade earlier. Did he simply not have time for a return blow when Musashi's wooden sword cracked down on his skull? We will never know. But the old swordsmen's saying, "To catch a tiger, you must enter the tiger's den," may apply here. In this one strike, Musashi must have been within an inch of Kojiro's very real and very sharp blade as it made its downward swing. His timing and sense of distance had to be perfect. As it was, his *hachimaki* was neatly severed by Kojiro's sword, and it was the knot of that towel that received the tip of the blade of the Drying Pole.

To say that Musashi had perfectly calculated the strikes of the two swords misses the point, however, for what brought him the victory was nothing so cerebral. Musashi himself addressed the matter in the Emptiness chapter of *The Book of Five Rings*, noting that all techniques and actions of either mind or body must have their foundations in Zen Buddhist Emptiness: "The heart of Emptiness is in the absence of anything with form and the inability to have knowledge thereof. This I see as Emptiness. Emptiness, of course, is nothingness. Knowing the existent, you know the nonexistent. This, exactly, is Emptiness."

The reader senses that in the absence of Musashi's intuition and discipline, language itself fails here. Thus we go back to Mukai Island (Mukaijima), now called Ganryu Island (Ganryujima; *jima* means "island"), time and again, looking for the key to the most famous one-on-one fight in Japanese history. Until we are able to enter Musashi's spirit that day, however, we will be left with only the sand and the sound of waves on this little island.

It is interesting to note that Musashi was asked years later why he did not deliver a *todome*, or coup de grâce, to Kojiro. His response was that such an action was for true enemies, and there had been no enmity between himself and his opponent. Their match was one of a "comparison of techniques."

There are two meanings to the word *todome* that might apply to this case. The first and more common meaning is a simple stab to the throat that quickly and reliably ends a fallen man's life, but this would make little sense in the context of this match: Kojiro had died immediately from the combination of Musashi's two blows. The more esoteric meaning, however, is to finish off the opponent in a manner that prevents his angry spirit from returning to take revenge. In this case, the *todome* would have been delivered by stabbing him "just below the left nipple and twisting the blade from edge up to edge downward as it was withdrawn."[18] Musashi's response indicated that he understood the question in terms of this second meaning, and that there was no need for such a *todome*. Kojiro himself had been eager for the match and, while his spirit might lament the result, it would honor Musashi for his victory.

But if Kojiro's spirit honored Musashi, there were those still living who did not. The surviving Yoshioka had slandered him, some declaring that Musashi had actually been beaten by Seijuro and then run away from a fight with Denshichiro. Others circulated a story that the fight with Seijuro had been a draw, or that both had cut each other's *hachimaki* but that the blood simply did not show on Musashi's persimmon-colored *hachimaki* and did on Seijuro's white one. How they accounted for the complete disappearance of the Yoshioka brothers and their school from the swordsmanship scene is unknown.

In the case of the fight at Ganryu Island, there were partisans in favor of Kojiro, or disciples of his, who claimed that Kojiro had only been knocked temporarily unconscious by Musashi's blow, and that Musashi's disciples, who had hidden themselves on the island, had rushed forward and finished Kojiro off when he started to regain consciousness. How Musashi's disciples might have managed to get onto the tiny island, evade detection by the Hosokawa verifying officials, and escape is not explained.

Some people may have stopped and listened to these stories,[19] but Musashi was not one of them. After returning directly to Shimonoseki, he wrote a letter to Nagaoka Sado Okinaga, thanking him for his graciousness and help, then left again for ports unknown.

The Way of the Sword
and the Way of the Brush:
Osaka Castle to Kokura

THE FIRE OF BATTLE

The fight with Sasaki Kojiro on Ganryu Island was a watershed for Musashi. Until then, he had focused his attention on matches of one swordsman against another, and had come to a preliminary understanding of his art. With his defeat of the Demon of the Western Provinces, he must have felt an intense confidence in his own innate abilities and in his readiness to turn to deeper and broader ground. In the opening chapter of *The Book of Five Rings*, after noting his sixty matches between the ages of thirteen and twenty-eight or twenty-nine, he writes:

> When I had passed the age of thirty and thought back over my life, I understood that I had not been a victor because of extraordinary skill in the martial arts. Perhaps I had some natural talent or had not departed from natural principles. Or again, was it that the martial arts of the other styles were lacking somewhere?

> After that, determined all the more to reach a clearer under-
> standing of the deep principles, I practiced day and night.

Hereafter there would be far fewer personal matches, and much more of the deeper discipline that would refine his art and clarify it to the point of articulation. Musashi's interests in the area of the martial arts were also expanding, and he began to look beyond one-on-one bouts to conflicts of a larger scale.

Although his tracks are by no means clear at this point, it would seem that he now made his way slowly up the San'yo area, along the Inland Sea, perhaps stopping off at Akashi and Himeji to visit the fiefs of the Ogasawara and the Honda clans on the way. Musashi was now famous, and any number of people—private sword practitioners and provincial lords alike—wanted to meet him and ask for instruction. His fame also gave him entry to observe other arts that he had found interesting, such as india ink painting, sculpture, and even formal gar-dening, and he may have met the famous artist Kaiho Yusho at about this time. At any rate, he slowly traveled on to Kyoto and eventually to Osaka, where the preparations for a large-scale battle were being made. There is little reason to assume that Musashi arrived at this location strictly by chance.

Although the Tokugawa forces had won a decisive victory at Seki-gahara, the Toyotomi family had remained wealthy, was firmly settled in Osaka Castle, and was not without allies. Slowly, however, the fam-ily's allies began to die off. Of the powerful men who had intervened between the two clans, Asano Nagamasa died in 1610, followed by Kato Kiyomasa in 1611, and Maeda Toshinaga in 1614. Other former sup-porters, like the Ukita, had been dispossessed and banished. These men and their armies were replaced, however, by thousands of the *ronin* who owed their masterless status to the destruction of their mas-ters' clans by the Tokugawa regime. By the late fall and early winter of 1614, there were over ninety thousand warriors inside Osaka Castle who felt nothing but rancor for Tokugawa Ieyasu and his son Hidetada. The Tokugawa knew that they would have to act soon to eradicate their only rivals to complete hegemony.

Strengthened by the troops of their feudatories and now considerably outnumbering the forces inside Osaka Castle, the Tokugawa attacked the fortification in mid-December, only to be repulsed and eventually stalemated. The fighting back and forth would last two months, but at last a truce was called, and the so-called Winter Campaign ended on 21 January 1615.

The Tokugawa then immediately set about filling in the castle's moats and destroying the outer ramparts, so that by mid-February the castle walls were directly exposed to attack. With this advantage established, however, they withdrew.

Despite the weakened state of the castle, *ronin* continued to pour in from the provinces and, by the spring of 1615, they numbered over a hundred thousand. This was, in a sense, a great boon to Ieyasu and his successors, as it gathered the most virulent of their opponents in one concentrated location that, regardless of its being a castle of great size, was also exposed on all sides. That so many men were willing to make a stand inside the castle speaks eloquently both about how they viewed the Tokugawa and about the selfless principles of the samurai code, now well known as Bushido.

By May of that year, the Tokugawa arrived with nearly twice as many men as were holed up within the garrison. The fighting was bloody, intense, and protracted, but by early June it was clear that the forces in the castle could no longer hold out. Hideyori, commander of the castle and heir to the Toyotomi, committed suicide when it was understood that his life would not be spared. His mother, Yodogimi, was dispatched by a loyal samurai to spare her any further humiliation at the hands of the enemy. In this way, Hideyoshi's only son, his favorite concubine, and all the hopes he had entertained in his rise to power vanished together under the early summer sun, and the blood of the clan washed away in the monsoon rains. The Summer Campaign was over—and the Toyotomi, as realistic rivals, were gone forever.

Musashi actively participated in these events, possibly in the position of a unit commander, and surely wearing armor and wielding his weapons. Years later, Musashi wrote Hosokawa Tadatoshi:

> Since I was young, I have gone out on the battlefield six times. On four of these occasions, there was no one on the field before me. This fact is widely known, and there is also proof.
>
> I have set my mind on the make-up of arms and how they are appropriately used on the battlefield since my youth.

One of these six battles was clearly the Campaign at Osaka. In the *Nitenki*, we find this: "There was proof of his military abilities at the Osaka Campaign in 1614. He was thirty-one years old. The castle fell the following year."

The "proof," unfortunately, has not been handed down, but the *Musashi kenseki kensho ehon* notes: "Musashi participated in both the Winter and Summer campaigns at Osaka. Though he despised the Tokugawa side no little bit, we know none of the details."

Although he "despised the Tokugawa no little bit," it is likely that Musashi fought on the side of those investing the castle.[1] At the age of thirty-one, he was still a *ronin*, an independent without sworn allegiance to anyone. His former commanding clan, the Ukita, was gone, its great commander, Ukita Hideie, now a priest on a lonely island off the Izu Peninsula; and the remnant of the Shinmen clan, led by the old lord, Shinmen Iga no kami, now served in Kyushu under the powerful Kuroda, also originally from Banshu and allies of the Tokugawa.

While there is no proof, it is most likely that Musashi "borrowed the battlefield" from the Ogasawara clan and fought alongside its troops. His actions in combat must have impressed the clan heir, Ogasawara Tadazane, for two years later, when the latter was moved from his fief in Shinano Matsumoto to Akashi, the man he put in charge of designing the town around his new castle overhanging the coastline—according to the records of the Ogasawara clan—was Miyamoto Musashi.[2] During the Summer Campaign at Osaka, Tadazane, his father, Hidemasa, and his eldest brother, Tadanaka, had left together for the action at Tennoji and opened the fierce attack on the forces of Mori Katsunaga of the Toyotomi side. His father and brother were both killed in action, and Tadazane was badly wounded. It seems unlikely that a man who had suffered losses this great would hire one of the enemy for such important work.

ARTS OF PEACE, ARTS OF WAR

Tadazane had recognized a variety of Musashi's talents. Not only was Musashi an extraordinarily talented swordsman and strategist, but his years as a wandering *shugyosha* had given him the opportunity to visit a number of the castle towns now growing under the Tokugawa regime. In addition, his astute powers of observation provided him with a deep understanding of how a town might best be organized for both everyday functioning and for defense in an emergency. It would not be laid out in a simple grid as had the capital, Heian-kyo, in the late eight century. That city, now Kyoto, had been fashioned on a Chinese model, and its designers had not been overly concerned with attack from the outside. The castle towns, on the other hand, and especially the samurai sections within them, were designed with narrow winding streets that the inhabitants would know well enough to maneuver through, but which any invading troops would find hopelessly confusing. In this light, it is not difficult to imagine Musashi in the middle of the bloody action of the Winter and Summer Campaigns, observing a scene that was much larger than any question of simply his own survival. Much later, in *The Book of Five Rings*, he would discuss the difference between broad "observation" and just "seeing."

It is interesting to note also that Musashi did not just work on the design of the castle town during his stay in Akashi, but also had a hand in designing the temple gardens at Enkakuin and Honshoji. Garden design is generally associated with Zen monks like Muso Kokushi and Kobori Enshu, but for Musashi to have been similarly engaged in this art is not as strange as it may first seem.

The first garden designer in Japan's recorded history was a Korean immigrant, Michiko no Takumi, a man with such mottled pigmentation that some people thought him a leper, or at the least, an unlucky figure. When it was suggested that he be taken to an uninhabited island and left to himself, Takumi responded that if people were offended by spotted skin, they should not raise horses and cattle with white spots. He also noted that he possessed a talent for depicting mountains and hills in landscapes, and that this talent would be a blessing to his adopted country. Those in charge decided to put Takumi to work, and not long thereafter he created a Chinese-style garden for Empress Suiko (r. 593–628). The empress must have enjoyed the artistic reshaping of nature, for it was her relative, Ono no Imoko, who went to China with Japan's first delegation there and brought back the art of flower arrangement—an art that had developed from floral displays on Buddhist altars.

From these modest beginnings, the art of garden design flourished among the Japanese aristocracy, so much so that, by the eleventh century, books were being written on the subject. All who could afford it had gardens with lakes, tiny mountains, and even waterfalls installed within the precincts of their mansions. These were gardens intended primarily for pleasure—viewing the seasonal change of foliage, watching the various birds attracted to the grounds, and even boating on the small lakes while accompanied by musicians.

As time went on, however, garden design came under the heavy influence of Buddhist and Taoist nature scrolls, and the garden itself became an object of contemplation. Natural phenomena were beginning to be seen as replete with deeper meanings of the universe. Garden design now tended to concern itself with displaying the essence of nature, rather than nature in its fullest array. By Musashi's time, the aristocracy had been experiencing a long decline, and gardens had tended—both because of the increasing population in limited urban space and the aristocracy's impoverishment—to become smaller and more appropriate to temples and relatively more modest residences. Thus, the best gardens were located at Buddhist temples and the homes of the *daimyo*. By this time, garden design had shifted almost completely into the hands of the Zen Buddhist priests (and, in some cases, their workers), with the result that the purpose of the garden—broadly speaking—was as a catalyst to meditation and contemplation. Gardens had become strictly understatements and suggestions of the larger natural world. Emphasis was often placed on space, or Emptiness, rather than on a multitude of foliage. The Buddhist concept of *mujo*, or transience, was suggested by the artistically arranged elements of the garden, manifesting the world in its state of eternal change.

The garden designer, then, had to be a man who both understood the Buddhist concepts involved and was well acquainted with the intricacies of nature. He must know what plants flourished where, how they would grow in sun or shade, and how they would react to the presence of water, whether flowing or still. What was more, he needed to be an artist who could distill the elements of nature to their most essential and abstract.

Thus, Musashi applied his hand with great interest in this work.[3] He was artistic by nature and had an intimate knowledge of the mountains and rivers, crags and springs, flowers and animals. His extended travel and keen sense of observation provided him with a familiarity with nature that very few people would ever gain. For as much as the Japanese love nature, most have been happy to observe it at a distance, or from within the confines of their residences or urban areas. Some of the most moving nature poems in traditional Japanese literature, for example, have been inspired not by the natural world itself but by depictions of nature on scrolls and screens.

Musashi, however, was in the tradition of the great Japanese traveler-artists—Saigyo, Enku, Basho, and Hiroshige, among others—and his artistic inspirations came from the heart of nature itself. As for his education on the restrictions of garden design, he would have had no trouble visiting the great gardens already established in Kyoto and elsewhere. As Musashi contemplated the small areas set aside for his garden projects in Akashi and later Himeji, he would have had no trouble reflecting on his memories of nature free from human restraints and then paring those memories down to their most abstract and aesthetic fundamentals.

But there is something more here.

At the end of the first chapter of *The Book of Five Rings*, Musashi encourages his students to meditate on certain rules for putting his martial art into practice. Two of these nine rules would seem to have little to do with the study of swordsmanship:

—Touch upon all of the arts.
—Develop a discerning eye in all matters.

Musashi's writing, however, is famous for its spareness and directness of expression. He was very careful about each sentence he wrote, and included nothing that we might currently consider "filler." When we consider his life, we see that he wrote nothing that had not been an integral part of his own experience.

Musashi constantly emphasized that the student must develop himself in the Way. The sword was his main vehicle, but he did not study it to the exclusion of all the other arts, or even "all matters." Each art was a discipline for Musashi, and each art informed the other. Another perspective of this same principle is a Zen Buddhist phrase with which Musashi would have been familiar: "Toss this away, and everything will be as it is" (*hoshin shizen*).

The "this" of this phrase is one's prejudice or preference for a single practice or article of that practice, or really anything at all. "Everything will be as it is" refers to the vision of the interior eye that grasps the essence of things.

Musashi had that interior eye, and so it is not surprising that the man who survived over sixty individual matches and the Winter and Summer campaigns at Osaka would be equally at home supervising the placement of rocks, sand, and plants in Akashi.

Musashi's work for the Ogasawara in the fields of defense planning and gardening did not go unnoticed—and, some years later, he would be employed by the Honda clan, who were related to the Ogasawara by marriage, in nearby Himeji. Once again he worked on the delineation of the castle town and designed the gardens of some of its temples, while continually developing his own sword style. Musashi was respected and much sought after by both the Ogasawara and the Honda, and it seems that he spent at least some of the years of his mid- and late thirties living alternately in the two new castle towns of Akashi and Himeji. One imagines that his fame and prestige must have been considerable, and that he was able to preserve the freedom he so loved by managing to maintain the status of "guest" rather than of "samurai."[4]

Both Akashi and Himeji had been the locations of castle towns for centuries. Akashi had been occupied by the Takayama, Hachisuka, Bessho, and Kuroda before the castle was rebuilt by the Ogasawara around 1617. Located near the northeastern end of the Inland Sea, with a mild and even relatively sunny climate, it is still famous today for the sea bream caught in the Akashi Straits between the main Japanese

THE WAY OF THE SWORD AND THE WAY OF THE BRUSH

island of Honshu and the small island of Awaji just to the north. This location also gave Akashi a strategic importance as a port near the entrance to both Kobe and Osaka.

Musashi's distant relatives, the Akamatsu, had built a castle in Himeji as far back as 1350, but the site had been controlled by a number of clans by the time Toyotomi Hideyoshi took control of the town and rebuilt the castle in 1577. Known today as the Hakurojo, or White Heron Castle, it is considered the most beautiful and graceful castle in Japan. After the Battle of Sekigahara, Ieyasu gave control of the castle to Ikeda Terumasa, who changed its name from Himeyama to Himeji. The Honda clan was established at this site in 1617, and it was from this time that Musashi began his work there.

———

During this period, as Musashi found himself with more and more students, he continued to develop his own sword style to include concepts that could be taught, rather than simply intuited by himself. As early as 1604, when he was in Edo (Tokyo), he had written a short "book" entitled *The Mirror of the Way of War*, which was an outline of the Enmei-ryu, or Perfect Enlightenment Style, that he was creating. The first edition of this book contained only eighteen articles, but it was later expanded to thirty-five and bore a strong resemblance to his later works, *The Thirty-five Articles of the Martial Arts* and *The Book of Five Rings*. It emphasized, in particular, taking the initiative—and it was probably a prototype for the latter two works.

The Enmei-ryu was clearly a precursor to Musashi's Two-Sword Style, but other than that, little is understood of it. The word *enmei*, in addition to its meaning of "perfect enlightenment," has connections to a phrase for two kinds of Buddhist wisdom, *daienkyochi* (大円鏡智) and *myokansatsuchi* (妙観察智), which translate respectively as "Great Perfect Mirror Wisdom" and "Wonderful Observation Wisdom." Interestingly, it is also a "pillow word" (or well-known literary referent) for

Akashi in classical poetry, a subject with which Musashi was beginning to be familiar.

One man who became acquainted with the Enmei-ryu at close range was a certain Miyake Gunbei. His story is related in great detail in the *Miyamoto Musashi monogatari nenpyo*, published in 1910. The year was 1621, and Musashi was thirty-eight years old:

In the town of Himeji there was a man famous for his Togun-ryu by the name of Miyake Gunbei. He was a very large man, was very good at the take-down techniques of the Araki-ryu, and had had many experiences in real battle. Gunbei had nothing but contempt for Musashi and laughed at him scornfully. One day, he finally petitioned for a match with Musashi and went to the latter's residence accompanied by three of his companions. They were led together into a fourteen-mat room.

Suddenly Musashi appeared from the narrow corridor that passed by the kitchen. He was casually carrying two wooden swords; one long, one short. Without changing his manner or position, he said, "Now!" upon which Gunbei and the others were thrown into confusion. Musashi added, "Taking on the four of you together would be all right, too." Chastened, Gunbei stepped forward indignantly.

The two faced off at a distance of about seven feet. Finally, Musashi slowly backed up to the corner at the doorway. Gunbei also gradually backed up and took a stance at the sliding paper door to the veranda. Suddenly, Musashi combined his swords into an *enkyoku* (circle), or *gassho* (steeple shape), and advanced toward Gunbei. Gunbei raised his sword over his head in the *jodan* position, advanced, and struck straight downward. Musashi separated his two swords and evaded Gunbei's blow. Combining his swords again and restraining Gunbei's attack, Musashi took a step backward. Gunbei swung his sword free from this restraint, and with a sort of leap, struck again. Musashi repeated his own maneuver, once again restraining Gunbei's sword and backing away. This action was repeated a number of times until Musashi had his back to the wall and appeared to be stuck. This time Gunbei pointed his sword directly at Musashi in the *chudan* position and, sure of his victory, stabbed forward with both hands on the hilt. Musashi yelled, "Watch yourself!", parried Gunbei with the short *tachi* he held in his left hand, and stabbed the man's cheek with the *tachi* he held in his right hand. Gunbei fell on the spot and his shocked companions ran up to him. Musashi calmly brought in some medicine and a strip of cotton cloth, and applied them to Gunbei's wound.

Later, Gunbei bowed to Musashi as a teacher, and held him in deep respect.

This Gunbei[5] was a retainer to Honda Tadamasa, the *daimyo* of Himeji Castle, and was the premier swordsman of the fief. He related later in life that he had known only two frightening moments in his entire career. One was at the Summer Campaign at Osaka Castle when the opposing armies were at the point of contact, and the other was when he first encountered Musashi—that instant when the swordsman appeared with his two lowered swords.

Gunbei had a number of things to be thankful for in this bout. The first was that it had not taken place ten years earlier, when Musashi was still deciding his matches with "extreme prejudice." The experience with Sasaki Kojiro affected Musashi deeply and, after 1612, his individual bouts would never again end in death or the terrible wounds that disabled Yoshioka Seijuro for life. No doubt his growing acquaintance with Buddhism and the arts of tea, poetry, and india ink painting was having an effect. The second was the fact that Gunbei himself was a retainer to the Honda clan, with whom Musashi was on excellent terms. Certainly he would not have seriously injured a retainer to that clan, regardless of the man's arrogance and bad manners. And third, one might say that Gunbei had been fortunate enough to have really seen a "comparison of technique" in this bout, as Musashi led, or actually, drew him around the room, demonstrating his style. It was only Gunbei's impetuousness that led him into the tip of the better man's sword; and had Gunbei not brought along his friends, in front of whom he could not back down, he might have gotten away with only a bruised ego. As it turned out, Musashi was even kind enough to tend to Gunbei's wound, an act of sympathy and concern.

Musashi was now walking steadily on the path that had been prescribed for the true warrior since Heian times in Japan, and in China even back to the time of Confucius. This was the path that included both the arts of war and the arts of peace (*bunbu no michi*), and he would become perhaps more accomplished in this ideal than any other warrior in Japan's history.

THE KYOTO RENAISSANCE

In the opening pages of *The Book of Five Rings*, Musashi states that "I have never had a teacher while studying the Ways of the various arts and accomplishments, or in anything at all." This is remarkable coming from a man who was not only one of the most singular swordsmen of his time, but also an extraordinarily skilled painter, sculptor, and metallurgist. As we have seen, he was also well acquainted with poetry—especially the classical style of the Heian period (794–1185)—and the Way of Tea; and he was adept at the recitation of Noh drama, garden design, and perhaps even carpentry. If he had had no teachers and lived his life in the solitary way that is so often depicted, how could he have become accomplished in so many of the arts?

It is important to note that Musashi, while eccentric and uncompromising in many ways, was certainly not the near-sociopath that his detractors have made him out to be. He was, after all, on good terms with Ogasawara Tadazane and both Honda Tadamasa and Tadatoki, and one of his still-extant letters indicates that he was friendly with one or two other *daimyo* as well. Such men were at the very top of the hierarchy in a very stratified world. Musashi, however, was an intellectually and artistically curious man of astonishing talents, and he lived at a time when communication among the various levels of society had been opened dramatically. Generals, wealthy merchants, and talented artisans might now sit together and mingle during the tea ceremony in a way that earlier would have been almost impossible. Artistic individuals like Musashi had many opportunities for contact with each other and with those who appreciated their talents. Art transcended social class in Japan of the seventeenth century as perhaps in no other time in history, and in the capital of Kyoto—an easy two or three days' walk from Himeji and Akashi—this tendency was concentrated like no other place in the world.

Musashi was active during a time aptly called the Kyoto Renaissance, a period of about a century, from 1550 to 1650. After suffering a devastating century and a half of civil wars during which countless art treasures were destroyed, ancient temples and buildings burned, and libraries lost forever, Japan was brought back to unification and eventual peace following the decisive battles at Sekigahara and Osaka. After so many years of social upheaval, this peace brought a surge in economic prosperity and a flourishing of the arts in almost every arena. Castle architecture blossomed, there was a renewed interest in classical poetry and painting, the art of the tea ceremony reached its height, the world of ceramics spread in new directions, and schools offering training in the martial arts proliferated, with every new disciple striking out on his own and hanging up his own shingle. How the various players of this period influenced Musashi is not documented, but considering his artistic talent and curiosity, his insistence that his students learn all the arts, and the time that he spent in the urban centers of the Kansai area, it is fitting that we look briefly at two men representative of the period with whom he is very likely to have associated.

At the aesthetic center of the Kyoto Renaissance was Hon'ami Koetsu (1558–1637), a man whom tradition, if not recorded evidence, links with Musashi. Koetsu came from a family of sword polishers and appraisers—well known in that field since the fourteenth century—and was much in demand for his skills in this work. Moreover, there were few other arts that he did not practice. Granted by the shogun an area of land—Takagamine, or Takaramine—just outside Kyoto, he established an art colony comprised of fifty-five friends and relatives that would act as a sort of launching pad for everything from papermaking to lacquerware to pottery. Koetsu himself is best known today for his calligraphy and pottery, but his strong ties to the samurai sword and his intense and friendly personality would have made him an engaging companion for Musashi. The swordsman's extraordinary talent, broad interests, and remarkable character, on the other hand, would likely have seemed to the older artist like a fresh breeze on a hot summer day.

Koetsu's wide-ranging artistic pursuits were likely an inspiration to Musashi. The refined aesthete's ties to Noh recitation may have sparked Musashi's later participation in that art; and one of Koetsu's friends, Sakon Tayu, was head of the Kanze school of Noh. It is not unlikely that Musashi would have made his acquaintance, along with many others in the arts. Among Koetsu's associates were also Tawara Sotatsu, the cloth designer and painter; Furuta Oribe, the warrior and tea master; Raku Don'yu, the potter to the tea masters; and Hayashi Razan, the Confucian scholar. Musashi could not have helped being influenced, even if only peripherally, by this society of talented men, and Koetsu's reputed strong character and intense dislike of greed would have fit well with the same tendencies in the swordsman's own personality.

Musashi insisted that through an intense study and practice of the Way of the Martial Arts, the Ways of all other arts would be understood. It is possible that these thoughts began to form in his mind as he talked to the old sword polisher-turned-aesthete at the Takagamine artists' colony at the edge of Kyoto, and that he found a certain confirmation of them as he sat down at a potter's wheel or took up a metallurgist's hammer himself. Visits to Takagamine would have given Musashi the physical material to work his own budding ideas into the reality of art. In this way, the shadow of Hon'ami Koetsu seems to pass over the pages of *The Book of Five Rings*, in subtle but convincing hues.

Takuan Soho (1573–1645), also traditionally linked with Musashi, was a Zen Buddhist priest of the Rinzai sect and another influential figure in the Kyoto Renaissance. Like Koetsu, Takuan was a polymath who excelled in calligraphy, painting, poetry, gardening, and the tea ceremony. He must have also enjoyed being in the kitchen, for it is said that he invented the pickle that is a constant in the Japanese diet and to this day retains his name. Takuan was a prodigious writer whose collected works fill six volumes. He was an advisor to the emperor and shogun alike, and became abbot of the Daitokuji, a major Zen temple in Kyoto, at the unlikely age of just thirty-five. Musashi would have appreciated the man's personality. Unlike a number of other Buddhist prelates who would, from time to time, feel a necessity to toady to the shogunate, Takuan stood his idealistic ground and got in trouble for it. In one such incident, the Purple Robe Affair of 1628,[6] he was punished and eventually sent to exile in the northern part of Japan; he was not pardoned until 1632. He had enough of the "bad boy" in him to have appealed to the former *gaki daisho* of Hirafuku and Miyamoto.

The tradition that names Takuan a mentor to Musashi is brought into focus in Takuan's essay, "The Mysterious Record of Immovable Wisdom."[7] This essay is written not to Musashi but to Yagyu Munenori, the head of the Edo branch of the Shinkage-ryu of swordsmanship.

It deals in part with the relationship of mind, body, and technique, a subject also covered extensively in *The Book of Five Rings*. In the essay, Takuan writes:

> When you first notice the sword that is moving to strike you, if you think of meeting that sword just as it is, your mind will stop at the sword in just that position, your own movements will be undone, and you will be cut down by your opponent. . . .
>
> What is called Fudo Myo-o [a wrathful manifestation of the Buddha Vairocana][8] is said to be one's unmoving mind and an unvacillating body. *Unvacillating* means not being detained by anything.
>
> Glancing at something and not stopping the mind is called *immovable*. This is because when the mind stops at something, as the breast is filled with various judgements, there are various movements within it. When its movements cease, the stopping mind moves, but does not move at all.
>
> If ten men, each with a sword, come at you with swords slashing, if you parry each sword without stopping the mind at each action, and go from one to the next, you will not be lacking in a proper action for every one of the ten. . . .
>
> [T]he action of Spark and Stone . . . underscores the point that the mind should not be detained by things; it says that even with speed it is essential that the mind does not stop. When the mind stops, it will be grasped by the opponent. On the other hand, if the mind contemplates being fast and goes into quick action, it will be captured by its own contemplation. . . .
>
> Putting the mind in one place is called *falling into one-sidedness*. One-sidedness is said to be bias in one place. Correctness is in moving about anywhere. The Correct Mind shows itself by extending the mind throughout the body. It is not biased in any one place. . . .

The effort not to stop the mind in just one place—this is discipline. Not stopping the mind is object and essence. Put nowhere, it will be everywhere. Even in moving the mind outside the body, if it is sent in one direction, it will be lacking in nine others. If the mind is not restricted to just one direction, it will be in all ten.

Not surprisingly, the relationship of mind, body, and technique is one of the main, mostly implicit themes running throughout *The Book of Five Rings*, and it is important to note that Takuan wrote these words during his exile at Kaminoyama in Dewa, sometime between 1629 and 1632. It was in 1631 that Musashi was also in Dewa, probably visiting Takuan and discussing exactly these matters, as well as giving a demonstration of his style to the *daimyo* Matsudaira Dewa no kami Ienaka. Thus, Musashi was likely every bit as influential on Takuan's writings on the sword as Takuan was on Musashi's writing on Emptiness in the final chapter of *The Book of Five Rings*. One can easily imagine Musashi and Takuan talking quietly together, each gaining from the other's experiences. Nor would they have limited themselves to discussions over tea. Both men believed absolutely in the value of actual experience, and the subject matter would inevitably have led them from the sitting mat to the *dojo*. Born into a samurai family, Takuan must have held his wooden sword with relish. Later, he would pick up the brush and write one of the most important works on Zen and the sword in Japanese literature.

While the passage quoted above from this essay in no way exhausts the subject of the relationship between the sword and Zen Buddhism, it certainly expresses the core of the subject, and it affected Yagyu Munenori so deeply that he paraphrased the work more than once in his own book, *The Life-Giving Sword* (*Heiho Kadensho*, literally, *The Book of Clan Traditions on the Martial Arts*). Later, we will take a closer look at the circle of influence that connected these three men.

In the end, Takuan may have had yet another effect on Musashi's life. As early as 1603, the year before Musashi defeated the Yoshioka clan, Takuan became good friends with Hosokawa Yusai, the general, diplomat, and man of great taste, whose approach to scholastics was strikingly similar to Musashi's approach to the arts in its eclecticism. The friendly relationship between the priest and the Hosokawa clan would span three generations of that warrior family, and Musashi's name no doubt came into their conversations and letters a number of times before Musashi himself went to live with the clan in his final years.

Musashi's association with the artists and Buddhist priests of the Kyoto Renaissance cannot be accurately documented, but neither can it be dismissed. It is clear in terms of his own development—from his rural birth to his rise to the status of both undefeated swordsman and multitalented artist—he would have had, if not teachers, then companions and associates on the Way. Kyoto is and always has been a closely interconnected society, with strong ties among people of high aesthetic abilities and tastes. Nor was this social network limited to Kyoto. Even in his wanderings around the country, from northern Kyushu to Edo, Musashi may very well have encountered eccentric Zen artists (his contemporary, the eccentric Zen painter Fugai, comes to mind), just as he encountered the sixty-odd martial artists he would fight and defeat.

FAMILY NAME

By 1619, Musashi began to have concerns directly connected with neither swordsmanship nor art. He had early on understood that having a family would be an impediment to his progress in swordsmanship and, in fact, to all other Ways. Having chosen the life of a perpetual *shugyosha* naturally precluded a long-term relationship with any woman, and having children was out of the question. Although Musashi was not an only son, he no doubt felt a certain duty to carry on the family line, for the importance of continuing the family name is paramount in Japan. It is, for example, not uncommon for a family without sons to adopt the husband of the eldest daughter, thus insuring continuity of lineage and the family name for at least another generation. The bridegroom, of course, would have to be the second or third son of his own family in order not to jeopardize his own family tree.

By the time Musashi was thirty-six, he too felt that he could no longer avoid this responsibility. Thus, at some point in time during this year, as he was riding a horse in the area of Amagasaki in Banshu, he encountered a young horse-pack driver by the name of Mikinosuke, who seemed to have ability far beyond his present station in life. Intuiting that the boy might present both a solution to his own succession problems and an opportunity to mentor a first-rate warrior, Musashi asked Mikinosuke if he would like to be educated as an apprentice under the swordsman's own tutorship. The youth cheerfully responded that he would be happy to do so if it weren't for the fact that he had two elderly parents to support. These were his circumstances, however, and he could by no means abandon his father and mother.

With this response, Musashi was even more impressed with Mikinosuke's qualities, and interrupted the progress of his journey to visit the home of the boy's parents. After some discussion and reassurances, he provided the old couple with enough money to take care of themselves, and departed with a new apprentice and heir.

Musashi's intuition had not been off the mark. Although less outgoing and aggressive than Musashi, Mikinosuke studied and practiced hard, becoming an excellent scholar and swordsman. He later became a page to Musashi's acquaintance, Honda Tadatoki, who relied on the youth for his many different qualities. Tadatoki had since become the second husband of Senhime, the daughter of the Tokugawa shogun Hidetada, and his stipend had been increased substantially. Among the responsibilities Mikinosuke held to this wealthy lord was that of sword instructor.[9] This job had formerly been Musashi's, but he had passed the position on to his adopted son.

Tragically for both Mikinosuke and Musashi, the young man's

career was cut short by the unexpected death of Tadatoki at the age of thirty-one on 7 May 1626. Mikinosuke was in Edo when Tadatoki passed away in Himeji and, upon hearing the news, quickly started his return to his lord's domain. Musashi, who was residing in Osaka at the time, somehow felt that Mikinosuke was coming to bid him a final farewell. To those around him he stated that if his son should come to visit him, he would be provided with "a grand meal as a memento of this life."

It happened exactly as Musashi had intuited. Mikinosuke stopped in Osaka, and the two of them exchanged farewell cups of saké without mentioning the event that would inevitably soon occur. The young man then left for Himeji, and committed *junshi*, or ritual suicide in sympathy for one's lord, on the following day. He was twenty-three years old.

Miyamoto Mikinosuke was known to be handsome, bright, and sensitive to the world of literature. He left the following death poem:

> Beckoned by the storm
>   on the peak
> of Mount Tatsuta,
>   the red leaves in the valley, too,
>   are falling.

———

Two years before Mikinosuke's death, Musashi adopted another young boy, Iori, whom he met while passing through an isolated plain called Shohojigawara in far off Dewa. Musashi first encountered Iori selling mudfish by the side of the road. When the swordsman said that he would like one, the boy replied, "Take the whole bunch," shoved the bucket of fish into Musashi's hands and left without looking back.[10] On the evening of the following day, Musashi lost his way on the plain, and stopped to ask for lodging at a small hut not far from the path. The

THE WAY OF THE SWORD AND THE WAY OF THE BRUSH

same boy, Iori, appeared and reluctantly gave him permission to stay. That night, as Musashi was lying sleeplessly awake, he heard the sound of a sword being sharpened in the next room. Suspicious of the boy who had already acted eccentrically enough, Musashi yawned loudly, as a warning that he was quite awake. At this Iori laughed out loud and accused the traveler of being afraid of a skinny twelve-year-old child. In the discussion that followed, Musashi came to understand that the boy's father had just died and, being too small to carry the body up the hill to bury it alongside the man's wife, the creative and dutiful child was preparing to cut the body in half, so that he could transport it to the proper place.

This was the second act of filial piety that Musashi had encountered in the youths he would adopt, and it must have impressed him deeply. He and his own father had not gotten along well, and, as we have seen, the young Bennosuke had left Munisai's house at an early age. Iori's determination and resourcefulness affected the swordsman so much that, after carrying the body of the old man up the hill in one piece and giving him a proper burial, he asked the young boy if he would like to become an apprentice. Iori mistook Musashi's intentions and declared that he would never take the status of a servant, for it was his dream to become a samurai with a horse and spear. If he could not attain that, he said, he was better off remaining as he was—alone but free. Musashi assured him that he would train him to become a great warrior and realize his dream, and so an agreement was reached.

Musashi did extremely well by Iori. Only a few years later, when he was offered the position of retainer in Akashi by Ogasawara Tadazane, Musashi felt confident enough to propose that Iori be employed in his stead. Musashi had no desire to become an official himself. To do so he would have to give up his freedom and the relative independence that warriors had enjoyed during the Warring States period (1333–1568). He realized, however, that very few men were cut out to live the life he had outlined for himself. Pouring all of his knowledge and training into Iori, he prepared the boy to be the best man he could for this new age of peace and bureaucratic management. In this way, Miyamoto Iori was taken into service as the *daimyo*'s personal retainer to Ogasawara Tadazane in 1626 in the castle town of Akashi, the same year that Mikinosuke committed ritual suicide in Himeji. Clearly, Musashi had accomplished more in those two cities than just town planning and garden building. His personality, circumspection, and many talents had brought him a tremendous amount of respect in the circles of political power as well.

Iori's career was destined to be a long and distinguished one. By 1631 he had risen to the position of chief retainer, although he was still barely twenty years old. Musashi had also taught the boy swordsmanship and courage, and at the Battle of Shimabara in 1637, to which we will return, Iori was given extraordinary praise by Kuroda Takayuki, *daimyo* of the neighboring Fukuoka fief, for rendering distinguished meritorious deeds. After this battle, his stipend was increased to four thousand *koku*, and when the Ogasawara clan was transferred to Kokura in Kyushu, Iori was granted land on Mount Tamuke, on the eastern side of the castle town. It was there that he would erect the Kokura Hibun, the monument engraved with the story of Musashi's life, eight years after Musashi's death.

Miyamoto Iori died on 8 March 1678. The Miyamoto family continued to inherit the occupation of senior retainers, but Iori's bloodline finally ran out in the sixth generation. In the end, the younger brother of the lord of the Nitta clan, a branch clan of the Ogasawara, was officially declared the seventh generation, taking over the family status of the house that Musashi had begun to build on the plain of Shohojigawara.

A REAL LIVE HUMAN BEING

In 1628, the same year that Takuan was punished in the Purple Robe Affair, Musashi was at Nagoya Castle in the province of Owari at the request of Tokugawa Yoshinao, Ieyasu's seventh son and the *daimyo* of that fief. Asked to give a demonstration of his sword style, Musashi had a match with a skilled martial artist of what was now called the Owari clan. Musashi used two wooden swords and, scissoring the sword of his opponent, kept him from performing any meaningful action at all. Without harming the man, he led him in a circle around the *dojo* and commented, "This is how a match should be conducted," demonstrating that with his style there was no need for injury. Yoshinao had been looking for something a bit more dramatic from the man who had defeated the Demon of the Western Provinces, however, and showed no further interest in Musashi's style.[11]

Just at the point of leaving Nagoya, Musashi saw a single warrior approaching from a distance and remarked to his disciples, "At last I've met a real live human being." As the two men came closer, they called out each other's names, even though this was the first time they had ever met. The records then state that

> [T]he two men quickly opened their hearts to each other as though they had been friends for a hundred years. The man took Musashi to his mansion, where they traded saké cups, played *go*, but never once crossed swords in a comparison of technique. Later, Musashi explained the psychology of their meeting: "This mutual recognition might be called a subtle mental attitude or a transcendental principle. The fact that we did not cross swords was a mutual acknowledgment in silence of one another's abilities."

The man in this short episode was Yagyu Hyogonosuke Toshiyoshi (1577–1650), head of the Yagyu-ryu in Owari and sword instructor to the above-mentioned Tokugawa Yoshinao. He is the only member of the Yagyu clan actually recorded to have met Musashi. It was his uncle, Munenori, who wrote *The Life-Giving Sword* and who was a friend to the priest Takuan. As the Yagyu family would become the premier clan in the world of swordsmanship during Musashi's time and for a number of generations thereafter, it is important to take at least a brief look at its rise to fame.

The Yagyu clan has traced its ancestry back to Sugawara no Michizane (845–903), the great saint of literature, thus tying it to arts other than the martial. It is not known when the clan actually moved into the village of Yagyu—partially hidden among the low mountains on the borders of Nara and Kyoto prefectures—but, by the 1600s, they seem to have resided there for centuries. The area had traditionally spawned men of great sword abilities, and the Yagyu figured strongly in this tradition.

Yagyu Muneyoshi Sekishusai (1529–1606) was considered the finest swordsman in the area around the capital of Kyoto when his friend, the spearman Hozoin In'ei, arranged to have him fight in a bout with Kamiizumi Ise no kami Nobutsuna (1508–77), a man whose stature is now legendary among sword practitioners. The contest, which some consider the inception of the Yagyu Shinkage-ryu, was held at the Hozoin temple and was over in minutes. Paralyzed by Nobutsuna's stare, the famous Sekishusai was unable to even raise his sword. He was thirty-five years old at the time; Nobutsuna, fifty-five. Both In'ei and Sekishusai begged to become Nobutsuna's disciples. Nobutsuna agreed, and then spent the following two years at Sekishusai's manor. At the end of that time, in April of 1565, the swordmaster awarded Sekishusai with a certificate noting that he had passed on all the hidden traditions of his style to the younger man. He also passed on his attitude that the study of swordsmanship was not to be used for the purpose of killing people, but rather to invigorate both a man and his opponent. Sekishusai would not forget this, and would later become famous, not only for his extraordinary ability and modesty,[12] but also for his philosophy of the "death-dealing sword" and the "life-giving sword." Sekishusai was already a master of the Toda Style of swordsmanship and, after Nobutsuna's departure, dedicated the rest of his life to developing an amalgamation of styles, the culmination of which was

THE WAY OF THE SWORD AND THE WAY OF THE BRUSH

his famous Muto-ryu, or No-Sword Style. In this style, the practitioner cultivates his intuitive powers and prowess to the point of being able to arrest his opponent's stroke just before its execution. This is done by grasping either the hilt or blade of the opponent's sword in one's own bare hands—joined in a prayerlike (fingers extended, not entwined) lock and, needless to say, requires an extraordinary sense of timing.

Sekishusai had eleven children—five boys and six girls. His eldest son, Yoshikatsu, had been devastatingly wounded in battle and was unable to follow his father as successor to his school. That honor would go, in part, to his youngest son, Munenori (1571–1646), a man skilled in swordsmanship and endowed with a superior sense of political tact. In 1594, Tokugawa Ieyasu invited the sixty-six-year-old Sekishusai and his son Munenori to Kyoto for an exhibition and was so impressed by the old man's skill that he quickly declared himself a disciple and wrote up a contract pledging his support for the Yagyu clan. Sekishusai, however, declined the offer for himself, wishing to proffer the position of instructor to his young son instead. Ieyasu agreed and, in this one stroke, the Yagyu became a part of the establishment, already setting a precedent for a hereditary position with the Tokugawa.

Munenori's career is well documented. After his appointment, in addition to instructing three generations of Tokugawa shoguns, he also performed meritorious deeds for them in battle—probably involving espionage at Sekigahara, but also actually saving Hidetada's life during the Summer Campaign at Osaka Castle. His stipend was steadily increased, as was his rank, and he eventually became a respected advisor, along with his old mentor, Takuan, to the third shogun, Iemitsu.

But although Munenori established the Yagyu lineage at Edo, he was perhaps not his father's true favorite. Sekishusai had devoted himself to the art of the sword and had involved himself with politics only when absolutely necessary for the continuance of the clan. Munenori, on the other hand, while showing a strong Zen Buddhist influence on his sword style, became progressively involved with the Tokugawa government, from Hidetada's shogunate through Iemitsu's. No public quarreling was ever recorded, but in his retirement, old Sekishusai may well have wondered where his son was headed with all these dealings outside the family's tradition of swordsmanship.

Regardless of the cause, it was Yagyu Hyogonosuke Toshiyoshi, Yoshikatsu's son, that Sekishusai initiated into the secrets of the Yagyu Shinkage-ryu, and it was to this grandson that he gave the manuscript of recorded secrets conferred on him by Nobutsuna. Thus it was Hyogonosuke, not Munenori, who became Sekishusai's successor. And, after a brief period of service under Kato Kiyomasa in Kumamoto, it was this same Hyogonosuke who would become the instructor of the Owari branch of the Tokugawa and who eventually would meet Musashi and enjoy an afternoon of saké, *go*, and conversation with the famous swordsman.

It is difficult to imagine the feelings or the conversation that must have passed between these two that afternoon. Hyogonosuke had mastered the Muto-ryu and had studied both the Shingon and Zen sects of Buddhism as roads that might lead to greater concentration in his art. His reputation as a swordsman surpassed that of even his more politically connected and famous uncle in Edo, and his school is considered by many to have been the orthodox Yagyu line. Musashi, meanwhile, had established his reputation as one of the absolutely finest swordsmen in the country and an artist of unique talents. For all the security that Hyogonosuke and others of his clan must have felt at the patronage of the Tokugawa, one wonders if this master of the Owari branch of the Yagyu did not feel a great respect—and perhaps a pinch of envy—concerning Musashi's independence and freedom.

At any rate, these two men, both accomplished in their arts and steeped in years of discipline, must have shared a deep appreciation of the other's experience. No doubt their disciples were anxiously waiting in the wings for the match that would prove one man superior to the other, but they would be disappointed. What the two swordsmen had understood was that each was a master who was truly beyond any dualistic consideration or comparison. There was no need to prove their skill, and so they simply passed the afternoon as they did. Any voyeuristic hopes that their disciples might have had—or any that we may have today—would go unfulfilled.

On to Kokura

Even after Sekigahara and the battles at Osaka Castle, the political map was changing. The Tokugawa were always seeking opportunities to bolster their own position and were constantly making efforts to secure total hegemony. One of those efforts would affect Musashi directly, and took place in Kyushu, not far from the very place where he had made himself so famous years earlier.

Kato Kiyomasa, who was one of the Toyotomi family's greatest allies and well known for his ferocity and courage in battle, had died, perhaps as early as 1611. Now, although Kato had sided with the Tokugawa at Sekigahara and was given a woman in marriage who had been brought up by Ieyasu, his real feelings and loyalty toward the shogunate were never quite felt to be totally reliable. When he died, possibly by poisoning, his son Tadahiro took charge of their fief at Kumamoto in Kyushu, but with an uneasy status in regard to the Tokugawa. Finally, while traveling from Kumamoto to Edo in 1632, Tadahiro was arrested and accused of conspiring against Tokugawa Iemitsu. In the end, his fief was dismantled and he was sent into exile at Tsuruoka in Dewa, where he would die twenty-one years later.

In 1632, Musashi's old friend, Ogasawara Tadazane, was transferred by the Tokugawa from Akashi to Kokura, the geographically sensitive fief at the straits between the main Japanese island of Honshu and the island of Kyushu, which was the center of foreign trade and the point closest to Korea and the Chinese mainland. This fief was vacated in

October by the Hosokawa, who, it will be recalled, had ruled the area during the time of the fight at Ganryu Island. They, in turn, were moved into the larger fief at Kumamoto, to take over what the Kato had formerly governed.

In 1634, Musashi came to visit his adopted son Iori and his old friend Tadazane, and was received warmly by the new *daimyo* of Kokura Castle. Predictably, a sword match was arranged with one of Tadazane's own instructors, no doubt to satisfy Tadazane's curiosity about the man's ability. This was Takada Mataemon, who was five years younger than Musashi and a skilled practitioner of the Hozoin Style of spear technique. The bout was set up and witnessed personally by Tadazane—but, after three rounds, Mataemon suddenly threw down his spear and yelled, "I'm beat!" Tadazane was somewhat surprised and quickly reminded Mataemon that no victor had yet been determined. Mataemon replied that a spear, because of its length, should have a sevenfold advantage over a sword, and then continued, "I have the longer weapon, but am still unable to win in three rounds. This is the same as losing." Musashi had made no effort to injure the man, but had simply shown him the futility of his attacks. He was fifty-one years old at this time. Once again Tadazane offered Musashi employment, and once again the latter refused. Instead he accepted guest status at Kokura, with its concomitant freedom of movement.

Much has been said about Musashi's independence and, in many cases, these comments have been critical. Some writers ignore his desire for independence, and instead declare that he was too dirty and strange-looking to be hired by anyone. Here are descriptions of Musashi from the *Tanji hokin hikki* and the *Watanabe koan taiwaki,* respectively, that added fire to the fuel of this theory.

> When Musashi was young, he was afflicted with a carbuncle on his head, and for this reason, said it was unsightly to shave his forehead (as was the style at that time). He went his entire life

THE WAY OF THE SWORD AND THE WAY OF THE BRUSH

without shaving his forehead and instead went about with a full head of hair. His eyes were a yellowish brown and sometimes shone like amber. According to his disciples, he always cleaned himself with a damp towel and he never once took a bath.

———

Musashi's worst point was that he hated the foot and bathtubs and went his whole life without bathing. When he went outside barefoot and his feet got dirty, he simply wiped them off. For this reason, his clothes were soiled and, in order to mask how soiled they were, he wore clothing that was velvet on both sides.

But Musashi's constant association with the Ogasawara, the Honda, and later the Hosokawa *daimyo* would argue strongly against such stories. Rumors about Musashi were often repeated, embellished, and finally turned into stories bordering on the fantastic (see Appendix 1). It should also be remembered that Japanese culture places an extraordinary emphasis on personal cleanliness and that, with the way rumors are spread, any infraction of the rules would likely be discussed and exaggerated as the stories circulated from village to village. Nevertheless, the most reliable portraits that still exist of Musashi show him well dressed in normal garb. His storied aversion to bathtubs may have been a result of his early days as a *shugyosha* wishing to avoid sudden attacks, but it is doubtful that even Tadazane would have deigned to come close to him had he not been clean and presentable.

———

A number of events occurred during Musashi's stay with the Ogasawara in Kokura that give an indication of his character. One is the time that a cook who thought Musashi arrogant decided to defeat the swordsman by lying in wait for him and taking him by surprise. As it happened, the man did hide and wait for Musashi, but just as he saw his chance and made his attack, Musashi dodged the blow and struck the cook's arm with the back of his sword. The man never picked up a cleaver again, but escaped with his life and likely counted himself as lucky. Musashi had defended himself but had not dealt the cook as heavy a punishment for his presumptuousness as other swordsmen might have.

In another case there was a martial artist residing in Kokura by the name of Aoki Kuwaemon. This man was widely known to be very capable with the sword. When insulted by someone and moved to contest the provocation with a match, however, he would produce a gaudy red-lacquered wooden sword from a cloth bag as the weapon of his choice. Musashi felt that this sort of display was both pretentious and vulgar, and when he met the man, he told him in no uncertain terms that he was foolish, adding that using such a sword in a real match was unthinkable. As he could see Kuwaemon's anger rising, he put a grain of rice on the forelocks of a page, and then split the grain in two with one stroke. Musashi was well known for his ability in *tsumeru*, or "holding back" at just the right moment, and Kuwaemon was advanced enough to realize that this ability suggested even deeper ones that were far beyond his understanding. Musashi then left the younger man with a caustic but instructive remark: "Though your skill is ripe, it will be difficult to beat an opponent with such a sword. Having it lacquered red is outrageous." Swordsmanship was a serious business to Musashi. It was not something to be made into a sideshow or an amusement, and he was frankly critical of those who would make it such. In the Wind chapter of *The Book of Five Rings*, he wrote: "[O]ther schools get along with this [swordsmanship] as a performance art, as a method of making a living, as a colorful decoration or as a means of forcing flowers into bloom. Can this be the true Way if it has been made into a salable item?"

KUMOI

Guest status at Kokura assured Musashi the considerable freedom he required; indeed, his need to travel seems to have matched that of Matsuo Basho, the great haiku poet who would be born the year before Musashi died. Even after establishing a comfortable home base in Kokura, he continued his old life on the road.

While in the city of Matsue in the coastal area of Izumo in 1638, the swordsman was invited to give a demonstration of his skill by Lord Matsudaira Izumo no kami Naomasa. There he defeated the most skilled sword practitioner in the entire fief in a bout in which neither man was injured. Not quite believing that this had been accomplished with such apparent ease, Lord Matsudaira himself took up a wooden sword and declared himself ready for a match. Musashi took up two wooden swords and chased Naomasa around the area three times before driving him into a corner. The match finished, Musashi went on his way.

The year before this event, Musashi had traveled to the lively new capital of Edo on business that had nothing to do with swordsmanship at all.

———

Although he had emphasized that a man truly serious about developing his swordsmanship should stay away from women, and even wrote in his final advice, "The Way of Walking Alone," that one should "have no heart for approaching the path of love," about the time he was fifty-four, he seems to have been a frequent visitor to the Yoshiwara courtesan quarters in Edo, and to have even fallen in love with a young woman by the name of Kumoi. This Kumoi was classified as a *tsubone*, which was the second-lowest of the six classes of the fifteen hundred courtesans and prostitutes in the Yoshiwara at the time. This relationship was recorded by Shoji Kasutomi, the sixth-generation descendant of the founder of the Yoshiwara, Shoji Jin'emon, in his book, *Dobo goen*, published in 1720. According to this work: "Among the women of Kawai Kenzaemon in Shinmachi, there was a lady-in-waiting by the name of Kumoi. At the time, she became familiar with Miyamoto Musashi, the master of two swords. She also frequented the brothel of Jinzaburo in the same quarter."[13]

It should not be surprising that Musashi might have sought the affections of a woman,[14] however briefly, particularly in his middle age. He would write that we must know "all the Ways," and he had likely been invited to courtesan houses a number of times by artist friends in Kyoto and elsewhere. It is also not surprising that Musashi would choose a courtesan to dally with, as commitment to a family and other emotional and practical ties would be out of the question, and his freedom—given the restrictions of her trade and his limited income—would remain intact. Certainly, he was not "swept away" by this affair, and at a later date would write the following poem:

When it comes to love,
    Don't write letters,
Don't write poems.
    For even a single penny,
    Watch your money carefully.

Kumoi seems to have been playful and popular with the women of her trade, and considering Musashi's sustained interests in the arts, she was probably not entirely uncultured. But if we have been reading between the lines, we will have noticed that Musashi, too, had his lighter side, and may have developed his relationship with Kumoi strictly for the sake of the transient human pleasures it afforded.

While Musashi was in Edo, circumstances were conspiring to set the stage for a large and important battle in distant Kyushu. Matsukura Shigemasa, the *daimyo* of Shimabara in Hizen, had been another ally of the Toyotomi before that family's annihilation at Osaka; and, as in the case of Kato Kiyomasa, his loyalty to the Tokugawa government had never really been proven. When Shigemasa died in 1630, his son, Shigeharu, ruled the fief in such an economically and politically repressive way that it became an embarrassment even to the other *daimyo* in Kyushu. His extraordinarily heavy hand became too much for the peasants to bear and in 1637 they banded together in revolt. In this, they were joined by Christians of the nearby Amakusa area, who had found a messianic figure in the seventeen-year-old youth Masuda Tokisada, whom they called Amakusa Shiro. People of the new Christian faith were most heavily concentrated in Kyushu, and had been persecuted for some time under both the local laws of the *daimyo* of Amakusa, Terasawa Katataka, and the anti-Christian promulgations of the Tokugawa government. These two groups—the poorest farmers in Japan and the harassed Christians—which had probably never been completely distinct, now gathered together in Hara Castle in the Shimabara Peninsula for a last stand.

Given the Tokugawa clan's need for total control of the country, these actions alone would likely have caused the government to directly oppose those ensconced in the castle. But, adding insult to injury, included in the opposition forces were a number of seasoned veteran samurai of Konishi Yukinaga, a leader of the Toyotomi forces at Sekigahara and a man closely connected to Ukita Hideie. Yukinaga had been captured and beheaded after Sekigahara, but many of his troops, who had gained great experience during the invasion of Korea, the Battle of Sekigahara, and the Osaka Castle campaign, remained loyal to the memory of their lord (who, incidentally, had been baptized as a Christian as early as 1583). The time was ripe for their final obliteration.

This combined group of rebels in Hara Castle numbered over thirty-seven thousand men. The Tokugawa government ordered the *daimyo* of Kyushu to raise an army to attack the castle and put down the rebellion. The state-sanctioned troops eventually numbered over one hundred thousand, and the Ogasawara, of course, were among their numbers.

When, in the spring of 1637, Musashi received news of the imminent action in Kyushu involving troops with whom he was connected, he made immediate arrangements to join the fray. Just before departing Edo, he took his leave of Kumoi. According to the *Dobo goen*, "When he was about to leave for (Kyushu), he went to Jinzaburo's house in order to take his leave from Kumoi, and prepared his departure from the brothel."

Musashi put a bag that had been woven for him by the affectionate Kumoi on two "spatulas," and put it on his back as a sort of banner. Then, wearing a black satin *haori* she had also sewn for him, on the breast of which was a red fawn of wadded silk, he departed the Yoshiwara pleasure quarters. A crowd of courtesans came to see him off. After this rather unusual departure, which must have put a smile on everyone's face, perhaps even Musashi's own, he rode straight to Kyushu. It is not known if he ever returned, nor is anything about Kumoi recorded after this event. There can be little doubt, however, about what would have been in her heart as she turned back to Jinzaemon's when Musashi's figure had finally disappeared. She had had intimate access to the more tender side of a man who was to make so strong a mark on Japanese culture that his legend would live on for centuries. Kumoi had indeed known a "real live human being."

———

At Shimabara, Musashi was appointed, possibly in deference to his age, as an inspector of the shogun's staff under the Kuroda clan. His adopted son, Iori, was made a commander of one of the units of the Ogasa-wara, which, however, had been placed toward the rear of the action.

The action did not go especially well for the government troops. They may have suffered some overconfidence in their own ability and some lack of confidence in their Tokugawa-appointed commander, Itakura Shigemasa. But they would not have wished to rally with the unsavory Matsukura Shigeharu. The troops attacking Hara Castle lacked enthusiasm and sufficient coordination. When the Tokugawa government made a show of changing commanders, Itakura led a des-perate attack on the castle walls and was killed for his efforts. At this, the Tokugawa sent even more troops and gave the command to Mat-sudaira Nobutsuna, who, on 14 April 1638, stormed the castle and put all those who had survived the attack to the sword. Soon afterward, Mat-sukura Shigeharu was ordered to commit *harakiri*, probably as much for his connections with the Toyotomi as for causing the revolt with his severe oppression of the farmers. His son was subsequently banished to the island of Shikoku and his fief was awarded to others.

Both Musashi and Iori must have chafed at their relatively safe posi-tions among the attacking forces. Iori eventually was able to maneuver his troops to the front and achieved a number of meritorious deeds for which he was well rewarded. Musashi, on the other hand, as a staff inspector, had to hold back. Finally, unable to hold back any longer, he joined in the attack at the base of the castle. With this demonstration of gratitude and loyalty to the Ogasawara, however, he was struck and wounded by a rock hurled from the castle ramparts. His recovery would not take long, but it did remove him from the action for the rest of the siege.

After the fall of the castle, Musashi returned to Kokura and made it his base of operations for the next two years. In 1640, however, he received a visit from a man named Iwama Rokubei that would lead to the flowering of Musashi's last years and ultimately to our own knowl-edge of the man.

CHAPTER THREE

The Way of the Brush: Kumamoto

CONNECTIONS

Over the years, Musashi's relationships with a number of *daimyo*, particularly those of the Ogasawara and Honda clans, had grown stronger. Like many clans with close borders, these two families were also tied by marriage, Ogasawara Tadazane being married to the daughter of Honda Tadamasa. Such connections,[1] however, did not stop there: Tadamasa's son, Tadatoki, was married to the daughter of the second Tokugawa shogun, Hidetada, and Tadamasa's daughter was married to Arima Naozane, the *daimyo* of Nobeoka in Hyuga. This was a normal state of affairs for clans that desired to secure their relationships—and indirectly their territories—both nearby and farther afield, and had been so since the days of the Fujiwara in the ancient capital of Nara. And while the policy of marrying daughters off to other powerful men or their sons had never proved to be a fail-safe plan, it did bring clans together on a family basis, and so provided some insurance against aggression.

Musashi, too, was now connected to both the Ogasawara and Honda —not by marriage, of course, but by the fact that the lords of the clans had taken his adopted sons, Iori and Mikinosuke, respectively, as personal retainers. Indeed, he seemed also to enjoy the lateral connections, for he was on close terms with Arima Naozane and even exchanged letters with the man concerning the *daimyo*'s problems with the shogunate. Thus, Musashi, who was essentially a *ronin*, transcended social barriers in a way that even high-placed samurai could not. One suspects that this was not on account of his swordsmanship alone, but also because of his intellect, personality, and, as we shall see in this chapter, unique artistic abilities.

The other important connection in these circles was the marriage of Ogasawara Tadazane's sister, Chiyohime, to Hosokawa Tadatoshi. This man was the *daimyo* of Kumamoto, and the leader of a clan of astonishing military, political, and artistic achievement. It was from Tadatoshi that Iwama Rokubei had been sent with an offer to Musashi, whom the lord had met at a poetry circle in Kyoto some time before.

Musashi at a poetry circle? At this point it may be relevant to discuss briefly how a man who had spent the first part of his life involved in over sixty duels could also distinguish himself in poetry as well as in garden design, tea ceremony, Noh drama, and india ink painting. By so doing, we may be better able to understand what would have attracted Tadatoshi to Musashi, and why Musashi would have been interested in a clan like the Hosokawa.

THE WAY OF THE WARRIOR

In the Chinese lexicon there is a word, 斌, pronounced *uruwashi* in Japanese, that means "balanced" and refers to the proper proportion of interior content and exterior form. The left side of this character, 文 (*bun*), originally meant something like "pattern" in the sense of the patterns of birds in flight or ripples in water, but eventually came to mean "literature," or the patterns of human culture, and finally "culture" itself. The right-hand portion of the character, 武 (*bu*), means "martial" or warrior, and can be further broken down to the radicals 止, "stop," and 戈, "halberd," indicating a meaning of "to stop with the halberd." The entire character, *uruwashi*, then, connotes a balance of cultural and martial abilities in a single person, and this ideal was established early on in both the Chinese and Japanese cultures.

In the early Kamakura period (1185–1249) in Japan, this sense of balance was expressed in exquisite form in the *Heike monogatari*, the story of the conflict between the Minamoto and Taira clans. The warrior is described as beautifully attired, well-versed in literature or music, and able to write a death poem at the time of his own demise. This concept of the masculine ideal as a balance between military and cultural strengths would endure throughout the history of the warrior class, although particular clans or individuals would sometimes emphasize one aspect over the other. Shiba Yoshimasa (1350–1410), the great general and administrator during the Ashikaga shogunate, wrote in his book, the *Chikubasho*, "When a man has ability in the arts, the depth of his heart can be imagined, and the mind of his clan understood."

Other great warlords and generals wrote in a similar vein. Hojo Nagauji (Soun) (1432–1519), who built one of the first great castle towns in Japan at Odawara, declared in his "Twenty-one Precepts," that "a person who is lacking in the Way of Poetry is truly impoverished. The cultural and the martial are the constant Way of the warrior. It is hardly necessary to note that the ancient law has it that the cultured [arts] should be held on the left, and the military [arts] on the right." Even Takeda Shingen (1521–73), widely considered the greatest general of his day, said, "A man's learning is like the branches and leaves to a tree; he can not be without it. Learning, however, is not just in reading something, but rather is something we integrate with our own various Ways."

There were exceptions certainly, and Kato Kiyomasa (1562–1611), who was commander of Kumamoto Castle just before the Hosokawa, believed that any warrior who studied poetry would soon become "feminized." He famously declared that anyone who studied the dancing in Noh drama should commit suicide. But the ideal had been established long before, and most *daimyo* dabbled in poetry, tried their hands at art—or at least collected it—and participated in the tea ceremony as it came into vogue. These men considered such artistic activities not just as pastimes, but as actually legitimizing their positions of power. Imagawa Ryoshun (1325–1420), one of the most powerful and cultured *daimyo* of his time, put the matter quite clearly in his "Regulations." His very first sentence proclaims: "If you do not know the Way of culture, in the end you will be unable to grasp victory in the Way of the martial." He later states:

> It is written in the Four Books and the Five Classics [of Confucian learning] and in the military writings as well, that one will be unable to govern if he is lacking in the study of literature. In the same way that the Buddha preached the various dharmas in order to save all sentient beings, we [warriors] should rack our brains and never abandon the Two Ways of the Cultural and Martial [*bunbu ryodo*].

It was the Hosokawa clan that took this ideal to its extreme. Tadatoshi's father, Tadaoki, or Sansai (1563–1645), was a veteran of many campaigns, famous for his front-line courage and armor innovations. As a child, he was, from time to time, left to the care of his servants in a poor section of Kyoto, where, as his father intended, he learned self-sufficiency and frugality. With an ingenuity rare for the son of a *daimyo*, he could repair his own clothing and, later, show workers how best to shape the huge stones for castle battlements. Yet he was also a master of the tea ceremony, becoming one of the seven chief disciples of the great tea innovator, Sen no Rikyu; and commissioned black *raku* tea bowls from the famous potter, Chojiro. Tadaoki was a poet and a painter as well as a master of lacquerware who created exquisite works of extraordinary craftsmanship.

Tadaoki's father, Fujitaka, or Yusai (1534–1610), became the head of his fief at the age of twenty, participated in over fifty campaigns throughout his career, but was also well known as a poet and scholar of the *Kokinshu*, the classic anthology of poetry compiled by Ki no Tsurayuki about the year 905. As was typical of the man and of the Hosokawa in general, Tadaoki, when his castle was being attacked in 1600, feared for the loss of the notes and books he had collected on the *Kokinshu* over the years. A delegation of aristocrats who carried a message of this concern to his attackers was allowed to enter the castle and take out the manuscripts for safekeeping. As they left the castle, Yusai handed them a poem in gratitude:

> These words I bequeath:
>   the seeds of the heart,
> in this unchanging
>   world both past
>   and present.

The Hosokawa family's aptitude for balancing the literary and the martial, however, went back even farther. It was first demonstrated by its progenitor, Hosokawa Yoriharu, in about the year 1335. At an archery contest in honor of the emperor Godaigo, Yoriharu demonstrated almost unbelievable skill. Then, putting down his bow and taking up brush and ink, he composed a poem for the monarch, who was looking on in amazement. This level of skill in both the arts of war and the arts of peace would distinguish the Hosokawa clan for generations to come.

When Musashi met Tadatoshi at the poetry circle in Kyoto, he encountered a man whose interests were as broad as his own. Tadatoshi had been an avid swordsman from the time he was young, and at this point was intensely studying the Yagyu Shinkage-ryu, having been initiated into this style by Munenori himself. He had even received a certificate from the Yagyu—a blank sheet of paper indicating that "with a blank sheet of paper, the mind of the martial artist is transmitted." Three years younger than Musashi, Tadatoshi had heard all the details about the fight at Ganryu Island, and had nothing but respect for the man who had bested the instructor to the Hosokawa. Like his father and grandfather, Tadatoshi was a man of letters and was interested in several of the arts. Interestingly, he also concerned himself with garden design, and the garden that he established in Kumamoto in 1632, the Suizenji, is still considered today one of the most beautiful in all of Kyushu.

So their conversation that day in Kyoto likely ranged over a number of topics, and the two men must have recognized each other as Seekers of the Way who had a great deal in common. Tadatoshi, as the circumspect leader of a highly esteemed clan, would no doubt have then corresponded a number of times with his brother-in-law, Ogasawara Tadazane, to find out more about who this swordsman really was. Musashi was fifty-seven at this time; Tadatoshi, fifty-four.

A PLACE IN THE SEATING ORDER

In 1640, then, Hosokawa Tadatoshi sent one of his most diplomatically skilled retainers, Iwama Rokubei, to Kokura with a message inviting Musashi to reside at Kumamoto.[2] The retainer was to express Tadatoshi's intentions and inquire into the expectations and conditions that Musashi would have if he were to make the move. Musashi was well known to be somewhat eccentric, and Iwama realized he would need to put his heart and soul into this mission.

Initially, Musashi was shocked at the invitation. To reside on the Hosokawa fief was in itself an honor, but Tadatoshi seemed to be offering much more: friendship and an official sanctioning of Musashi's sword style, which Musashi was now calling the Niten Ichi-ryu. Thus he sent back a response to Tadatoshi in a statement carried by his intermediary, Sakazaki Naizen:

> Concerning your inquiry about my situation through the services of Master Iwama Rokubei, it is difficult to apologize enough for sending a verbal statement, but I bring these things to your attention with this note.
> —I have never held an office up to this time. I am already on in years and recently feel that I am sick. For this reason, I have no aspirations. If it turns out that I should stay [in Kumamoto], it would be enough if I were given the position of wearing proper armor and leading a single horse when my lord himself rides out. I have no wife or child and my body is old, so I entertain no thoughts about house or household goods.
> —Since I was young, I have gone out on the battlefield six times. On four of those occasions, there was no one on the field before me. This fact is widely known and there is also proof. Nevertheless, I do not bring this up to plead for a position.
> —As to the make-up of arms, how they are appropriately used on the battlefield, and, according to the occasion, the way of regulating the province, I have set my mind on these things since my youth and have trained diligently. Thus, if Your Lordship has any questions, I will humbly speak out.

February 1640
Miyamoto Musashi

Terms were quickly arranged, and Musashi left for Kumamoto in the spring of that year—but not without an ambiguous omen concerning his fate. In accordance with what he had written about his health to Tadatoshi, as he left Kokura, he erected a *juzo*, a sort of grave marker that one could put up while one is still alive, on Mount Tamuke, near Kokura Castle. Years later, in 1654, Iori and Shunzan, Musashi's instructor in Zen, erected a stone monument—now called the Kokura Hibun[3]—to him on this same spot.

Musashi was given an allowance for seventeen men and an annual stipend of two hundred *koku* of rice. His status was that of a guest, but his place in the seating order at meetings was equal to the head of a large military group. For his residence he was given land at the old Chiba Castle in Kumamoto.

There have been writers who have made critical remarks about these terms, especially the relatively low stipend of two hundred *koku*, stating that this was not much considering Musashi's status as a swordsman. But the conditions that were provided for Musashi were far better than he had requested, and the honor given him in terms of the seating order was surprisingly high. He was, after all, not a retainer but a guest, and his stipend was outside the fief's ordinary wage system. Musashi had lived his whole life in simplicity and he would insist on that ideal to the end. Just days before dying, he wrote "The Way of Walking Alone," his final words of advice to his students and disciples. Among the items in this short work are

> Do not ever think in acquisitive terms.
> Do not harbor hopes for your own personal home.
> Do not be intent on possessing valuables or a fief in old age.

Again, like the haiku poet Matsuo Basho, Musashi was an artist and his goals were not those of the common run. There is certainly no indication that he was anything but pleased with his new situation.

Indeed, Musashi seemed to thrive in Kumamoto, despite the fact that his health was on the decline. He was able to set up a *dojo*, take in a number of talented disciples, and devote himself to other pursuits for which he would become as well known as he was for his swordsmanship. Before looking into those pursuits, however, we should return briefly to his relationship with Hosokawa Tadatoshi.

LAST BOUTS

Before Musashi came to live with the Hosokawa, a man by the name of Ujii Yashiro had been dispatched by the Yagyu clan to Kumamoto, where he became personal instructor to the Hosokawa. Not long after Musashi's arrival, however, a match between the two swordsmen was secretly arranged by order of Lord Tadatoshi. Contrary to the usual arrangements for such bouts and suggesting the level of Tadatoshi's sensitivity, there was to be no judgment of winning or losing from either side, and even the lord's personal retainers were kept at a distance. Both men were to use wooden swords, and there were to be three bouts.

The result was predictable: Because he no longer fought to make an indisputable statement and because he was in the presence of Lord Tadatoshi, Musashi did not strike with strength, but only controlled Ujii's technique, not letting him move at will. Greatly surprised, Tadatoshi took up a wooden sword and engaged in a bout with Musashi himself, but he was able to get no further than had Ujii. The good-natured lord exclaimed that he had heard a great deal about Musashi's reputation, but had never thought that he was this strong! Although Tadatoshi had always treated Musashi as a respected teacher, from that time on, he began practicing the Niten Ichi-ryu himself, and in due time inherited its teachings.

Musashi's last bout was held this same year with a retainer of the Hosokawa clan, Shioda Hamanosuke. Hamanosuke had served the Hosokawa since the time of Tadaoki and excelled in the techniques of staff and take-down. He instructed the clan's warriors and received a stipend that was enough to support five men. This bout, too, had been arranged by Tadatoshi. Hamanosuke wielded his usual six-foot staff and Musashi carried a short wooden sword.

During the match, Hamanosuke swung his staff every time he found a chance, but the tip of the staff was invariably checked by Musashi's short sword. As in the bout with Ujii, Musashi's opponent was unable to make any advance at all, while Musashi himself made no move to put the man out of the contest. Finally, Musashi said, "Hamanosuke has no way of beating me, but if he can get within six feet of me, I'll consider the victory his."

Infuriated, Hamanosuke threw away his staff and went to grapple with the swordsman. And yet, despite Hamanosuke's expertise in this area, he was repeatedly maneuvered to the side by Musashi and was never able to get close enough to apply his skills. At this, Hamanosuke understood that he had been truly beaten. He bowed, set aside his own style, and asked to become Musashi's disciple.

Musashi, however, realized that Hamanosuke's techniques with staff and take-down were superb, and so he instead requested that the man teach them to his own disciples. Today these techniques are included in the Musashi style. Musashi was fifty-seven years old at that time. Hamanosuke lived on to teach the next generation of Hosokawa men, finally passing away when he was well past the age of seventy.

THE THIRTY-FIVE ARTICLES OF THE MARTIAL ARTS

As mentioned earlier, Tadatoshi was not only an enthusiastic martial artist, but a highly educated man, and it was likely from both of these standpoints that he was taken with the eccentric Musashi. The Hosokawa clan had long been considered one of the most cultured *daimyo* families in both the arts and literature, and one of the most sophisticated in governance and diplomacy. Thus it should not be surprising that Tadatoshi appreciated Musashi and put great stock in his abilities, beckoning him to his inner circle to discuss govern-mental matters, and often inviting him into his presence. Musashi, too, by the time he entered Kumamoto, was not only a famous mar-tial artist but a "man of taste," superbly accomplished in the arts of painting and sculpture.

Tadatoshi seems to have relied on Musashi's judgment in areas be-yond military affairs and governance. The *daimyo*, for example, once asked the swordsman if he had noticed any men of special ability among his samurai. Musashi said that he had noticed one, but that he did not know the man's name. When the warriors were brought out for inspection, Musashi identified the man, whose name was Toko Kinbei. This seemed strange because to all others, Kinbei appeared to be a perfectly run-of-the-mill retainer who had never stood out from the crowd. When Tadatoshi looked quizzically at Musashi, the latter asked Kinbei if he practiced any special discipline beyond the usual martial arts. Kinbei replied only that he slept every night with a sword sus-pended tip-down just over his head, and that this helped him to be resolved about the fine line between life and death and to be unwaver-ing in the service of his lord. Tadatoshi was once again amazed at Mu-sashi's perceptive observation.

Years later, when he was employed in the repairs of Edo Castle, this Kinbei was appointed supervisor of the Hosokawa group of workmen. At one point, his subordinates took stones from a setting done by another clan and fit them into their own setting. Kinbei was accused of the crime, and a Tokugawa official tortured him horribly for it on a daily basis. Kinbei continued to calmly declare his own innocence, and he was finally released. The figure he had cut while enduring torture, however, had not gone unnoticed, and he was considered extraordi-narily manly and heroic. Musashi had not been amiss in his assess-ment of the man.

Added to Musashi's other skills was the thorough education that he had somehow given himself in literature and in writing itself. With very few exceptions, most of the top-notch martial artists who had established their own styles could neither read nor write, and those who could were not sufficiently educated to write about the styles they had established. This job was usually left to either Buddhist priests or later disciples. Thus Musashi was far above the majority of his peers in his literary abilities as well.

Within a year of his coming to Kumamoto, Musashi was asked by Tadatoshi to write down the essence of his style. This he did in a short work entitled *The Thirty-five Articles of the Martial Arts*, which he presented to Tadatoshi in February of 1641.

The work, which actually contains thirty-six articles, is a tersely worded treatise on the fundamental principles of Musashi's Niten Ichi-ryu, barely covering fifteen pages of modern Japanese print.[4] It is now considered to be the outline or prototype for *The Book of Five Rings*, and its basic premises will be covered later in a discussion of that book. Its headings—such as Movement of the Feet, Use of the Eyes, and The Three Initiatives—are much the same as in Musashi's masterpiece, but the explanatory paragraphs lack the detail of the later work. The arrangement of the contents is also somewhat different. In the opening paragraph of *The Thirty-five Articles*, he wrote,

> Having trained myself daily in the Two Heavens, One Style, I now take brush to paper. Though the sequence is inadequate and the words difficult to express, in the following I have written out my general understanding of the sword of the martial arts, into which I have always put great effort.

Despite Musashi's apologetic phrase that "the sequence is inadequate and the words difficult to express," Tadatoshi was overjoyed at receiving this small book, and felt that he had obtained one of the great treasures of his life. The next step would be to officially sanction Musashi's style and to place it under the full patronage of the Hosokawa clan, much as the Yagyu Style had come under the patronage of the Tokugawa. Sadly, this was not to be.

AN END AND A BEGINNING

On 17 March 1641, about one month after receiving *The Thirty-five Articles*, Tadatoshi passed away from an illness. He was just fifty-five years old, and his death was a blow for people from Kumamoto to Edo. This was a man who was well respected, a trusted advisor to the shogun Iemitsu, and on friendly terms with the powerful Nabeshima and Kuroda clans in the neighboring provinces. He was also on intimate terms with the famous Zen priest, Takuan Soho; with Ishikawa Jozan, the eccentric literati poet who created the Shisendo hermitage in Kyoto; and with the scholar, Hayashi Rasan. All of these men wrote notes to the Hosokawa family expressing their grief at the passing of this educated and cultured man.[5]

The Hosokawa clan chronology (*Hosokawa-ke nenpu*) states that "Lord Tadatoshi was a famous general, proficient in both the military and literary arts. He excelled in the Six Accomplishments."

One of Tadatoshi's greatest "accomplishments" was the art of the sword. To have had Musashi as an advisor and sometime companion in the last two years of his life must have been a happiness for him beyond compare. For Musashi, Tadatoshi had been an incomparable friend. For a while after his lord's death, Musashi stayed in his room with the door closed and mourned the passing of the man who had been closer to him than anyone else at any point during the fifty-eight years of his life. In due time, he opened his door and reentered the world, but it would not be as it had been. Nor would Musashi be as he had been. While still teaching his disciples as before, he now directed his life toward concentrating more on the arts: the tea ceremony, Noh recitation, poetry, and, above all, painting.

THE BRUSH AND THE MIND

Monochrome india ink wash painting, or *suibokuga*, was imported to Japan from China during the Kamakura period (1192–1333) along with Zen Buddhism, with which it is closely connected. At its simplest, this style of painting requires only an ink stone, ink, brush, and paper. Necessitating intense concentration and control, it is said to be the perfect art for the student of Zen. In this style, everything unessential is shorn away and each irreversible stroke is fueled by the intensity and disciplined energy of the artist. The mind must be harmonized with the artist's brush, exactly as it must be harmonized with the samurai's sword: the stroke, once executed, cannot be withdrawn.

It should be no surprise, then, that the first practitioners of *suibokuga* in Japan were Zen monks and the warrior rulers of the thirteenth century. The warriors, newly in control of the nation, were searching for both the proper mental framework with which to govern the country and a sense of culture that would add an aura of legitimacy to their rule. The Chinese Zen priests who were immigrating at that time from the deteriorating Sung Dynasty provided both. Zen meditation and philosophy helped to foster the spontaneity necessary to conduct military affairs and also to eliminate the fear of death, while the study of continental culture and administrative skills gave the warriors a basis from which to direct national affairs.

Of all the Buddhist sects, warriors seemed to relate best to Zen, with its emphasis on self-reliance, or *jiriki*. Both esoteric Buddhism, which was primarily taken up by the aristocracy, and the Pure Land Buddhism of faith that was embraced mostly by the masses, tended to rely on the Other, or *tariki*, whether that other be mantras and mudras or the grace and compassion of the Buddha Amida. This breakdown of class and sect was by no means rigid—all types of Buddhism were, at least in theory, open to all classes of men. However, the paradox of Zen—that through one's own disciplined and strenuous emptying of the mind, the self is transcended—was one that the warrior could deeply appreciate, for obvious good reason.

This trend—the study of Zen and its accompanying arts and letters—would continue through the Muromachi period of the Ashikaga shogunate (1338–1573) until it became the predominant cultural and religious force in the country, and resulted in the flowering of nearly everything we associate with the classical culture of Japan: Noh drama, tea ceremony, garden and landscape design, and, quintessentially, the monochromatic india ink painting, *suibokuga*. The Ashikaga shoguns were patrons of the national cultural scene, which centered in Kyoto, culminating with the third Ashikaga shogun, Yoshimitsu (1356–1408), who was brought up, incidentally, largely by Hosokawa Yoriyuki. Yoshimitsu not only studied Zen but built the Sokokuji (which is today the largest Zen temple complex still extant in Kyoto) and constructed the Temple of the Golden Pavilion on the outskirts of the capital. With the deterioration of Ashikaga control and the near-destruction of Kyoto during the Onin War (1467–77), however, the Zen priests and artists fled to the relatively stable capitals of the provincial warlords. These warlords in turn practiced meditation and cultivated the arts associated with Zen, spreading the culture throughout the entire nation.

By the early seventeenth century, however, after years of civil wars and disturbances, the new Tokugawa shogunate turned its focus toward strict control of national affairs, and neo-Confucianism—predominantly ethical and social in outlook—became the dominant national philosophy. Attention now turned to the great ateliers of the Kano school and Tawara Sotatsu; and Zen and its arts, while still widely practiced, lost the patronage of the central government, and took on the status and character of the outsider.

It was the Zen art of *suibokuga* that was the medium of the ultimate outsider—the artist, Niten, also known as the swordsman Miyamoto Musashi.

PAINTING WITH THE MIND OF THE SWORD

It is not known exactly when Musashi first began painting, although at the age of thirteen he executed a painting of Daruma at the Shoren'in temple in Hirafuku in Harima, where he stayed after leaving his father's home. It is clear, however, that he was already an extraordinarily talented artist by the time he entered Kokura in northern Kyushu in 1634, and all of his extant paintings date from this period until his death in 1645.

Musashi clearly stated in *The Book of Five Rings* that he had no teacher for his study of the Way of the sword or for any of the other Ways that he practiced, and we can only surmise that this was true for the art of *suibokuga* as well. Quite obviously he applied the same dedication and discipline to this art as he did to his sword technique: in his words, training himself morning and night, and investigating it thoroughly. Although he once signed his name to a register of the disciples of Yano Kichiju, a painting master employed by the Hosokawa clan, this would have been done during a courtesy call. Musashi himself was a fully mature artist by this time.

If Musashi did have a teacher, it was his own Way of the Sword. The *Kaijo monogatari*, published twenty years after his death, gives this interesting account of his approach to the brush. This account also shows quite clearly that his relationship with Tadatoshi was not simply defined by instruction in the sword:

> Once Musashi was ordered by his lord to do, in the lord's presence, a painting of Daruma, but his skill was not forthcoming

and he was unable to finish it that day. That night he turned in, but suddenly the solution came to him and he leapt out of bed, finishing the painting beneath a lamp. It came out exactly as he desired and was, indeed, exquisite. Musashi then turned to a disciple and said, "My painting is still not up to my sword technique, and the reason is this: under the gaze of my lord, I painted with the intention of doing the work well, but in fact it turned out to be quite inferior. I did the work just now, however, using my martial art, and it turned out just as I wanted. In my martial art, when I step out grasping my sword, neither I nor my enemy exists. My viewpoint is one of destroying both Heaven and Earth, and thus I have no fear. Well, I can see now that my painting is as yet no match for my skill with the sword.

Later, Musashi would write in *The Book of Five Rings*: "With the principles of the martial arts, one makes a Way for all the arts and accomplishments, and will not misunderstand them."

He would surely have agreed with the Chinese calligrapher who wrote:

When the Mind is correct, the brush will be also.
心正即筆正

Despite the setback described in the story above, Musashi handled the brush with astonishing clarity and strength, and seemed to grasp the very spirit of his subject matter. He was a remarkably keen observer of nature and of the nature of things. His victory in over sixty individual matches, his survival through six major campaigns, and the paintings he left to us all speak of this in different tongues, but to the same effect.

It was the assessment of the Zen Buddhist painters that in *suibokuga* the mind was translated spontaneously to the brush, and that the character of the artist was seen clearly in the brush's stroke. Musashi, in his insistence that the Way of the Sword provided a path for all other Ways, said in essence that the stroke of the sword and the stroke of the brush were the same: that with each stroke, the mind of the practitioner could be observed with certainty.[6]

With his paintings, then, we may add yet a sixth chapter to *The Book of Five Rings*, and observe what the master was indicating as his ink and brush demonstrated the Fundamental Way.

THE PAINTINGS

Underlying Musashi's prolific output at this time was the fact that he was now living in the extraordinarily cultured domain of the Hosokawa; the artistic milieu in Kumamoto was far beyond even what it had been with the Honda and Ogasawara. Through his friendship with Hosokawa Tadatoshi and his father, Tadaoki, he would view some of the best art in the country, periodically drink tea using the exquisite utensils collected by the older Hosokawa lord, and engage in discussions of art with the two of them. Tadatoshi's death, however, brought several major changes that would influence the intensity of his creativity. The first, of course, was his grief. The loneliness of his solitary search for the Way that Musashi must have felt throughout his career surely multiplied exponentially with the loss of this close friend and patron. Now Musashi devoted himself all the more to the more introspective arts. At linked poetry meetings, his voice was so low that it could not be heard by people in the next room, despite the thinness of the walls. He spent more time chanting from the librettos of Noh drama and dedicated more time to the quiet ceremony of tea. If Tadatoshi's absence drove Musashi ever deeper inside himself, however, it also gave him more time to concentrate on these arts. The hours he had spent at his lord's side were now given over to working with brush and ink.

Second, and no doubt connected to the *daimyo*'s death, was Musashi's increased study of Zen meditation. At about this time, he was befriended by the two monks who were responsible for the Hosokawa's family temple, the Taishoji. The older of these, Obuchi Genko, talked with him about the depths of Buddhist thought, while the younger, twenty-year-old Shunzan, was his companion in *zazen*. Accompanied by Shunzan, Musashi would often walk out to the mountains to sit atop the boulders there that overlooked the expansive scene beneath, meditating. During one such retreat, as the two sat deep in meditation, a snake crawled up over Shunzan's lap and made its way towards Musashi. When it got within a foot of the swordsman's knee, however, it raised its head and remained still for a moment, then turned and veered off into the rocks. Musashi laughingly took this as an admonishment: his commitment to Zen meditation had not yet overcome his adversarial nature, it seemed. Yet his study of Buddhism and the practice of *zazen* were serious matters for him, and his intense involvement in this discipline was sharpening both the concentration and spontaneity he needed for the work he was now doing with brush and ink.

Finally, Musashi was ill. He had had inklings of this even before coming to Kumamoto, but at this point the disease—believed now to have been some sort of thoracic cancer—was progressing. There were days when this was apparent: once, when he went to Nagaoka Okinaga's mansion, everyone was making their greetings at the entranceway and Musashi was about to ascend the steps. For some reason, his steps faltered and he put his hand to the hip of his *hakama* and gave a groan as he started up. Okinaga's retainer, Yamamoto Gen'emon, came forward and asked if he could use a hand; but Musashi declined the help, saying that it wasn't that bad, and continued up the steps.

On the other hand, Musashi at times exhibited an inner strength that demonstrated the superiority of mind over matter. Shortly after that same meeting at Okinaga's, there was a large fire in a section of Kumamoto called Yaoyamachi. During the confusion, someone was seen leaping from rooftop to rooftop, helping to put out the encompassing flames. Later it was revealed that it had been none other than the old man who had stumbled at Okinaga's mansion.

Generally speaking, however, Musashi realized that his once almost invincible body was growing more and more frail. This did not stop him from continuing to take his long walks through the forested sections of Kumamoto, or from instructing his students at the *dojo*. Decreasing physical strength, however, gives all but the most superficial an increased sense of mortality, and Musashi's illness no doubt led him to meditate all the more deeply on the world of nature around him and its connections to Buddhist truths. These insights into nature would be some of the major themes of many of the more than forty of his art works still extant.

In the tradition of Zen Buddhist painters, Musashi painted mostly portraits of the Zen patriarchs and scenes with birds and animals. He did not paint larger landscapes in the style of Sesshu, the great *suibokuga* artist of the fifteenth century, or in the style of Hasegawa Tohaku or Kaiho Yusho, with whom he is often compared.

Some of his best-known paintings are of birds and, of these, *Shrike on a Withered Branch* (Figure 1) is his signature work.[7] In the single, unhesitating swordlike stroke of the branch and the concentrated stare of the shrike into the void, the viewer feels as though he is looking directly into the spirit of swordsmanship itself. The shrike seems to be in a state of what might be called intense repose, and brings to mind the opening words of the priest Takuan in the "Annals of the Sword of Taia":[8]

> Presumably, as a martial artist, I do not fight for gain or loss, am not concerned with strength or weakness, and neither advance a step or retreat a step. The enemy does not see me. I do not see the

FIGURE 1. *Shrike on a Withered Branch* by Miyamoto Musashi, signed
with his artist name Niten. Scroll. Ink on paper 22 x 50 inches
(54 x 125 cm). Kuboso Memorial Museum of Arts, Izumi.

enemy. Penetrating to a place where heaven and earth have not yet divided, where Yin and Yang have not yet arrived, I quickly and necessarily gain effect.

The intense, concentrated quality of this painting cannot be overstated. In the unblinking eye and hooked beak of the shrike, one can sense the almost nonexistent border between life and death—a reminder that its creator had experienced over sixty individual matches and six major battles. And yet, with a slight shift of the imagination, it is a perfect scene of nature: a bird on a branch. This is the perfect quality of Musashi's Zen: nothing is as it seems; nor is it otherwise.

Another work that demonstrates Musashi's skill at the brush and his keen observation of nature, while also providing insight into his view of swordsmanship, is his painting of a cormorant (Figure 2). The long-necked bird is perched on a small ledge, no doubt over an unseen river, with a look of a Zen priest who has seen the Other Side.[9]

Cormorant fishing was at one time a popular trade in the Far East and it can still be observed in some parts of China and Japan. In this practice, the fisherman goes out into the river at night with large lanterns or torches suspended from his boat. When fish, attracted by the lights, approach the boat, the fisherman "releases" his cormorants into the water to catch the fish. Throughout, the cormorants are leashed with cords around their necks that allow them to take fish into their beaks, but not to swallow them. Once the birds are retrieved, the fish are taken from their captors and placed in the hold.

Musashi would have seen these birds many times in his travels about Japan—both wild and captive fishers—and likely saw them often on his walks along the Tsuboi River in Kumamoto. Surely he must have admired their skill and singleness of purpose. And he may very well have had an old Japanese phrase in mind when he first perceived one as a possible subject for his art. The phrase is worth remembering for both the sword practitioner and the layman:

FIGURE 2. *Cormorant* by Miyamoto Musashi, signed Niten.
Scroll. Ink on paper. 22 x 47 inches (56 x 119 cm).
Eisei Bunko (collection of the Hosokawa family).

> The crow imitating the ways of a cormorant
> *U no mane suru karasu*

A crow imitating a cormorant cannot swim and so will nearly drown. In the same way, every man should be true to his own craft or, in swordsmanship, his own talents and training. Musashi would have us be the cormorant if we are the cormorant, and the crow if we are the crow. On this principle stands life and death. As he wrote over and over again in *The Book of Five Rings*, "You should investigate this thoroughly."

————

Musashi's painting of an owl on an oak tree may have been conceived with a related concept in mind. Musashi's owl—a small horned owl called the *konoha-zuku* in Japanese (or in English, the Scops owl)—perches among a number of oak leaves, its eyes fixedly watching something below our sight and its ear tufts extended out to the sides, indicating a relaxed curiosity. This small owl—all of eight inches tall—would have wintered in Kumamoto and no doubt come to Musashi's attention on the swordsman's rambles along the river or other warmer paths.

Owls are well known for their ability to strike silently. Musashi, however, may have been inspired for this work by a line from Ch'uang T'zu, a Chinese Taoist author from the third century B.C.E. whose writings were widely read by Zen adepts: "The horned owl catches fleas at night and can spot the tip of a hair, but when daylight comes, it cannot see a mound or a hill. This refers to a difference in nature."[10]

The cormorant and the owl both teach us that we all have different natures or abilities developed through our own training, and that we should be true to them. Musashi states this clearly in *The Book of Five Rings*: "Without imitating others, you should take what is appropriate to yourself and use a weapon you can handle. It is wrong for either general or soldier to have a preference for one thing and to dislike another. It is essential to make efforts in these things."[11]

Both of these paintings were executed to be *kakejiku*, or hanging scrolls, to be placed on the wall in the recessed alcove for tea houses or the like. Musashi, however, did not paint only on this small scale. In what was likely either a response to a request by one of the members of the Hosokawa clan or a gift to the same, Musashi illustrated two large folding screens, each about eleven-and-a-half feet long by five feet high, with flocks of geese among the reeds at the edge of a river.[12] This is a monumental work that might have been ordered from a professional atelier and that demonstrates not only the high level of Musashi's skill but also the degree to which his works were admired by the cultured Hosokawa.

In these large-scale paintings, Musashi portrays the beauty of these birds and their social character as well. One of them is caught perfectly in mid-flight while being watched with intense interest by others in the flock. In China the goose was believed to have great spiritual qualities and was a symbol of the male principle. Such factors may have been considered by the Hosokawa, who were well acquainted with continental art, when they asked Musashi to do the work. At any rate, paintings of geese and reeds were popular among the Zen priests in China, and such paintings were among those brought to Japan in the fourteenth and fifteenth centuries. Musashi surely encountered a number of these in his travels around the country.

For live models, he needed to go no further than the river that still runs to the east of Kumamoto Castle. During his time, the natural scene along this river was far more extensive than it is today; ducks, geese, and other birds must have flourished there in great numbers. This work—like many other paintings by Musashi—is still greatly admired by the Hosokawa family, and is housed today in the Eisei Bunko, the building that has served as the repository of the Hosokawa family treasures from the fourteenth century to the present. First opened to the public in 1972, this collection is housed on the grounds of the Hosokawa family estate in Tokyo. In this way, the relationship

THE WAY OF THE BRUSH

between Musashi and the Hosokawa that formally began in 1640 has continued on to this day.

A painting that may indicate Musashi's peace of mind in this last part of his life is that of a dove in a red plum tree. The plum blooms in late winter, and is a symbol of purity and of the ability to endure hardships. Although the dove is a symbol of peace in the West, it is dedicated in Japan to Hachiman, the god of war. It is also a symbol of filial piety in the Far East, and the saying *Hato ni sanshi no rei ari* concludes that young doves will perch three branches below their parents out of respect for their elders. Musashi, who had been parentless for years, certainly held this same kind of respect for the Hosokawa.

The tranquility of this scene, with the dove basking in the sunshine of the late winter/early spring, expresses a calm that the old warrior must have felt about the final home provided him by his patrons in Kumamoto. And after so many years of conflicts, wounds, and living on his own, Musashi must have felt a serenity from time to time that he would not have known as a young man. The observer, however, will not miss the swordlike stroke of the top plum branch, nor forget that Musashi continued to teach and write until his dying day. The dove in this painting is clearly at ease, but it seems also to be intently observing the long vertical branch directly before it.

Although he painted other animals—squirrels, horses, even dragons—Musashi seems to have had a special affinity for birds. He did not, however, collect and cage rare or colorful ones as did a number of the *daimyo* of his age. Musashi was interested in the wild ones, admiring them for their intensity, play, economy of movement, and, above all, freedom.

———

During this period, Musashi was committed to a regular practice of *zazen*. Now in his late fifties, one can imagine him pulling his legs up into a painful lotus position, approaching this practice with the same intensity and concentration he applied to everything.

As was mentioned earlier, the older, more scholarly priest Obuchi likely discussed the Buddhist dharma with Musashi in the brisk, energetic manner typical of priests of the Rinzai sect, while Musashi's training in seated meditation fell to the guidance of the much younger Shunzan. Although he had always studied Zen and other forms of Buddhism, Musashi was now making it an integral part of his life. It was only natural, then, that one of his favorite subjects for the *suibokuga* that he was painting at this time would be the founder of the Zen sect, Daruma.

Daruma (in Sanskrit, Bodhidharma) was born in either southern India or Persia, reportedly to a royal family, and went to China to teach Buddhism as the twenty-eighth patriarch of the religion around the year 520 C.E. One of his most famous dialogs was with Emperor Wu of the Liang Dynasty, a devout Buddhist, who asked how much merit he would acquire for his good works in promoting the faith. "None whatsoever," was Daruma's reply. Somewhat daunted, the emperor then asked about the sacred doctrine's first principle. Daruma responded, "It's just a vast emptiness, and there's nothing sacred." Finally, the emperor asked, "Then who are you to stand in front of me?" Daruma's answer was, "I don't know." After this unsuccessful, elliptical interview, Daruma left the court and eventually arrived at the Shaolin Temple, where he spent nine years meditating in front of a rock wall in a cave. Legend has it that at one point he fell asleep during meditation. When he woke, he was so angry with himself that he cut off his eyelids and threw them on the ground. Later, the first tea plants grew from them.

Daruma's abruptness and eccentricity appealed to the Zen sect, which adopted him as their first patriarch, and paintings of his image are hung reverently in places of honor during ceremonies of that sect.

Daruma also held great appeal for Musashi. His answer to the emperor, "A vast emptiness and nothing sacred," could stand as a summation of the philosophy of swordsmanship Musashi gives in *The Book of Five Rings*, and Musashi would surely have appreciated Daruma's subtle humor as well. And there was more. In Daruma's lectures, Musashi would have found confirmation of his thoughts on swordsmanship and concepts that led him to a deeper understanding of those thoughts. In his essay "The Bloodstream Sermon," Daruma wrote:

> Once you hold on to something, you'll be unaware. If you truly want to encounter the Way, don't hold on to anything. All practices, all actions, are impermanent.
>
> But this mind isn't somewhere outside the material body of the four elements. Without this mind, we can't move. The body has no awareness. Like a plant or stone, the body has no nature. So how does it move? It is the mind that moves.
>
> Apart from motion there's no mind, and apart from the mind there's no motion. But motion isn't the mind. And the mind isn't motion. Motion is basically No-Mind. And the mind is basically No-Motion. But motion doesn't exist apart from the mind, and the mind doesn't exist apart from motion.

Musashi would have read this passage and inwardly nodded in vigorous assent, and it is interesting in this connection that Musashi painted more *suibokuga* of Daruma than of any other subject except Hotei, another Zen saint. Two of his most famous renditions of the first Zen patriarch are quite arresting. One shows Daruma in full Zen concentration, his eyes intensely focused toward his nose, and his mouth pulled downward in unflinching determination (Figure 3);[13] the other is a three-quarter view of the Zen master, with enigmatic lines that could suggest anything from anger to self-reproach.[14] In both paintings, the heavy, grounded lines of the robe, the lighter and more sensitives lines of the face, and the "vast emptiness" extending above

FIGURE 3. *Daruma* by Miyamoto Musashi, signed Niten.
Scroll. Ink on paper. 15 x 36 inches (38 x 91 cm).
Eisei Bunko.

the figure of Daruma reflect Musashi's own intensity, reverence, and, once again, little-noted sense of humor.

After the less-than-satisfying interview with Emperor Wu, Daruma is said to have left the area, crossing the Yangtze River on a reed leaf or branch of reeds. Wet-blanket scholars have pointed out that during the Sung Dynasty, when this story began to circulate, the Chinese character for reed (芦) also meant "reed boat," but the anecdote had a life of its own. Zen-sect artists picked it up quickly, and it has been a popular subject for them ever since. Apparently Musashi was unable to resist it either, and painted a number of *suibokuga* on this subject. In one of his renderings of the *Reed Leaf Daruma*,[15] a triptych, he made Daruma the central figure and added paintings of single ducks on either side, floating lightly among the reeds, as if to give Daruma some cheerful companions along his Way.

There are a great many other stories about Daruma, but one worth mentioning here concerns doing *zazen* for nine years—sitting facing a wall the entire time—at the end of which time his legs are said to have fallen off from disuse. It is indicative of how thoroughly Zen Buddhism and such stories have pervaded Japanese life that a popular round, legless doll of the patriarch is seen almost everywhere and is accompanied by the saying,

Life is falling down seven times, getting up eight
Jinsei nanakorobi, ya'oki

Musashi continued to practice *zazen* through the physical pain and the psychological disappointments known to every Zen adept who has continued to practice for any length of time. Again, it must be remembered that Musashi was ill even before coming to Kumamoto, which must have added an extra dimension of difficulty to this discipline. He persevered, however, deepening his understanding of Zen doctrine and leaving a spiritual statement in his paintings and other arts.

Fearlessness, detachment, and humor are all considered to be attributes of the enlightened human being, one engendering the other in an endless cycle. Musashi's life story, writings, and paintings all indicate that he lived well inside this circle. Of his paintings, there are more of Hotei, the humorously rendered Buddhist priest, than any other subject, and this fact may hint at a side of Musashi that is often overlooked—that he was not the ever-serious swordsman we may imagine from reading *The Book of Five Rings*, but a man who could laugh good-naturedly and out loud. Indeed, had Musashi left only his paintings to posterity, we would have a very different view of him today, as many of them exhibit the humor for which Zen Buddhism is well known and which is fundamental to its worldview. Certainly Musashi found in Hotei an image to express a part of himself that would have been difficult to do with a sword.

Hotei, the corpulent priest known to the Chinese as Ch'ang Ting-tze or Pudai, lived in the ninth and early tenth centuries, dying in 912. An eccentric, he would at times utter strange, cryptic words, but at other times he would eloquently preach the Buddhist scriptures. Hotei roamed the marketplaces of China, carrying a huge cloth bag and a cane, and begging for money and food. He would eat anything, including meat and fish—foods that were forbidden to the Buddhist clergy. Among other wonders, Hotei was able to predict the weather, and was seemingly immune to cold and even death: not long after he passed away at a place called Fengchuan, he was seen wandering through a neighboring province. While it is not recorded that he was a member of the Zen sect, he is noted in *The Transmission of the Lamp*, a thirty-volume work on the ancient patriarchs compiled in 1004, as one of ten men who had "arrived at the gate of Zen."

By the twelfth century, Hotei had become a common subject of Zen artists. He is always depicted as a happy, corpulent monk, nearly naked, and often in odd surroundings for a Buddhist priest. The large bag in his possession is said to indicate his magnanimity, and to hold countless treasures. His bald, unshaven, often slovenly visage camouflages the fact that he is considered to be an incarnation of the bodhisattva Maitreya, the Buddha of the Future. Zen artists, however, were often happy to use the humor of the unexpected to break us free of our preconceptions. Musashi's renderings of Hotei do much the same.

It should not be too surprising, then, that Musashi's most striking painting of Hotei has the old priest intently watching a cockfight (Figure 4). This decidedly un-Buddhist scene was not original with Musashi, having been painted by both the Chinese painter Liang K'ai (c. 1210) and Musashi's older contemporary Kaiho Yusho (d. 1615), but the swordsman's version is by far the most striking.[16] In this painting, Hotei watches the cockfight with concentration, amusement, and perhaps a bit of irony, his scruffy chin resting on the top of his cane. Much as Musashi must have watched many sword matches with detachment but great interest, so Hotei looks on as the cocks—perhaps representing all of us, the sentient beings of this world—get ready to peck and leap at each other. Musashi brings the perspective of a highly focused swordsman to this scene, portraying a situation of life and death with humor. It is a painting—like the shrike on a withered branch—that only Musashi, the truly Zen-imbued swordsman, could have produced.

Musashi was often tempted, in various paintings he did of Hotei, to insert his favorite subjects—birds. Two sets of triptychs include both a sparrow and a bird Musashi obviously enjoyed observing, the kingfisher. The center scrolls of both sets are of Hotei. One has him —heavy as a sumo wrestler—fanning himself and stepping lightly in a sort of jig; the other has him taking a nap, elbows resting on his huge bag, chin supported by the palms of his hands.[17] In the left scroll in both cases, a kingfisher perches above a pond, its gaze raptly held by whatever is in the water beneath it. The inscription over the kingfisher with the napping Hotei reads:

FIGURE 4. *Hotei Watching a Cockfight* by Miyamoto Musashi, signed Niten.
Scroll. Ink on paper. 13 x 28 inches (32 x 71 cm).
Matsunaga Collection, Fukuoka Art Museum.

A single lonely form, next to the lotus leaf wilted by the late year chill,
A green light shines over the water in the full evening sun,
Its entire body unmoving in the autumn wind,
Its mind following the golden scales filling the single pond.

This inscription, added by a Zen priest of the Tenryuji who lived about fifty years after Musashi passed away, has caught not only the spirit of the kingfisher but a certain sense of Musashi's mind during his time in Kumamoto. This pair of scrolls (the one with the sparrow is lost) expresses two seemingly paradoxical characteristics of Zen meditation: a light-hearted relaxation and a highly focused attention. Apparently Musashi did not find these mutually exclusive.

As an interesting aside, the triptych in Buddhist art usually has as its center a major Buddhist figure such as the historical Buddha or one of the main Bodhisattvas. The scrolls at the right and left ordinarily portray the central figure's attendants: lesser Bodhisattvas, avatars, or the like. In Musashi's work, the central figure is often the happy and eccentric Hotei, while his attendants are the animals generally considered the freest in nature: birds. This tells us as much about Musashi's inner life as any book on swordsmanship.

A number of those who were fortunate to own works by Musashi were moved to either write their own inscriptions on the backgrounds of the paintings or to ask others to do so. One work containing such an inscription shows a fat, happy Hotei, his huge bag supported by the stick over his shoulder. High in the void over his head is written a poem:

To find many joys
    in not being confused
is likely not so sophisticated.
    Be that as it may,
    the dancing Hotei.

Although the writer of this poem was Hoshina Masayuki (1609–72), a scholar and administrator in Aizu Wakamatsu, the sentiment—in its essence not very different from that of the poem above the kingfisher —may be a reflection of Musashi's own feelings at the time. Surely he had obtained some measure of enlightenment from his intense studies of Zen, and his happy portrayals of Hotei indicate a lightness of heart far removed from the ferocious intensity of the young Bennosuke of so many years before.

Other of Musashi's unique paintings of Hotei include one that is sometimes called *The Yawning Hotei*,[18] although "belly-laughing" could just as well be substituted for "yawning"; another is of the fat priest astride a huge ox,[19] with the wary grin of a man uncertain as to where his bottom will land at the next step of his mount. But all of Musashi's *suibokuga* are unique and—it bears repeating—provide us with an account of his spiritual life that we cannot find in his life history or his writings.

Musashi's insistence that he had no teachers in any of the arts he practiced, whether swordsmanship, painting, calligraphy, metallurgy, or sculpture, has been met with thinly veiled skepticism from a number of writers who are often quick to mention Kaiho Yusho, Yano Kichiju, or even Hon'ami Koetsu as possible teachers, and Liang K'ai and Hasegawa Tohaku as definite influences. Yet there is no evidence for such teaching other than one visit that Musashi made to Yano's school. All of these suggestions are interesting, however, and give the reader a bit more latitude in trying to understand how Musashi's talent could have developed to the heights it reached. All of the men who are sometimes mentioned as his teachers had some formal training, as did nearly all the famous swordsmen of this period. Thus, some skepticism in the face of Musashi's claim is probably understandable.

It may be interesting to mention here another artist who was Musashi's contemporary and who may have been an influence on the artist-swordsman, in spirit if not in technique. Their lifestyles and subject matter were certainly quite similar, and the possibility of their meeting and discussing art and Zen does not stretch the imagination too far at all.

Fugai Ekun (1568–1654) was a Zen priest who demonstrated his own independence by rejecting the tradition of residing in Zen temples. He first studied esoteric Shingon Buddhism, then turned to Zen, in which he trained intensively for ten years. Completing this training, he stepped out on the road and did not look back for the next two decades. In this independent wandering, his life was similar to Musashi's; and like Musashi, Fugai was strongly antimaterialistic, carrying with him only a few bare essentials, his brush and other tools of his trade, and an unwavering intention to perfect his art. Food was sometimes procured by trading a painting for it, and his lodging was likely to be whatever hut or lean-to he could find. Like Daruma and Musashi, he sometimes lived in caves.

There are no records of Fugai ever having trained under a particular teacher of *suibokuga*, but he, like Musashi, was influenced by the Chinese Zen artists of the Sung Dynasty and his favorite subjects were also Daruma and Hotei. Again, like Musashi, he not only painted but also practiced calligraphy, was a talented sculptor, and carved the seals that he used to sign his brushwork pieces.

In a striking parallel with Musashi, Fugai was also invited toward the end of his life to live in a castle town under the patronage of a local lord. Unfortunately, the lord of Odawara Castle did not seem to have possessed the same degree of culture and integrity as did the lord of Kumamoto Castle. Fugai soon departed and lived for another three years in a small temple on the Izu Peninsula. He was an original to the end: just as he felt death approaching, Fugai asked some local villagers to dig a large hole. He then stepped into it, stood up and died.

Fugai's paintings of Hotei bear the mark of a wonderfully light and independent spirit, and while his style is in no way similar to Musashi's, both men's paintings seem to emanate directly from their own individual Ways. It is easy to imagine the two of them camping out in an abandoned hut for a few days, sharing tea and talk and their own particular brand of Zen.

CALLIGRAPHY

Like the Zen artists and scholars of both China and Japan, Musashi also practiced calligraphy, and with the intensity that was customary for him. He had an interest in both the sword and the brush from an early age, and we may recall that he was on his way home from a calligraphy lesson at the age of thirteen when he saw the invitation to a sword match from Arima Kihei. One wonders if the young Bennosuke was as outraged at Arima's poor calligraphy as at the audacity of the swordsman's challenge.

At any rate, to gain a better measure of how his calligraphy might reveal the inner workings of Musashi's mind, it is helpful to review the differences in the Western and Eastern concepts of the art. For this, it may be interesting to compare the etymologies of the English word and its Sino-Japanese counterpart, *shodo* (書道). The English word "calligraphy" is a combination of two Greek words, *kallos*, meaning "beautiful," and *grafos*, meaning "something written." Thus, calligraphy in the West is something beautifully written, a linear grouping of individual letters in a graceful or ornate style, and it can be used apropos to anything from wedding invitations to diplomas to the Book of Kells.

Shodo, however, is another matter. In contrast to English words which are linear and composed of letters representing sounds rather than meaning, each Sino-Japanese character is itself a concept or a full word. In this sense, the character has a visual meaning of its own, and the goal of *shodo* is to express that visual meaning in way that is both beautiful and significant and manifests the artist's intent or state of mind. The first character, 書, means "to write," "writing," or "book," and its roots are a stylus or brush over a nominative (or possibly over a mouth exhaling), indicating something written. The second character,

道, means "street," "road" or "Way," and shows a head (intelligence) bounded by a character root indicating activity. Thus, rather than being a Way in the sense of a specified series of steps, it suggests a constantly moving intelligence; and the term *shodo*, like *kendo* (剣道), *karate-do* (空手道), or *sado* (tea ceremony; 茶道), includes within it a Way of life, or a Way of becoming more fully human.

So it is understandable that calligraphy would play a much more important role in everyday life in the Far East than in the Western world. In Japan, it is displayed on shop signs in the street and in the alcove in the entryway to the home, and *shodo* is a popular extra-curricular study for people of all ages. Calligraphy was no less important for the warrior class in feudal times. In *Hagakure*, Yamamoto Tsunetomo wrote that one should always be mindful of the way he writes, and that a man should write even a receipt with the understanding that it might be hung in someone's alcove.

Like *suibokuga*, the ink of each line of calligraphy is immediately absorbed into the paper or silk and cannot be corrected. Thus, each stroke of the brush is said to give insight into the character of the artist.

Although a number of Musashi's calligraphic works survive, by far the best known is a scroll upon which is written 戦氣 (*senki*), or "the spirit of battle," in large characters. These are followed by smaller characters reading "The cold current holds the moon, its clarity like a mirror," which is the first line of a couplet by Po Chu-i, the T'ang Dynasty poet. The entire couplet reads:

> The cold current holds the moon, its clarity like a mirror;
> The evening wind merges with the frost, piercing like a sword.

———

The large characters for "battle" and "spirit" are in the unmistakably bold and decisive style that one might expect from Musashi; and it may be interesting that the character for "battle" is made up of the elements used to write "simple" and "spear." That the "spirit of battle" could be reduced to the "spirit of a simple spear" would not have been lost on Musashi. He was, after all, a practitioner of Zen (禅), the character for which can be reduced as well to "manifesting [the] simple." At any rate, the balance of motion and stability in Musashi's characters are reminiscent of the gourd floating downstream that Takuan equated with the mind of Zen—moving along with water, but always itself. The smaller characters of Po's poem are much more loosely fluid, reminding one of the cold current itself.

The first line of Po's couplet reflect Musashi's insistence (and Takuan's as well) that the swordsman not have his mind catch or be caught by anything during conflict. The mind should be as clear and ungrasping as a cold stream, reflecting the opponent's activities, intentions, and morale. This is the clearing away of the clouds of confusion, the Emptiness of the final chapter of *The Book of Five Rings*.

Finally, the very choice of a line from a tenth-century Chinese poet shows us yet another dimension of Musashi's character. It is well known that he studied linked Japanese poetry, and we are reminded that he likely met Hosokawa Tadatoshi for the first time at a poetry circle in Kyoto. But Po Chu-i's poems were in classical Chinese—a language quite different from Japanese and one that Musashi had taught himself sometime during his life as a *shugyosha*. He found this particular couplet in his copy of the *Wakan roeishu*, a popular source since the eleventh century for the study and recitation of both classical Chinese and Japanese. Po Chu-i, who was called Hakurakuten by the Japanese, was one of Musashi's favorites among the old Chinese poets. One of the poems Musashi liked best was from Po's "Song of Unending Sorrow," and was perhaps, for him, the perfect expression of the Way of Nature and the turning of all things:

> In the spring breeze, the plum and damson blossoms open at night;

In the autumn frost, the leaves of the parasol and paulownia fall
in their season.

Thus, there were many nights when the old swordsman stayed up alone in his simple residence, only a candle lighting the text. In his famous low voice, he would have quietly chanted the bits and pieces of poems that so well reflected the sixty years that had brought him to his final home.

Fudo Myo-o

The range of the arts in which Musashi excelled was nearly as broad as that of the Kyoto sword polisher Hon'ami Koetsu. His abilities were founded in swordsmanship but encompassed *suibokuga* and calligraphy, both of which were further refined by his study of Chinese poetry and his practice of Zen meditation. He became quite expert at metallurgy, fashioning a number of sword guards that are still extant, and producing an elegantly simple saddle, which he gave to Nagaoka Yoriyuki, Nagoka Okinaga's son, and which remains in the Matsui family collection to this day.

One of his most remarkable works, however, was produced when Musashi returned his hand to the blade. This is a wooden statue of the deity Fudo Myo-o (literally, the "Immovable Brightness King"), who is ever ready to strike down the enemies of Buddhism.[20] This small wooden piece has Fudo Myo-o with his feet firmly planted on level ground, holding a single sword vertically at his right side. Eyes flaring and mouth set into a determined frown, he manifests an astonishingly palpable tension and wrathful energy. As if to underscore these qualities, his back and side are surrounded by flames. Japanese commentators have described this statue as having *kankei*, or "strength in spite of small stature," which can be further defined as strength contained in conciseness or brevity.

What would an "immovable" deity have to do with Musashi, whose swordsmanship required an absolute freedom of movement? For a concise view of Fudo Myo-o and his significance, we once again turn to "The Mysterious Record of Immovable Wisdom" by Takuan:[21]

> Although wisdom is called immovable, this does not signify any insentient thing, like wood or stone. It moves as the mind is wont to move: forward or back, to the left, to the right, in the ten directions and to the eight points; and the mind that does not stop at all is called *immovable wisdom*.
>
> Fudo Myo-o grasps the sword in his right hand and holds a rope in his left hand. He bares his teeth and his eyes flash with anger. His form stands firmly, ready to defeat the evil spirits that would obstruct the Buddhist Law. . . .
>
> What is called Fudo Myo-o is said to be one's unmoving mind and an unvacillating body. *Unvacillating* means not being detained by anything. . . . Glancing at something and not stopping the mind is called *immovable*.
>
> If ten men, each with a sword, come at you with weapons slashing, if you parry each sword without stopping the mind at each action, and go from one to the next, you will not be lacking in a proper action for every one of the ten.

This is one of the very foundations of Musashi's swordsmanship, and it is interesting that this commentary was given by Takuan, a Zen sect priest. But given the connection of the title and the structure of Musashi's *The Book of Five Rings* with Shingon Buddhism, and the fact that worship of Fudo Myo-o was introduced by that sect in the ninth century, it is worth taking a further look at this interesting deity who inspired Musashi.

There are a number of sutras devoted to Fudo Myo-o, giving various descriptions of him, but he is most often described as having

THE WAY OF THE BRUSH

a blue-black body, and being either standing or seated on a Diamond Seat and surrounded by the purifying flames of the Kali-yuga. In his right hand he holds the double-edged Sword of Wisdom (often with a dragon winding up around the blade) to cut through our ignorance, and in his left hand the ropes to tie up our passions, thus defeating the enemies of Buddhism—ignorance, greed, and hatred. Fudo's brow is covered with wavelike wrinkles, his left eye is often squinting, and from his curled upper lip one fang protrudes downward while another protrudes upward from his lower. Over his left shoulder hangs a braid of hair.

Fudo's title in Sanskrit is Vidyaraja, and the word *vidya*, at its root, means "wisdom" or "knowledge." The Sino-Japanese translation, *ming* (明), means "bright" or "clear," but connotes both wisdom and knowledge, and both the Sanskrit and the Sino-Japanese terms suggest that this knowledge is supernatural. As an esoteric sect, Shingon Buddhism holds that the repetition of spells or magic formulas (dharanis and mantras) is part of the key to enlightenment, and one of its main holy works, the Mahavairocana Sutra, indicates that these magical formulas are the active nature of Emptiness itself. Thus, the supernatural knowledge of the "Brightness" or of the "Wisdom Kings" like Fudo is the magical formula of a dharani or mantra. There are, in fact, five vidyarajas, each a manifestation of one of the five Dhyani Buddhas, all of whom possess the supernatural knowledge contained in these spells. Fudo is a manifestation of Vairocana, the central Buddha of Emptiness and the source of all the world's phenomena. What better deity for the writer of the Emptiness chapter of *The Book of Five Rings*?

Did Musashi engage in the practices of Shingon Buddhism as well of those of Zen? There is no evidence other than this sculpture, the title and structure of his book, and the tradition of the swordsman to sometimes ritually purify himself by meditating beneath waterfalls, all of which are closely associated with Fudo in Japan.

Musashi kept such things strictly to himself. What seems most likely, however, is that he did not adhere to any one sect in particular, Zen included. A staunch individualist, Musashi took from each sect that which was to him the most useful and true, and made it his own. The animals of nature, the patriarchs of Zen, the mystical deities of Shingon—all became manifestations of the spirit that moved and directed his Way.

————

Even as a Zen-inspired artist, Musashi is difficult to categorize into one particular school or group. He does not exactly fit into the classical mold of men from a century earlier, nor does he fall into the almost cartoonish style of the Zen priests Hakuin or Sengai, who would follow him. But his stature as an artist was never in doubt and, starting with the patronage of the powerful and cultured Hosokawa clan (which still owns the majority of his paintings today), his reputation only grew. By the end of the nineteenth century, however, the fate of traditional Japanese art itself was in jeopardy.

With the Meiji Restoration and the opening of the country in 1868, Japan turned its eyes overseas for the cultural and scientific knowledge from which it had effectively barred itself since the first half of the seventeenth century. Promising young men were sent to Germany to study medicine, to England to study technology and the parliamentary system, and to America to study the educational system. Soon, Western clothing and even Western haircuts came into vogue, and "things Japanese" came under suspicion of being "unenlightened."

In particular, the artistic heritage of Japan, of which painting was the primary expression, lost prestige dramatically, often with drastic consequences. Traditional paintings were given far less value and were sometimes thrown away; *ukiyo-e*, the hand-printed classic illustrations of the Edo period (1603–1868), were crumbled up and used for stuffing in sending exports overseas; and in the scramble to catch up, important cultural works were lost entirely or sold cheaply to foreign buyers. An anecdote from the *Record of Praise of Floating Waterweed* by a Viscount Fukuoka (1835–1919), coincidentally concerning a painting of Musashi's, illustrates the situation well.

> At the time I was amusing myself in Asakusa, and passed through the Raimon Gate. There was a roadside stand that had hung up a portrait of Daruma. The paper was dirty and sooty, and I could just barely see the heroic strength of the brush. I thereby put down twenty *sen*, and it was mine. I still didn't know whose painting it was. Later, I carefully inspected it and found a small seal on the bottom which read "Niten." For the first time I realized it was signed with Miyamoto Musashi's artist name, which was Niten. It was enough to observe the character of this painting to understand that he was the swordsman known to all.

In 1915, however, an interesting event occurred. When the new emperor attended the graduation ceremony at Tokyo Imperial University, he was invited, as was the tradition, to observe artistic and cultural works selected by the Department of Literature. That year, the department selected three works by Musashi: *Reed Leaf Daruma, Shrike on a Withered Branch,* and *Wild Geese and Reeds,* arranging them together and accompanying them with an explanation by a professor of art history. This caused no small excitement among both academic circles and the public at large, and it is indicative of the level of Musashi's artistic genius that his paintings were in the vanguard of what became a reevaluation by the Japanese of their own artistic traditions.

Musashi, however, had always been appreciated as an artist as well as a swordsman. His works were highly valued by the warrior-artists Watanabe Kazan and Tanomura Chikuden, and have been noted with extreme praise as being unparalleled in terms of observation, insight and precision by both Japanese and foreign art historians from the Edo period to the present. Even during the Meiji period (1868–1912), when Japanese art was held in low esteem by so much of the populace, Musashi's works were considered fundamental in the art history of the country by a number of important historians, including Okakura Tenshin, who worked with Ernest Fenellosa and wrote the famous *Book of Tea*, and Fujioka Sakutaro, who published Japan's first systematic history of art.

It may be interesting to finish this section with an evaluation by Fujikake Shizuya, a former professor of art at Tokyo Imperial University. In 1951, he wrote an article on the *Dancing Hotei* for the art magazine *Kokka*.

> Niten was praised as being pre-eminent in the Way of the Sword, and he was extraordinary as a swordsman. Although his painting was fundamentally an avocation, he surpassed the specialists in his artistic technique and was, once again, extraordinary. It can be thought that there exists in Niten's paintings the deepest meaning of his swordsmanship, and a sublime transcendence that communicates to the two disciplines. The strength of his spiritual originality is obvious. Niten's technique was truly in his ability to express the strength of this originality as artistic works in painting. This was not simply strength of character. Niten was extraordinarily skilled as a painter as well.

CHAPTER FOUR

The Way of Life and Death:
Reigan Cave

OLD AGE

A lthough he could feel his disease progressing, Musashi did not take up the life of a shut-in. On a typical day he went out accompanied by a retinue of six samurai and provisioned with a horse, a spear, and a carrying-pole box. At times he practiced *zazen*, either at the Taishoji or at the Reigan Cave on Mount Iwato, a steep hill at the foot of Mount Kinpo, some miles west of Kumamoto. Musashi reached the cave by following a narrow path that starts from behind the Unganzenji, the temple near the peak of the hill, then rises and cuts through the boulders to just below the cave's entrance. At the top of the precipice is a large boulder called "Black Rock," and it was while sitting on this that Musashi practiced Zen meditation. On clear days, he could see the peaks of the distant mountains and the Ariake Kai, the "Sea of Dawn."

Musashi also participated in everyday affairs and, of course, the training of his disciples, among whom were Terao Magonojo Katsunobu, Terao Kumanosuke Nobuyuki, and Nagaoka Yoriyuki. Yoriyuki, it will be remembered, was actually a son of Hosokawa Tadatoshi, but was given in adoption to Nagaoka Sado no kami Okinaga; and Musashi, too, seems to have become a sort of father figure to the young man. Yoriyuki often came to the old swordsman for advice, and their relationship had lighter moments as well. Once, Yoriyuki came to Musashi with a question and the response showed that Musashi, despite his sickness, had not lost all of his former strength. Bringing a number of heavy bamboo poles to Musashi, Yoriyuki asked how to determine which ones would be best to use as banners. Musashi replied that this was a relatively easy problem to solve. He grasped each bamboo pole by the base, went to the edge of the veranda and swung it down sharply with such force that some of the poles split and others broke off at the joints. Finally, he laid out all of those that had not broken and said, "I suppose these are all right." Yoriyuki laughed and said, "An unquestionable method, Sensei, but one that seems limited to a man a bit stronger than myself."

Musashi clearly stated his method of instructing his disciples in the Wind chapter of *The Book of Five Rings*:

> My way of teaching the martial arts is to take a man who is a beginner in the Way; have him learn according to those skills that he may develop well; teach him the principles that he will quickly understand first; see through the places where his mind may be suitable for matters not easily understood; and gradually, gradually, teach him the deeper principles later.
>
> Nevertheless, this is a matter of having him learn how to cross swords in battle, so there is no point called "the entrance to the interior."
>
> ———
>
> In my style, there is neither entrance nor depth to the sword, and there is no ultimate stance. There is only seeing through to its virtues with the mind. This is the essence of the martial arts.

In this way, Musashi taught each of his disciples individually at his *dojo*, judging each man for what would be appropriate or inappropriate for him to learn. Hating the hypocrisy and showmanship of other schools, he refused to make his disciples sign the usual blood oaths of secrecy and did not titillate them with promises of hidden principles and techniques to come. He was honest and understanding and did not push students to the point of collapse, as some teachers did then and do today. His approach was simple and direct.

Stances, for example, are limited to five: the Upper Stance (*jodan*), the Middle Stance (*chudan*), the Lower Stance (*gedan*), the Left-side Stance (*hidariwakigamae*), and the Right-side Stance (*migiwakigamae*). "There are no other stances than these five. No matter which of these stances you take, you should not think of the stance itself, but rather that you are going to cut down your opponent." Moreover, the stances are not essential in themselves, but can be adapted to suit the circumstances a practitioner encounters; as necessary, stances may be substituted one for another, or subtly altered. The point Musashi constantly drove home to his disciples was the importance of not becoming attached to even the simplest of techniques. Thus, all stances became one (or none) in his teaching of the Stance/No-Stance.

The same principle applied to the Two-Sword techniques that Yoriyuki, the Terao brothers, and the others all learned. Some of these, which have now been taken up and given names by styles that splintered off from the Niten Ichi-ryu Musashi taught, are as follows:

- The Jumonji ("cross") technique: The long and short swords are combined to make a cross. The practitioner waits for his opponent to attack, then pushes the opponent's sword aside with the short sword and at the same time strikes with the long sword.

- The Taka no Ha ("hawk wing") technique: The practitioner advances with both swords crossed in front of him. That is, the tip of the short sword held in the left hand points to the right, and the tip of the long sword held in the right hand points to the left. The instant the opponent attacks, the cross of the two swords is opened up. The form of this move is like the spreading of a hawk's wings.

- The Hiryuken ("flying dragon") technique: This was also called the Shuriken-uchi ("*shuriken* throw"). The practitioner throws the short sword like a *shuriken*. The short sword can either be brandished in front and then thrown or, while the long sword is revolved above, thrown from the left. This is meant not so much to hit the opponent as to destroy his stance.

- The Ryusetsuto ("snow on the willow") technique: The practitioner takes a stance in which the left side of the body is in front, with the short sword thrust forward, and the long sword is held to the right and back. When the opponent strikes in an effort to brush away the short sword, one drops that sword on purpose. In other words, losing the sword does not matter; rather it should fall from the hand "as the snow would fall from a willow branch." The opponent's blade will cut through a void without resistance, and at that instant, one strikes him with the long sword.

None of these techniques, however, was absolute. What was important in their execution was the same as in *suibokuga*: keeping the body fluid and the mind totally unmoved.

———

Thus, Musashi spent his late fifties teaching, painting, meditating, practicing tea, and writing poetry, among many other endeavors. He also advised Tadatoshi's son, Mitsuhisa, from time to time and participated in the activities of the fief. One interesting episode indicates that, although old and sick, he was still a man to be reckoned with.

On the third night of the New Year during this time, a ceremony of the first recitation of Noh drama was held at Mitsuhisa's Flower Garden Mansion, and Musashi attended. Before the standard formalities had begun, a certain Shimizu Hoki, who held the rank of group leader, yelled over from his seat to Musashi, "There's a story going around that when you fought Ganryu years ago, Ganryu managed to strike first! What do you say to that?" Musashi said nothing, but picked up a lamp and went straight to where Hoki was sitting. "When I was young, I had a kind of abscess on my head called a 'lotus root,' " Musashi said. "Because of the marks from that abscess, I've been unable to shave my forehead and have had to keep a full head of hair. In my fight with Ganryu, he used a real sword while I used a wooden one, so if he had struck first I would still have a scar. Take a good look." So saying, with his left hand holding the lamp, he pulled his hair back with his right hand and thrust his head into Hoki's face. Hoki drew back and said, "There's no scar that I can see." Musashi, however, pressed him further and in a quiet voice ordered, "Take a careful look, please." When Hoki said, "I have checked and I am sure," Musashi adjusted the lamp and returned to his seat, smoothing down his hair, calm and composed. The records note that "of all the samurai in attendance, there was not one whose hands were not sweating in breathless suspense."

By the early fall of 1643, however, when Musashi was sixty years old, he understood that his remaining time was limited. On October 10, he once again climbed Mount Iwato, prayed to the Iwato Kannon, "bowed in veneration to Heaven and stood before the Buddha" in an act of purification, and began to compose his literary legacy, *The Book of Five Rings*. He would now spend two years in meditation on his life and experiences, writing what he felt could be transmitted in words in the five short scrolls that made up this work. As he dipped his brush into the ink and wrote out the characters in his unique hand, he would have had no idea of the kind of interest that would be garnered by this effort, not only in Japan, but far beyond his own place and time.

THE FIVE-STORIED PAGODA

Musashi wrote *The Book of Five Rings* as a harmony of five chapters, with the image of the five rings of the title being related to the five-storied pagoda or stupa. The structure of the stupa traditionally symbolizes the true reality or expression of the universe, from the fundamental to the ethereal: earth, water, fire, wind, and the Void. None of these elements can exist independently, and all make their transformations according to circumstances and in accordance with each other. The chapters—actually individual scrolls—of Musashi's book were composed with this same interdependence in mind.

In the first chapter of his book, the Earth chapter, Musashi gave a brief summary of the contents of each chapter. The Earth chapter, he says, is an outline of the Way of the Martial Arts and of his own style. The Water chapter contains the principles of swordsmanship ("With the one, know the ten thousand"). The Fire chapter is concerned with victory or defeat in battle. The Wind chapter is on the other martial arts and their various styles. The Emptiness chapter is written so that readers "might naturally enter the Way of Truth."

A fuller summary is as follows:

In the Earth chapter, Musashi explained the significance of the martial arts as he had come to know them over the course of a half century, stressing the utter necessity of knowing the advantages of the weapons used and the fundamental principles of using them. Likening the martial artist to a master carpenter, he pointed out the relative levels of skill and explained the necessity of knowing one's tools. As Musashi himself had learned first-hand in his more than sixty bouts and six major military engagements, the martial artist must be practical: partiality towards (or bias against) one weapon or another is anathema, as is one-sidedness of any kind. On the one hand, he urged the student to wield the weapon that would be "fitting to his own abilities." On the other, he stressed the need to be ambidextrous and the advantages of being able to use two swords at once. The fundamental point of the martial arts, he declared, is to win: "Your real intent should be not to die with weapons uselessly worn at your side."

Musashi closed this chapter with rules for putting his martial arts into practice, and they are the bedrock of practicality supporting the entire book:

1. Think without any dishonesty.
2. Forge yourself in the Way.
3. Touch upon all of the arts.
4. Know the Ways of all occupations.
5. Know the advantages and disadvantages of everything.
6. Develop a discerning eye in all matters.
7. Understand what cannot be seen by the eye.
8. Pay attention to even small things.
9. Do not involve yourself with the impractical.

In the Water chapter, Musashi related the philosophy and the practice of his own style of swordsmanship, the Niten Ichi-ryu. This included the practical measures and practices for mental attitude, body posture, use of the eyes and feet, and the various ways of striking with the sword. In other martial arts, instructors taught their students to make extraordinary changes in both their mental attitudes and their body postures to adapt to the extraordinary circumstances of combat. Musashi, however, concluded that one's mind and body should be changed very little, if at all, from everyday attitudes. According to his experience, both body and mind "should be at peace and unwobbling."

This is to say that Musashi cautioned the student against being needlessly tense or lax, and advocated adaptability to any situation. Concentrate on a ploy, a stance, or a place on the opponent's body, and your actions will coagulate and bring about your defeat. This was

THE WAY OF LIFE AND DEATH

a teaching he held in common with the Zen priest Takuan, the fundamental point being to let both body and mind work freely, and not to allow them to be "caught" anywhere at all.

In the Water chapter, Musashi taught various stances and strikes that the student was to practice day and night. Still, the culmination of these was to be in the above-mentioned Stance/No-Stance and in the No-Thought/No-Concept Strike. Perhaps he was remembering the fight at the Ichijoji temple with the Yoshioka clan when he wrote, "It is best to think that one will cut a man down without considering a stance."

In the heat of battle, one does not have time to think about form, but only strikes his opponent down; and the practitioner's aim is not correct movement, but winning. Thus the student leaves by the same door through which he entered, and is no different than before. Yet, having internalized all of his practices, he is totally changed.

In the Fire chapter, Musashi wrote about the strategies and practical applications of combat, and developed the extrapolation of the "large martial art" from the "small martial art." This chapter begins with a section entitled "On Place," which considered the advantages and disadvantages of light sources and obstacles in the immediate area of an encounter. Musashi described this with such concrete examples that the reader can visualize situations the swordsman had experienced and the ways that he might have come to these insights. He made a subtle shift here, however, demonstrating that geographical advantages are psychological, and not just physical advantages, and he quickly moved to an emphasis on psychological techniques that continues throughout the chapter.

Taking the initiative, breaking the opponent's rhythm, checking stalemates, agitating or confusing the opponent, beating him down beyond his ability to recover—all of these are stressed as the psychological components of battle necessary to gain the victory. And yet, much as in the previous chapter on stances and strikes, he advises: "In order to win, do not select a method."

This is psychology at its best. It is also the foundation of Musashi's martial art and its very point of departure.

A reading of Musashi's life shows that he was a master of psychology as a technique, and that he used it time and again. The Yoshioka fell to it, as did even the Demon of the Western Provinces, Sasaki Kojiro. Although Musashi could have relied on strength and speed—recall that he was described as being big-boned, remarkably strong, yet nimble—he used strategy instead. As he wrote in the Wind chapter, "In my martial art, it is essential . . . that you bend and warp your *opponent*, taking the victory by twisting and distorting your opponent's mind."

———

When Musashi was sitting high up in the Reigan Cave writing *The Book of Five Rings*, there were a great number of competing schools of swordsmanship, each claiming superiority over the others by virtue of some hidden way of grasping the sword or some secret stance. In Kyushu, both the Shinkage-ryu and the Taisha-ryu were popular; it will be remembered that Hosokawa Tadatoshi himself had studied the former style and been very satisfied with it, leaving it only when Musashi defeated his own Yagyu-appointed sparring partner. In Higo Kumamoto, a sizeable and strategically important castle town, there were any number of stylists who had hung out shingles and were doing their best to attract students with flashy techniques and promises of the "deepest hidden traditions." In his Wind chapter, Musashi exposes the failings and contrivances of these other schools, with the undercurrent of thought that is expressed clearly in the *Sun Tzu*, the ancient Chinese classic: "If you know the enemy and know yourself, you will not be endangered in a hundred battles."

The danger Musashi alludes to here, however, was more concerned with what the swordsman might do to himself if he considered the "heresies" of other schools to be the True Way. In the beginning Musashi states the thrust of the chapter quite concisely: "The other schools get along with this as a performance art, as a method of making a living, as a colorful decoration, or as a means of forcing flowers to bloom. Yet, can it be the True Way if it has been made into a saleable item?"

This is followed by a very crucial point: "Moreover, the other martial arts in the world only give fine attention to swordsmanship: teaching ways of handling the sword, body postures or hand positions. Can you understand how to win from such things? None of them is the unfailing Way."

Thus, in exposing the faults of other styles, Musashi criticized hypocrisy, the kind of thinking that limits the martial arts to sword technique and, most importantly, the deep attachment to form and equipment that could scotch a student's freedom of movement and mind. Other schools taught absolutes in terms of a certain length of the sword, a special stance, or in a secret way of fixing the eyes. Musashi pointed out the failings in techniques themselves and in the insistence on using a certain technique or weapon regardless of the circumstances. Musashi's main concern was practicality, and in this chapter he demonstrated the impracticality of some of the more esoteric approaches to the martial arts.

———

The Emptiness chapter provides in very few words a frame of meditation for the philosophical foundation of the preceding four chapters. It is a description of the Great Way in which Musashi's Way is deeply rooted. Emptiness is Existence, Existence is Emptiness, and attachment is the great heresy. *The Book of Five Rings* has been an article of daily meditation and recitation for sword practitioners over the centuries, much as the Heart Sutra has been for Buddhists all over the world; and the Emptiness chapter is the perfect parallel to the mantra at the end of that sutra.

It is natural that this chapter would be Buddhist in its orientation.

Musashi lived within the context of Buddhism all his life, from the Pure Land Buddhism of his parents to the Rinzai Zen of his friend Takuan and the Hosokawa clan. Moreover, his students would have been familiar with the concepts in this chapter, as would most educated and cultured people of his time.

Yet, if the vocabulary is Buddhist, the phrasing is pure Musashi, each sentence supporting and deepening the principles of his Way. At its center, the chapter points directly to the martial arts, to the art of Musashi's life, and to the mature understanding that he gained by the final years of his life. The Emptiness chapter[1] brings *The Book of Five Rings* around in a full circle to the Earth chapter again. It is the perfect *enso* (circle of enlightenment),[2] giving the work a center that is everywhere and that cannot be pinned down. The Emptiness chapter is the blade and the grip of the sword, the hand that grasps it, and the mind that informs it all.

> Make the heart of truth your Way, . . . Accordingly, you will make Emptiness the Way, and see the Way as Emptiness.

THE CONCEPT OF THE FIVE RINGS IN ESOTERIC BUDDHISM

Traveling the backroads of Japan or wandering through the temple precincts there, one often finds five-tiered stone monuments called stupas. These can range from two to more than ten feet high and they are often made of plain granite or some other hard stone. Stupas are descended from original monuments that held relics of the Buddha and, later, his saints. Believers consider them to hold the actual presence of the Buddha or his Truth. There is an interesting connection between this ubiquitous monument and *The Book of Five Rings* that is worthy of note.

When the monk Kukai returned to Japan from China in C.E. 806, he brought with him an understanding of a new, esoteric form of Buddhism that he called the Shingon, or True Word, sect. Kukai was

THE WAY OF LIFE AND DEATH

not only a devout Buddhist but a brilliant teacher, and an artist. He is credited with having created the *kana* system of Japanese orthography (the syllabaries that are used together with *kanji*), and is considered the patron saint of calligraphy. The Shingon sect grew rapidly in importance during his lifetime and gained favor especially among the aristocracy, who loved its rituals and artistic representations. Kukai taught that the esoteric meanings of Shingon could be conveyed not in wordy explanations, but rather through art. This notion of Truth through Art had a direct appeal to Japanese sensibilities, and the basic assumptions of Shingon have always been a strong undercurrent in Japanese culture, despite the later ascendancy of the Zen and Pure Land sects of Buddhism. Even the tea ceremony, with its well-known connections to Zen, probably in fact owes its aesthetic foundations more to Shingon than to Zen.

Among the tenets of Shingon Buddhism is the assertion that the esoteric teachings were taught not by the historical Buddha, Shakyamuni, but by Vairocana, the cosmic Buddha, who is in fact the universe itself. Vairocana is manifested in a number of artistic forms, but in Japan he is often represented by the five-tiered stone pagoda, or *sotoba*, also called the *gorinto*, or Tower of Five Rings (*Gorin no sho* is the Japanese title of Musashi's book; *sho* means "book). This *gorinto* is usually constructed as follows: a square stone at the bottom represents the Earth Element, or stability and the fundamental element of being; next, a round stone represents the Water Element, or permeation and vacuity; a triangular stone represents the Fire Element, or purity and perfect activity; a crescent-shaped stone represents the Wind Element, or growth and perfect awareness; and, at the top, a stone in the shape of a mani-jewel (wish-fulfilling gem) represents the Void Element, or space. The stones are inscribed respectively with the Sanskrit letters A, Vi, Ra, Hum, and Kham, which together represent Vairocana himself, the very essence of the universe.

According to Kukai, these five elements are constantly interfusing to form the various manifestations of the universe, and hence Vairocana. We see the forms, but we are too unenlightened to recognize them for what they are. The outward result of this eternal interplay is impermanence, but what is inherent in every single form, no matter how small or large, earthy or ethereal, is Emptiness.

Each of the five rings also represents one of the Five Dhyani Buddhas, and each of these has its own corresponding element (Earth, Water, Fire, Wind, and Void), color, location (south, east, west, north, and center), mudra (meditative hand gesture), meaning and transformational wisdom. Shingon teaches that constant meditation on these Buddhas and their aspects will eventually result in the unification with Vairocana, and thus in enlightenment.

The parallels of this system with the title and structure of Musashi's work are too obvious to pass over. Each chapter does indeed echo, reflect, and fuse with the others, as do the Five Elements in Shingon. One chapter cannot be read to the exclusion of the others, or the full meaning will be lost.

Shingon Buddhism[3] is not specifically mentioned in *The Book of Five Rings*, nor is Pure Land or Zen. Musashi, however, was too inquisitive about the world and too intense an artist to have ignored this system of thought; and indeed he urges us to know the various Ways of the world. What kind of austerities Musashi performed in the Reigan Cave while meditating on his life work is not known, but the burning eyes and taut muscles of his sculpture of Fudo Myo-o, the manifestation of Shingon's central Buddha, Vairocana, suggest that we might look for meanings that lie deeper than the words on the page.

BASIC PRINCIPLES

Musashi's structure of *The Book of Five Rings* provided an outline of various themes: a general look at the martial arts, his own particular style, the problems of combat, other styles, and philosophical foundations.

There are a number of fundamental principles established throughout the book, however, that, although emphasized strongly in certain chapters, are not particularly tied down to any one chapter. These principles form the essence of Musashi's martial art—what the Japanese term the *shinzui*, the true pith or marrow—and from them develop the skeleton, muscles, and skin of everything he taught. Like his life and his art, they are another window through which we have a glimpse of Musashi's soul.[4]

THE WAY OF THE MARTIAL ARTS IS TO WIN

Some eighty years after Musashi's death, Yamamoto Tsunetomo, a samurai of the Nabeshima clan in nearby Hizen, dictated what would become the most famous words of his book, *Hagakure*, and gave expression to one of the major tenets of the warrior's way of life:

> The Way of the Samurai is found in death. When it comes to either/or, there is only the quick choice of death. It is not particularly difficult. Be determined and advance. To say that dying without reaching one's aim is to die a dog's death is the frivolous way of sophisticates. When pressed with the choice of life or death, it is not necessary to gain one's aim.

This was not so radical as it may seem. The samurai served a master, and his master supported not only the samurai's own life but the lives of his entire family. The clan was the samurai's prime identity and he was expected, as a warrior, to lay down his life for it. Tsunetomo's conclusion that giving up one's life was "the substance of the samurai Way" was, while given remarkable expression here, not all that remarkable an idea.

Musashi, however, completely rejected this concept. For him, the

Way of the Warrior was to wear two swords into battle, to be able to use those swords well, and to defeat the enemy. Death would eventually come to everyone, and resolve in the face of death was not the crucial point distinguishing the samurai from other classes in society.

> Generally speaking, when people contemplate the heart of warrior thought, they consider it simply a Way in which a warrior learns to be resolute toward death. But this is not actually the essence of the Way: what distinguishes the warrior and is most basic in the Way of the Martial Arts is learning to overcome your opponent in each and every event.

———

> The true Way of swordsmanship is to fight with your opponent and win.

Why else, Musashi asked, would a lord give a man two swords and a stipend?

Musashi's motive for writing *The Book of Five Rings* was to give his students—and their students after them—a Way to defeat their opponents.[5] His Way was one of victory, not of death in battle, and to that end he encouraged the student "to practice in the morning and train in the evening."

> Your real intent should not be to die with weapons worn uselessly at your side.

———

> Moreover, my Way of the Martial Arts is to know the Way of victory with certainty when you are fighting for your life alone against five or ten men.

Closely connected with his opposition to a warrior's stepping into battle simply to die was Musashi's contention that many of the martial arts schools taught useless, showy techniques. He declared that if students relied on such techniques, it would be the same as fighting only to die with attractive form, but without victory. What was important to Musashi was not so much the flower as the fruit, and the fruit was clearly defined as the defeat of the enemy:

> The other schools get along with this as a performance art, as a method of making a living, as a colorful decoration, or as a means of forcing flowers to bloom.

———

> In the way of the martial arts, especially, form is made into ornament.

———

> While other schools look good to the eye, none of them contains the heart of Truth.

It would seem to be common sense that the reason for being involved with the martial arts during this period was the goal of defeating one's opponent. Musashi considered this common sense, but some martial artists clearly did not.

DISCIPLINE

It is not uncommon in Oriental literature for major themes and propositions to be given away in the very beginning of a work. Kamo no Chomei, the writer of the thirteenth-century *Hojoki* (*Record of a Ten-Foot-Square Hut*), for example, expressed his entire theme in the first line, "The flow of the river is unending, but the water is never the same."

Musashi also provided the reader with one of his most fundamental themes in the very first line of his book: "[A]fter many years of discipline, I have thought to describe [my own Way of the Martial Arts] for the first time." This was not a light entry. The absolute necessity of discipline and practice is repeated over and over again in *The Book of Five Rings*, and it is no accident that phrases like "You should take up the sword and practice," "You should investigate this thoroughly," "You should make great efforts in this," or "This is something you should practice thoroughly" appear at the end of almost every section of the work. Musashi's realization of the Way was not given to him all at once in a dream or a moment of satori. It was acquired only through a never-ending discipline.

Without discipline, one would never forge himself into a true swordsman and never make the art his own; Musashi made it clear, in his Water chapter, that transformation comes only with practice: "The journey of a thousand *ri* [6] proceeds step by step, so think without rushing. Understanding that this is the duty of a warrior, put these practices into action, surpass today what you were yesterday, go beyond those of poor skill tomorrow and exceed those who are skillful later."

It is strongly implied in *The Book of Five Rings* that discipline is far more important than any lesson on fancy footwork or on how to gain the advantage of length with a particular grip on a sword. Musashi felt that techniques have little value unless they are internalized and verified by constant practice and investigation. To express this principle, he wrote the now-famous line, "See to it that you temper yourself with one thousand days of practice, and refine yourself with ten thousand days of training."

Musashi defeated over sixty men between his thirteenth and twenty-ninth years, and these statements leave us with little doubt as to how he otherwise spent his time.

Closely linked to the subject of discipline is Musashi's insistence on gaining direct, not theoretical, knowledge. We know with certainty that Musashi was deeply involved in Zen practice in the last years of his life, but we do not know just when this involvement began. However, Musashi undoubtedly had a strong penchant for many Zen principles from the very beginning. His repeated dictum, "You should investigate this thoroughly," echoes the common Zen phrase, "See everything for yourself" (*issai jikan*). He did not survive his personal bouts and major battles on armchair knowledge. Early in *The Book of Five Rings* he states, "Learning these principles indoors, studying all the minor details but forgetting the Way of actuality will likely be of little use at all." He also insisted that "You should train in the Way of the Sword with your hands."

Musashi's pragmatic emphasis on real knowledge led to his disdain for partiality of any sort in the practice of the martial arts. To him, real knowledge meant real efficiency in every situation. He spoke derisively of practitioners whose view was too narrow: "[N]ot knowing how to defeat others in any situation, they put virtue in the length of the sword and think they can win by their distance from their opponent."

Real knowledge implies real freedom, and any prejudice for one weapon over another or one stance over another, or for anything at all, does nothing more than hobble a man or put blinders on his gaze: "But with weapons as with other things, you should not make distinctions or preferences. It is wrong for either general or soldier to have a preference for one thing and to dislike another."

Musashi illustrated the positive approach to this principle with the example of a carpenter. Just as a carpenter must have real knowledge of his tools in order to succeed in his various projects, he wrote, so must the warrior have an intimate knowledge of his weapons for the various virtues they will have in real situations: "When you put your life on the line, you want all your weapons to be of use."

Musashi wrote that the swordsman should know all the Ways, and not just theoretically. Preference or prejudice is akin to untried theory, and both are detriments to real knowledge. Real knowledge understands that an oar may be more efficacious than a naked blade, or that a simple change in technique may determine the outcome of a battle. In this sense, Musashi's style was one of expediency, but such a style cannot be successfully executed with a one-track mind. In the end, "The Way of this style is the mind that obtains the victory with anything at all."

EVERYDAY MIND

Musashi despised the showy techniques and "hidden meanings" taught by other schools. Not only did they transform the study of the sword, its implements and even its instructors into commodities to be bought and sold, but they put students in a false frame of mind. Musashi's understanding of the Way of the Martial Arts was similar to the approach of Zen Buddhists to their practice: he considered it nothing extraordinary, nothing that would require mysterious or flashy leaps of either body or mind.

Concerning the mind, he wrote in the Water chapter: "In the Way of the martial arts, do not let your frame of mind be any different from your everyday mind."

Neither too taut, nor too lax, the mind was not to depart from its normal condition. Musashi no doubt discovered this principle on his own, but he would not have failed to notice its similarity to Zen when he studied the *Gateless Gate*, the thirteenth-century Chinese collection of koans that was almost required study for serious practitioners of that sect. In the nineteenth case of that book are these famous lines:

"Nansen was asked by Joshu, 'What is the Way?' He replied, 'Your everyday mind is the Way [*Heijoshin kore do*].' "

For Musashi, the body was to be regarded in the same light: the outstanding was unnatural, and the unnatural was not real. If a practice was not built on a foundation of reality, it would only become an obstruction, mere baggage on the way to victory or, more likely, to defeat: "In all things concerning the body in the martial arts, make the everyday body the body for the martial arts, and the body for the martial arts the everyday body."

Feet, eyes, hands, and general stance: nothing was to be moved, concentrated, or arranged in an unnatural fashion. To give one example, "In the use of the feet, you should walk as usual." No leaping or running—nothing to get the mind "caught" or distracted from the work at hand. Both body and mind must be released from concentration on extraordinary feats and be allowed to function in an everyday mode. Musashi regarded every unnatural stride, hand maneuver, or fixing of the eyes as abnormal attention to trivia. He urged his students to remain free. As the popular seventh-century Chinese Zen manual, the *Hsinhsinming* urged: "Let go of the mind, and it will be natural [*hoshin shizen*]."

FLUIDITY

As already mentioned, Musashi's most famous sculpture is a small statue of Fudo Myo-o, and his knowledge of the symbolism of Shingon Buddhism indicates that he had a deep understanding of this Buddhist deity. It is probably no coincidence that his friend, the priest Takuan, also had an affinity for Fudo Myo-o. Takuan wrote in "The Mysterious Record of Immovable Wisdom":

> The man who is close to enlightenment understands that [Fudo Myo-o's image] manifests immovable wisdom and clears away

all delusion. For the man who can make his immovable wisdom apparent and who is able to practice this mental dharma as well as Fudo Myo-o, the evil spirits will no longer proliferate. This is the purpose of Fudo Myo-o's tidings.

Takuan is again referring to his "unmoving mind and unvacillating body." This is exactly the same as letting go of the mind (and body), and means that both are to be in a state of fluidity. Musashi hints at this principle throughout *The Book of Five Rings*, but discusses it most explicitly in the Water chapter. Consider the following:

Water follows the form of either an angular or round container; it becomes either a drop or a great sea.

———

Do not let your mind stand still, even when you are in repose.

———

Let [the mind] sway peacefully, not allowing it to stop doing so, even for a moment.

And, echoing Takuan's writings, "Even when the action is extraordinarily lively on the battlefield, you should take the principles of the martial arts to the extreme and keep your mind unmoved."

Musashi and Takuan both believed that the great mistake was being slowed or rendered immobile by what one sees, hears, feels, or thinks. For them, even an instant's preoccupation could be fatal. Both body and mind must be free to flow and to respond to whatever the situation demands. Again, in the Water chapter Musashi wrote specifically of the hands: "In all things . . . immobility is undesirable. Immobility means a dead hand; mobility means a living hand." The same might have been said of the body and mind.

In "The Lesson of Stance/No-Stance," Musashi discussed how, with just a slight movement, one stance becomes another, and this invokes a constantly fluid situation: "This is the principle in which there is, and there is not, a stance. At its heart, this is first taking up the sword and then cutting down your opponent, no matter what is done or how it happens."

Fluidity means having no obstruction, and particularly no obstruction from one's own mind. We must be careful not to create our own fetters or our own inflexibility. Musashi expresses this principle in the following passages from the Wind chapter:

> The knowledge of sword techniques . . . is undesirable in the martial arts. Thinking of the various ways of cutting someone down confuses the mind.

> It is harmful to specialize in stances with the sword. Establishing hard and fast rules is not the Way of victory.

> As they fix their mind on one special place, they confuse the mind and inflict a malady on the martial arts.

There is an interesting story about Musashi and Takuan that illustrates this principle quite well. Once when they were discussing the virtues of Zen as it applied to everyday life, the priest invited Musashi to attack him with a wooden sword. He would defend himself, Takuan said, with only a fan. Musashi, the story goes, grasped his wooden sword and took several stances facing Takuan, but the priest simply stood there with his arms lowered, one hand grasping the fan. After a long while, Musashi threw away his sword in disgust and declared that he had been unable to find an opening in which to strike. Takuan's mind had been everywhere and therefore nowhere, and in this perfect state of fluidity he had become unassailable.

Musashi must have thought over this "bout" for many years, and internalized the lesson. In the end, he could write from his own experience, "Without putting your mind anywhere, strike him quickly and directly."

This gives a slightly different slant to Chomei's line—"The flow of the river is unending, but the water is never the same"—one that may have shocked the old recluse in his lonely hut.

PSYCHOLOGY

About two thousand years before Musashi's time, Sun Tzu, the Chinese philosopher of war, wrote, "Warfare is the Way of deception."

The word "deception," or *ki* (詭; *kuei* in Chinese), is etymologically derived from "what is not correct" and, interestingly enough, can also mean "to cheat," "to be cunning," or "to be perverse." The *Sun Tzu*, popularly known as *The Art of War*, became required reading for every general, warlord or politician from the fourth century B.C.E. through the time of Mao Tse-tung in China, and for every feudal lord, commander, and literate samurai in Japan. Musashi would have known this work well.

About ten years before *The Book of Five Rings* was completed, another famous Japanese swordsman, Yagyu Munenori, wrote a phrase very similar to Sun Tzu's in his own work, *The Life-Giving Sword*: "Duplicity is the foundation of the martial arts."

"Duplicity" in this case is *hyori*, literally "inside and outside," but it also means "double-dealing," "treachery," and "dishonesty." So the meaning is, perhaps, not far from that of his distant Chinese predecessor, and Munenori would certainly have studied Sun Tzu's writings as well. As the Yagyu-ryu was one of the most important schools in Japan, and Munenori himself was the instructor to the Tokugawa shoguns, this germinal maxim was likely on the lips of many a student of the martial arts.

Musashi did not use either phrase in *The Book of Five Rings*, and his personality was such that he may have found the words themselves repugnant. He had a strong sense of his martial art being founded on principles, not tricks or dishonesty, and his vocabulary reflected this. In *The Book of Five Rings* he wrote, "The Way of the martial arts is direct and true, so it is essential that you be intent on pursuing others and subjugating them with true principles." His choice of words like "direct," "true," and "true principles" reflects Musashi's sense that the martial arts is to follow the straight and narrow. His were the "principles of life and death," and he had no patience with trivial tricks or lading the mind with strategies.

That said, it is quite doubtful that any swordsman ever used psychology more often, or to better effect, than Miyamoto Musashi. He constantly reflected on the relationship of the opponent's frame of mind to his own, and that of his own frame of mind to combat itself. As we have seen, the histories of his bouts give us several examples of how he used this psychology in life and death situations.

The classic example is the celebrated bout with Sasaki Kojiro at Ganryu Island on 13 April 1612. It will be recalled that Musashi slept well beyond the agreed time of the match, making even the proprietor of his lodging nervous. Meanwhile, Sasaki and his entourage, in formal dress, waited on the island in the hot sun and speculated about whether their opponent might have fled in fear. By the time Musashi's boat appeared on the horizon, Sasaki was outraged that he had been made to wait for so long and in such discomfort. As his opponent's craft drew near, Sasaki ran to meet it, angrily accusing Musashi of disrespect. Musashi met this outburst with blank silence. As if this weren't unnerving enough, Sasaki then saw that Musashi's weapon was not the standard wooden sword, but an oar carved into the shape of a sword, slightly longer than his own sword. Sasaki was known for the length of his sword, and with this turn of events his confidence took a further slide. Impatiently, Sasaki unsheathed his sword and dramatically flung the scabbard away, into the waves. At this, Musashi spoke for the first time: "You've lost, Kojiro. Only the loser will have no need for his scabbard."

Sasaki's frame of mind can be imagined, and the result of the ensuing contest is the stuff of legend. As the Demon of the Western Provinces lay in the sand, blood flowing from his mouth and nose, Musashi approached with care. Suddenly, the fallen man struck out with a sweep of his sword, cutting into his opponent's *hakama*, but not piercing the flesh. At this point Musashi gave a final blow, crushing Sasaki's chest and ending his life.

Musashi must have given deep thought to Sasaki's character: to the sense of dignity that could be bruised, putting him off balance; to the pride in and perhaps dependence on the length of his sword, and the offense he would take at Musashi's lack of a proper weapon; and to the impatience he might feel at having to wait, the way that his calm would slip away bit by bit. In the section of his Fire chapter called "Agitating Your Opponent," he wrote: "There are many kinds of agitation. One is a feeling of danger, a second is a feeling that something is beyond your capacity and a third is a feeling of the unexpected. You should investigate this thoroughly."

And in another section: "In my martial art . . . you bend and warp your opponent, taking the victory by twisting and contorting your opponent's mind."

Perhaps what he learned in this bout was expressed in the following comments. Certainly they give the reader a vivid impression of Sasaki's last desperate strike:

> You must cut him down with such vigor that he cannot recover.

――――

There may be times when you appear to be winning on the

surface, but hostility remains in your opponent's mind. In such situations it is important that you adjust your own mind, destroy your opponent's spirit, and make sure that he has been defeated in the very bottom of his heart.

Another series of matches in which Musashi demonstrated his understanding of the importance of psychology was, as we have seen, his fight with the Yoshioka clan in 1604. In the first two matches with Seijuro and Denshichiro, Musashi arrived late, putting his opponents off guard with feelings of resentment, offense and anger. So unsettled was Denshichiro at the defeat of his older brother that Musashi was able to quickly take the Yoshioka warrior's own sword (a very long one) away and turn it against Denshichiro, killing him. In the final match with Matashichiro, Musashi reversed his psychological tactic and arrived early. Thus, when the large Yoshioka force arrived and began grumbling about their opponent's likely late arrival, Musashi suddenly appeared, saying, "Did I make you wait?" As they reacted with fear and surprise, he took advantage of their disarray and cut them down one after another. Here, Musashi demonstrated his understanding of the principle of warping the opponent's mind. In the Fire chapter, he gave this yet another dimension:

> The heart of Mountains and Seas is that it is wrong to use the same tactic repeatedly during a fight between you and your opponent. Using the same tactic twice is unavoidable, but you should not use it three times. Thus, if your opponent is thinking "mountains," attack with "seas;" and if he is thinking "seas," attack with "mountains." This is the heart of the Way of the martial arts.

These are only a few of the psychological insights Musashi discussed in *The Book of Five Rings*. He wrote further on the advantages of such tactics as making the opponent think that you are larger in stature than he is, making him flinch, convincing him that you are an expert in the martial arts (and so convincing him of his own imminent defeat), or conversely, appearing weak at first and then attacking with ferocity. All might be summed up in the short phrase toward the end of his book:

The Way [of victory] is in devising difficulties for your opponent.

Musashi had won over sixty bouts by the time he was thirty, and by his own reckoning this feat was not due to extraordinary strength, speed, or skill. As he traveled the country alone, however, he must have thought deeply about what had been in his opponents' minds and, just as important, what had been in his own. It was this deep capacity for reflection, his natural curiosity, and his constant search for insight that set Musashi far beyond his contemporaries. This is in part why we still read his slender book today.

———

In addition to these principles, Musashi also discussed in great depth the importance of taking the initiative, having an impeccable understanding of the tools of the trade, being able to grasp the various kinds of rhythms used in the martial arts, having the ability to see both broadly and closely, and, above all, being able to see through the opponent's mind but not letting him see through your own.

Musashi believed in principles, not tricks, and in substance over form and flashiness. As indicated at the beginning of this section, the principles he discovered are discussed in *The Book of Five Rings* both explicitly and between the lines. Informing us that he bowed in veneration to the gods and Buddhas while not invoking them for help is in itself a lesson on the principle of self-sufficiency. This in turn enjoins us to believe in the principles we make our own and in the abilities we develop from putting those principles into practice. When he wrote

"Though I fought as many as sixty matches," he was clearly addressing the necessity of real experience.

To grasp the book, one must read it thoroughly on one's own. To quote Musashi once again:

> You will not reach the essence of the martial arts by merely looking at this book. Think that what is written down here was done just for you, and do not consider simply looking at it, familiarizing yourself with it or trying to imitate it. Rather, you should consider these principles as though they were discovered from your own mind, and continually make great efforts to make them a physical part of yourself.

FINAL DAYS

By the early spring of 1645, Musashi could barely walk the pathway leading to the Reigan Cave, and climbing up to the cave racked his body with pain. In April, understanding that his life was nearly over, he wrote a polite letter to the senior retainers of the Hosokawa clan:

> I have felt sick prior to this, and since the spring, both hands and feet have been difficult to arouse. I no longer have any desire for a stipend. As the last generation, Lord Tadatoshi, had a refined taste for the martial arts, I came to this province strongly hoping he would voice judgement on my style. Just as Lord Tadatoshi had almost kindly grasped the moves of the Two-Sword Style, he suddenly passed away, and the chance of attaining my long-cherished desire was completely lost. As it was my lord's wish, I wrote down a summary of the principles of the martial arts, and presented it to him.
>
> For what I have judged the laws of Two Swords, I have not used the old words and phrases of the Confucianists or Buddhists,[7] nor have I used the old stories of the military arts. I have

thought through the ways of all the arts and accomplishments together. This should be understood in accordance with the principles of the world, but it has not been in accord with the times. This is truly regrettable.

Well then, when I look back now on my own way of life, it would seem as though I lived too much to the letter of the martial arts. This is because I was taken by the true "martial arts disease." I have pursued fame, and would seem to be leaving my name as a sort of famous person to this floating world. But now, neither hands nor feet will function, and I cannot directly teach the secrets of my style. It appears to be difficult to plan out my life any longer. It is my intention now to seclude myself in the mountains, and await my own death, even if I last but a single day. I hereby ask for your permission.

April 13
Miyamoto Musashi

Soon after sending this letter, he made his last painful climb up to the Reigan Cave to wait peacefully and alone for death.

The three retainers to whom Musashi had addressed his letter were at first willing to comply with the sick man's wishes, and they may initially have felt too intimidated to reject his proposal. But soon they became uncomfortable with the idea of simply discarding a man who had been so respected by their late master, Tadatoshi. Moreover, there were all sorts of stories coming into Kumamoto. People who lived not far below the cave were reporting seeing lights emanating from the cave at night, and an eerie atmosphere that seemed to whistle around its entrance. No one, of course, dared to climb up and look into the cave under these circumstances, but it may have been that Musashi was practicing intense *zazen*, and perhaps some of the more esoteric forms of Shingon meditation. Was he communicating with the spirit of Ganryu Sasaki Kojiro?[8] The cave was, after all, named for Kojiro's spirit. No one knew, but the combination of these reports and the guilt felt by the three Hosokawa retainers resulted in some action.

The man who looked after Musashi's affairs in his later years was Matsui (Nagaoka) Sado no kami Okinaga. Okinaga's grandfather, Matsui Hiroyuki, had served the shogunate governments of both Ashikaga Yoshiharu and Yoshiteru. Okinaga's father, Yasuyuki, had served as an important retainer to both Hosokawa Fujitaka and his successor, Tadaoki. Yasuyuki's eldest son, Okiyuki, was killed in battle. It was then that his second son, Okinaga, who inherited the family headship, took Hosokawa Tadaoki's second daughter as his wife and adopted his sixth son, Yoriyuki. Thus, their connection with the Hosokawa clan was a close one, and by the time of the fourth-generation lord, Mitsuhisa, Okinaga received the rather large stipend of thirty thousand *koku* and was warden of Yatsushiro Castle.

Considering these ties and the fact that Okinaga had been a disciple of Musashi's father, it is not surprising that this particular vassal and his adopted son, Yoriyuki, were appointed to look after Musashi at this time. Knowing that the damp and isolated cave would not help Musashi's deteriorating health, they began sending up a doctor who could attend to the swordsman and supply him with medicine when it was needed. Musashi, however, meant to meet death on his own terms and refused even these solicitous advances. Finally it was decided that Yoriyuki would have to bring Musashi back.

On a fine day at the beginning of May, Yoriyuki went out into the hills on the pretense of hawking, and dropped by the cave. There he found Musashi in such a weakened state that the old man could no longer put up any resistance. Yoriyuki knew what he had to do, and despite Musashi's protests, "persuaded" him to come home.

It is difficult to imagine the feelings of these two men that day— one, the independent old swordsman who had always lived on his own terms, and the other, his young disciple and a relative of the two men who had so helped Musashi in his career—stumbling down the mountain in late spring. The young man carried the older on his back at least part of the way. The cherry blossoms, symbol of the warrior in Japan, had already fallen, and the new, light green leaves were everywhere. The sun in Kyushu would have been quite warm by May, but Yoriyuki did not falter. Soon Musashi was lying on his futon at his residence on the grounds of the old Chiba Castle, made as comfortable as possible by his disciples Terao Kumanosuke and Nakanishi Magonosuke.

On May 12, Musashi called his disciples into his room for his last formal instructions. First he presented his swords as a memento to Okinaga Yoriyuki. To his favorite disciple, Terao Katsunobu, he gave the work he had just completed, *The Book of Five Rings*; to Katsunobu's brother, Kumanosuke, *The Thirty-five Articles of the Martial Arts*. After dividing up his possessions and putting his affairs in order, he picked up the brush for the last time and wrote out the heart of his philosophy in one short manuscript. Musashi gave this the title of "The Way of Walking Alone," which could alternatively be translated as "The Way of Independence." The twenty-one maxims read like a bare-bones outline of Musashi's life, both historical and spiritual.[9]

- Do not turn your back on the various Ways of this world.
- Do not scheme for physical pleasure.
- Do not intend to rely on anything.
- Consider yourself lightly; consider the world deeply.
- Do not ever think in acquisitive terms.
- Do not regret things about your own personal life.
- Do not envy another's good or evil.
- Do not lament parting on any road whatsoever.
- Do not complain or feel bitterly about yourself or others.
- Have no heart for approaching the path of love.
- Do not have preferences.

- Do not harbor hopes for your own personal home.
- Do not have a liking for delicious food for yourself.
- Do not carry antiques handed down from generation to generation.
- Do not fast so that it affects you physically.
- While military equipment is another matter, do not be fond of material things.
- While on the Way, do not begrudge death.
- Do not be intent on possessing valuables or a fief in old age.
- Respect the gods and Buddhas, but do not rely on them.
- Though you give up your life, do not give up your honor.
- Never depart from the Way of the Martial Arts.

On 19 May 1645, Musashi died at his residence on the grounds of the old Chiba Castle. He was sixty-two years old. In accordance with his last request, his body was dressed in armor and helmet, provided with the six martial accoutrements, and placed in the coffin. According to the promise made beforehand, he was buried in Handa-gun, 5-cho, Tenaga Yuge Village,[10] with Abbot Shunzan of the Taishoji temple as officiating priest. When the abbot had finished his address to the departing spirit, a single crack of thunder rang from the clear sky. Musashi's grave marker remains to this day.

Others closely connected with Musashi were not slow to follow. In December of the same year, both Hosokawa Tadaoki and the priest Takuan passed away. In March of the following year, Yagyu Munenori died in Edo. In January of 1650, Yagyu Hyogonosuke passed on. In 1654, Musashi's adopted son Miyamoto Iori, now a retainer of great prestige to the Ogasawara clan at Kokura, raised a stone monument to Musashi at Mount Tamuke. Abbot Shunzan wrote the script. In 1678, Iori himself passed away at the age of sixty-six.

———

Besides the disciples mentioned in these pages, other men known to have studied under Musashi were Furuhashi Sozaemon, Ishikawa Chikara, Aoki Joemon, Takemura Yoemon, and Matsui Munesato. All were excellent swordsmen. Terao Katsunobu, being his senior disciple and having inherited *The Book of Five Rings*, was in a sense the true heir of Musashi's lineage. His best student, however, was said to have been Terao Kumanosuke, and on one occasion Musashi stated:

> I've traveled around the more than sixty provinces of this country and have taught those willing to learn, but I've yet to have another disciple like Kumanosuke. I've taught this style without holding back on the smallest secret. Among my many disciples, however, I have taught the Way of Manifesting One's True Mind to Kumanosuke alone.

There were, however, no special secrets of swordsmanship passed on to special students. His disciple Furuhashi Sozaemon makes this clear in the following statement:

> Musashi passed away on May 19, but he called the three of us [Furuhashi and the Terao brothers] together on the twelfth. He told us that he supposed we had written down various things he had discussed every day concerning the martial arts and that we would be using them as memos. Nevertheless, there was to be no secret book for us and so he asked us to burn those notes and to throw away the ashes.

Thus, while *The Book of Five Rings* and *The Thirty-five Articles of the Martial Arts* were given as gifts and mementos to the Terao brothers, what Musashi really passed on to each student was his own spiritual resolution to solve the matter of life and death.

With such a legacy, a true school with rules, degrees, and diplomas could not be founded. Musashi could teach his techniques and give advice, but in the end each disciple was required to assess his own strength, find his own Way, and make that Way truly his own. So while the "Musashi style" is still taught today, the actual lineage of the Niten Ichi-ryu died with its founder. It could have been no other way. As Yagyu Hyogonosuke observed when he was teaching in Owari: "Musashi's sword is for himself alone; it is not something that could be taught to other people."

MUSASHI'S CHARACTER

Except for short periods when he stayed in Kyoto or various castle towns and the last five years of his life in Kumamoto, Musashi spent his life on the road. Travel broadened his perspective on his environment and on human nature, as it would for the traveler-poet Basho nearly a century later. Although many people traveled the roads of Japan at this time, Musashi was far more observant than the average sojourner. His paintings, *The Book of Five Rings*, and the story of his life all bespeak a man who dismissed no experience and who noted everything that crossed his path. When he enjoined his disciples not to turn their backs "on the various Ways of this world," he was speaking of far more than just formal studies. The life of a traveler was Musashi's way of ensuring that he would continue to have broadening experiences. A safe position with a local *daimyo* could never have provided him the same opportunities. For Musashi, it was not happenstance that the Chinese character 道 (in Japanese, *do* or *michi*; in Chinese, *tao*) meant both "Way" and "road."

The great amount of time Musashi spent traveling points to another facet of his character that has often been ignored; that is, that he must have been a congenial man who made an interesting and valued guest. With the self-confidence of a superb swordsman, the sensitivity of an artist, and the experiences of a well-traveled man, he was no doubt as welcome at farmers' homes as at the castles of the Ogasawara and

Honda. As a *shugyosha*, he carried no money for room and board. Thus in more humble lodgings, he no doubt paid for his meals of rice, country vegetables, and maybe a dried trout by "chopping wood and carrying water," or, because he was highly literate, writing letters for uneducated farmers to their relatives. For townsmen, he might have left small paintings, much as Buson and Basho did on their journeys, and it is not difficult to imagine him polishing the floors of the long wooden corridors at temples where he passed an evening. Local *daimyo* would surely have had work for him in their *dojo* teaching their retainers swordsmanship, strategy, or both. What is certain is that a man could not survive long on the road without the goodwill of those who might provide lodging and food. Most *shugyosha* looked toward that happy day when they would no longer have to put up with such insecurity, but Musashi seemed to relish these conditions. No doubt many of his benefactors were sorry to see him leave and looked forward to the next time he might be passing through. Since he continued these peregrinations for about forty years, it is safe to say that his reputation would have preceded him everywhere he went.

Although Musashi's detractors have described him as hot-blooded and even sociopathic, a more measured consideration of his life argues otherwise. Surely he was hot-tempered as a teenager and surely he killed a number of men during his lifetime. But those who died by his sword were all men who would have killed him if they had been able. The *shugyosha* who wandered the country were looking for bouts to perfect their martial arts, and the understanding was that the bout, if to be a true lesson, might well result in either man's death (or the death of both, in some cases). Such men were not practicing safely in the *dojo*, but were out in the world truly testing their skills against one another. Thus the death of one man was not necessarily an indication of any particular ruthlessness of his opponent.

Moreover, psychiatrists inform us that the corner to true maturity—both physically and psychologically—is turned at just about the age of thirty. This seems to have been true in Musashi's case as well, for far fewer of his duels resulted in fatalities after his match with Sasaki Kojiro, the Demon of the Western Provinces. It will be recalled that a number of times Musashi simply led his opponents around until they realized the futility of the match, and that once he even tended the wounds of a man who had arrogantly challenged him against his will. Even the famous Tsujikaze's death was caused not by Musashi's sword, but by a fall from a balcony. Also consider the way he taught his students: with a spirit of understanding and with no abuse. These were not the actions of a man bent on seeing blood flow.

It seems clear, however, that Musashi was an idealist and as such could be strict and unbending, especially with himself. That he refused to leave the Reigan Cave and had to be carried down the mountain is an example of this. Musashi had come to his ideals through his life experiences and believed in them as we believe boiling water is painfully hot. If he swayed from his principles from time to time, it might have been simply because he was human.

His idealism notwithstanding, Musashi had his character weaknesses, perhaps the greatest of which was pride. He is considered to have had his fair share of this trait, even into old age. Witness his reaction to the hapless Hoki at the Noh performance. Unable to turn his cheek to a public insult, Musashi humiliated his tormentor in front of all present. Throughout his life, Musashi was quick to defend his honor—sometimes, as in the case of Yoshioka Matashichiro, with dismaying results. Still, he certainly had cause for pride: he had made his way completely on his own, a feat that few samurai could claim.

Paradoxically, at times Musashi seems to have possessed a self-deprecating sense of humor, as displayed in the get-up he wore when leaving Kumoi for Shimabara. His paintings of the smiling Hotei likewise display a humor that could only have come from deep within the artist himself.

In the end, we cannot fully know Musashi's character. Widely differing assessments and conjectures have been made about the man, from his own day to the present, and this in itself is an indication of his complexity. If we need a final image of him, however, we might see him as he no doubt was from time to time: seated informally on the tatami in a ten-foot-square tea room in Kumamoto Castle, speaking respectfully but openly in his low, quiet voice with the *daimyo* Hosokawa Tadaoki and the young Zen priest Shunzan. It is a crisp autumn afternoon, and of the three men, only Musashi can identify the bird that sings in the garden outside. The black Chojiro tea bowl that Tadaoki so highly regards and which Musashi has carefully examined rests momentarily in the swordsman's calloused hands, while in the alcove hangs a scroll with a short line of calligraphy taken from the Kannon Sutra:

An unending sea of blessings
福寿海無量

AFTERWORD

1

It is about ten o'clock in the morning in late October, and I am standing on a seawall near the Straits of Kanmon in the city of Shimonoseki. This is on the southwestern tip of Honshu, the main island of Japan. The sun has been intermittently covered and then uncovered by a combination of white and deep purple clouds, but the wind is down and the air is cool. Maybe a dozen antique fishing boats a little less than twenty feet long are tied up, bow toward the seawall, wooden sides and trim nearly colorless from long exposure to salt water and air. I wait patiently for the captain of my boat to arrive, which he does after ten minutes or so. He is round-faced and sixtyish, with close-cropped gray-and-white hair; and he is riding a rusty, creaking old bicycle.

The captain boards his boat from a plank extended from a seawall, but pulls the craft around lengthwise to a larger boat tied to a floating dock so that I can step on over the other boat and avoid the precariousness of the plank. Once I am seated on a board in the front of the boat, the captain stands behind his tiny enclosure of a cabin and pulls out into the straits. Although swift currents run through these waters, the dark surface is relatively calm, and the only waves are the periodic wakes from other passing vessels. Nevertheless, you can feel that the mid-morning wind is picking up.

The green mountains above Kokura on the island of Kyushu immediately appear, and I am struck as to how close the two great islands are. Far to the left the more distant blue mountains of these two islands come even closer together at the Bay of Dannoura. Musashi would have boarded his own boat from a neighborhood of Shimonoseki a mile or two farther to the left.

In less than ten minutes, a small island appears in front of us, perhaps 750 yards in length. A small hillock covered with pines and a few deciduous trees rises near its northern shore, but for the most part, the island is flat. Here and there are groves of short-statured pines, goldenrod, and tiny purple wildflowers. Some of the shore has been sea-walled, some is still sand and rocks. Again, it is surprising how close this island is to the starting point, and that Kokura itself must be only two or three times that short distance away. This island is still called Funa Island, as it was four hundred years ago, but anyone you ask will tell you that, yes, it is also well-known as Ganryu Island. Then they will often extend their forearms as if holding a sword, and smile.

Walking over and around the island, I try—as any visitor would—to gain some sense of what happened on this place, 13 April 1612. The wind is now a little stronger, and the clouds seem to be moving faster. As I walk, I am again struck as to how small the island is, and how, except for the small tree-covered mound, the entire area is visible from any one point. How could a man's life have climaxed here? How could one short bout on this little island have brought about an end to a career of deadly matches, and started a career of reflection and art? Although the captain has told me that the island has changed shape even in his time, I wonder just where Musashi and Kojiro would have met. The scabbard thrown into the water in anger.

"Kojiro yaburetari."

168

As I move on, I inevitably look for something to take with me—a rock, anything to hold on to, to have in front of me. Everything else would be ancient records, stories, hearsay—all carried far away on the salt air.

———

I am still wandering around over the stony beach when the captain finds me, and the two of us head back toward the boat. On the way, he shows me a well from a natural spring—the water is sweet and cold—and the former location of an old Korean temple that has been torn down and removed some fifty years ago. He knows the island well, he says: he came here to play often as a child, although he never thought to bring along a bamboo or wooden sword.

Just as we approach the boat, the captain leads me to a low rise. We push aside the thin trees and bushes and walk up a short path to a two-yard high memorial stone, now hidden in the overgrowth. The Chinese characters engraved on the stone are weathered and lichen-covered, but you can still make out the name: Ganryu Sasaki Kojiro. A few old coins lie in the rusted offering box at the base of the stone, and next to it has been placed—some time ago—a One-Cup Ozeki saké can, now half-filled with murky water. Who still comes here to offer such things?

The sun is higher now, and the captain, watching the current, turns the boat back toward Shimonoseki. A few plovers work the shore behind us. By this time of day, Musashi would have already won his match and left the island. The light is surprisingly bright on the wavelets running over the water, and the wind has picked up still a little more. The tide has turned, and crosscurrents agitate the surface of the deep.

2

To the west of the city of Kumamoto rises Mount Kinpo, not particularly high at seven hundred and thirty yards, but rather steep. The road leading up its western slope—itself called Mount Iwadono—has been constructed with a great number of switchbacks, some of which look over precipitous drops, and, so perhaps the mountain seems higher than it truly is. The atmosphere of the place is softened, however, by grove after grove of *mikan* trees, and, in the autumn, the entire scenery is dotted in orange by this seedless Japanese tangerine brought to Kyushu from China some four hundred ago.

As my bus winds farther and farther up the mountain, I am impressed that this would not have been an easy trip from Kumamoto in the seventeenth century, either by foot or on horseback. This would have been a place to come only if you had wanted to get far away from centers of activity and perhaps from people altogether.

I get off the bus at the highest pass and see that I still have some distance to go. The road curves up through still more *mikan* groves, and here and there flocks of large Japanese crows are enjoying the fruits of the farmers' labors. Their laughter and sharp cawing are the only sounds to be heard.

Eventually the road runs outs, becoming a trail, and I continue on up the mountain until suddenly the Ariake Kai—the "Sea of Dawn"—is visible between the slopes of the lower peaks. Although the sky is bright blue, a thin mist obscures the line between sea and sky, causing the two or three boats in the offing to appear to be resting on a void. After a moment of struggling to find detail that will not reveal itself, I turn down the path on a descending slope, and soon emerge in the small compound of a Zen Buddhist temple, Unganji. In the thirteenth century, a Chinese priest established this as a place of worship after finding a statue of a four-faced Kannon that had apparently floated to shore on a wooden plank. This statue was the Iwato Kannon that Musashi prayed to before taking up his brush to write *The Book of Five Rings*.

But the statue is not in the temple, and neither did Musashi linger here.

After passing through the temple gate, the path becomes a narrow stony outcropping that winds around the steep slope of the mountain. You must watch your footing, as a twisted ankle would make for a long and painful trip down, even just to the bus stop.

Finally, the rocky path goes over a low rise, and I am standing beneath the Reigan Cave. Its mouth is expansive—perhaps forty feet or so—but after climbing the twenty-odd stone steps that now offer entry, I find that inside it is remarkably small: only ten feet high and thirteen feet deep, and the shrine enclosing the statue of Kannon takes up a good bit of that depth. A light drizzle has begun to fall, and it is immediately clear that during even a halfhearted storm, you would not be entirely comfortable here. Nevertheless, this must have been a very good place to be alone.

Ink, inkstone, a brush, and paper to be made into five scrolls. What else did Musashi have here as he began to reflect on the fifty-nine years of his life? And two years later, when he selected this cave as his place to die, what would have comforted him other than his life of intense discipline? In the tree-lined ridge opposite the mouth of the cave, a few tiny birds—Japanese buntings—play among the branches and leaves.

I stay for a while, not knowing what to do other than to examine each fold in the surface of the rock, but after placing some coins in the offering box and signing the guest book that rests on a small wooden table, I begin to navigate my way down the steep steps. The light rain has stopped momentarily. Reaching the bottom of the steps and looking back, I am suddenly aware of the dark energy residing in the cave above.

3

Four hundred years ago, the main road currently running through the eastern suburbs of Kumamoto was the way taken by the Hosokawa lords on their way to and from Edo, now called Tokyo, the capital city of the Japanese empire. Today it is lined with shops, gas stations, and private residences, although a few hundred yards from the pavement there are still rice and vegetable fields and even some open and unused land. Turn off this road and go down a narrow street lined with bright blue Higo morning glories, for which Kumamoto is famous. As the street becomes shaded with camphor, juniper, and pine trees, the morning glories thin out, and you come to an old wooden gate topped with loose cedar shingles. Carefully pushing the gate open and going through it, you are faced with the smooth back of a large grave marker rising out of a small mound. Go around to the front of the marker and you can see that the Chinese characters are quite clear, the early morning sun casting shadows inside the chiseled indentations: Shinmen Musashi. This is the place Musashi was finally laid to rest, dressed in full regalia to greet the Kumamoto *daimyo* on the way back from their biannual attendance upon the shogun. Lord Hosokawa Mitsunao, Tadatoshi's son, is said to have selected this location himself.

It was a thoughtful selection. Situated on a small rise, the shaded area around Musashi's tomb opens to an expansive valley bounded by blue mountains in the distance. Dappled sunlight filters through the trees onto the large marker and several smaller ones nearby; and just below the area of the tomb, a clear quick-flowing stream runs down the slope, headed for the valley below. The atmosphere is one of intense quiet and peace. On the morning of my visit, no one is there except an old man and woman sweeping the grounds with brushwood brooms.

I sit for a while on a low concrete bench, once again trying to absorb the moment and feeling of gratitude for having been able to come this far. How much farther had it been for Musashi from his birthplace near the Inland Sea to the Battle at Sekigahara to Kyoto and his wanderings throughout Japan? To Ganryu Island, Kokura, Kumamoto, the Reigan Cave, and finally to this place?

What, really, do we do with our lives?

At last I stand up, walk to the offering box, and light incense before Musashi's tomb. Placing my hands together in the Buddhist *gassho*, I recite the mantra of the Heart Sutra.

Gyate, gyate, haragyate . . .

The old couple has finished their sweeping, and soon other visitors will begin arriving to pay their respects as well. But for now, all that can be heard are the faint shouts of the *kendo* practitioners in the *dojo* across the stream and beyond the wall.

Life After Death

Stories about Musashi began to circulate around Japan very early in his life. The name of the young boy became well known in Harima and Mimasaka soon after he defeated the Shinto-ryu swordsman Arima Kihei, and this tale was followed only two years later by that of the downfall of Akiyama from Tajima at the hands of the same boy, still barely a teenager. These stories would have traveled the roads, albeit only to the contiguous provinces, with other *shugyosha* attuned to such information. Some might have disparaged this young swordsman when they heard about him at their inns or the local drinking establishments at the end of a day's wandering; the more discerning would have listened with quiet interest.

But if information about the youth Bennosuke had remained only in the provinces, the news of Miyamoto Musashi swept through urban areas with his defeat of the entire Yoshioka clan. Although the events connected with this story occurred on the outskirts of Kyoto, the shock and sensation of each match would have quickly made the gossip rounds throughout the capital, to nearby Osaka and beyond. And not just at the swordsmanship schools, but at any place where people gathered for the most recent news. Here was a young man barely twenty-one years old who seemed to come out of nowhere to defeat an entire school! Where did he come from? What was his style? Hadn't he defeated over sixty men at Ichijoji? Or was it a hundred?

In this way, Musashi not only gained a reputation, but also became the focus of what would become a growing legend even while he was alive. His victory over Sasaki Kojiro, the Demon of the Western Provinces and sword instructor to the revered Hosokawa clan, helped to guarantee that his story would continue far beyond his lifetime. His eccentricity in dress and his nonconformity in refusing the binding status of a samurai were additional ingredients for a tale that would be too good to let go.

By the time Musashi passed away on 19 May 1645, stories about him had been told and embellished for at least forty years. As the Tokugawa government gained political and cultural control, and Japanese society was increasingly marked by conformity, the reputation of a man who had become possibly the best swordsman of his time without patronage, lineage, or compromising his freedom only grew. Just as important to the growing legend was the entertainment factor. With government control seeping into so many social institutions, the Pax Tokugawa, and the concomitant economic prosperity—particularly among the merchant class—brought a certain restlessness and demand for diversion from everyday affairs. New forms of public entertainment proliferated, and, although Japan's long history provided a plethora of heroes for plot lines, there was always a need for something new. Musashi's legend fit the bill. In less than a hundred years from the time of his death, his story—at times almost unrecognizably embellished—was being dramatized in kabuki, *bunraku*, and professional storytelling; and he was featured in the new styles of woodblock prints produced for a public well-acquainted with the theme. In these genres, Musashi's popularity continued for well over two hundred years.

Modern times and new media have only broadened Musashi's fame. Beginning with Yoshikawa Eiji's perennially popular novel, *Miyamoto Musashi* (in English translation, *Musashi*, by Charles S. Terry), the swordsman, artist, and writer has been the subject of countless novels, movies, television series, television specials, and quiz programs, and even a very serious, long-running comic book series. The core of Musashi's spirit was also too good not to embellish. Everybody, it seems, wanted their own Musashi. Through the years and changing forms of communication, the Japanese public, and more recently the Western world as well, have been unwilling to let the story die.

KABUKI AND *BUNRAKU*

On 23 October 1604, the year Musashi came to Kyoto and began his series of matches with the Yoshioka clan, a theater opened in that city for the performance of a new style of drama, kabuki. The premier of this new form of entertainment had been given some years before, in 1596, when a priestess by the name of Okuni came from Izumo and performed a number of dances in the Kamo riverbed. What Okuni performed is not clear, but it is thought to have been a combination of Buddhist dances called *nenbutsu-odori* and folk dances, laced with erotic gestures. Whatever it was, it was so successful that she was summoned to perform at the Imperial Palace in 1603, and this was followed by the construction of a semipermanent theater the following year. By the end of the century, kabuki theaters were everywhere. The origin of the word itself is obscure, but the old verb, *kabuku*, suggests a strange or willful inclination.

Very early in its development, kabuki began to take plot lines from historical romances and the like and thus became legitimate drama. Not unlike the classic Noh drama, kabuki performers acted out words chanted by a narrator, but with far more animation and exaggeration.

Unlike Noh, however, kabuki was never meant to be highbrow entertainment, and it has remained popular theater in that sense to this day. Costumes range from colorful to gaudy, and the accompanying instrumentation is far less subtle than the stark music of Noh. Broadly speaking, it is a theater of action rather than nuance.

During the same period, the puppet theater—termed *bunraku* or *joruri*—was developing in a parallel and even symbiotic way with kabuki. This art form originally began as a story—*The Tale of Joruri*—chanted by blind musicians who accompanied themselves on the *biwa*, a four-stringed lute. By the middle of the sixteenth century, however, the Okinawan samisen, a sort of three-stringed banjo, was substituted for the *biwa*, and by the end of the century a musician by the name of Menukiya Chozaburo hired a puppeteer to act out the story with wooden hand puppets as Chozaburo played and chanted the narrative.

By the end of the seventeenth century, the puppet theater had evolved into serious public drama. Like kabuki, it used plots taken from various classical sources, but eventually embraced tragedies of the day, including—perhaps especially—love suicides. Once only hand-puppets, the "actors" have gradually become ingeniously flexible and almost doll-like in aspect, three-and-a-half to four feet tall and each one operated by three "handlers" dressed in gauzy black shrouds. Two chanters now deliver both narrative and dialogue, and the literature has been written by such revered playwrights as Chikamatsu Monzaemon. Kabuki and the puppet theater have traditionally shared a number of plays and styles, and kabuki actors will even, at times, imitate the stiff-jointed movements of the puppets.

Both kabuki and the puppet theater were well attended during the Edo period (1603–1868), as they are today, and stories of swordsmen and vendettas were extraordinarily popular fare. As might be expected, the swordsman Miyamoto Musashi was a great draw.

In 1737, ninety-two years after Musashi passed away, part of his legend was turned into drama as the kabuki play *Revenge at Ganryu*

Island, written by Fujikawa Fumisaburo and performed at the Ayameza theater in Osaka. The play was a success and still saw production at the Kadoza theater in Osaka in 1848. So popular was this play that printmakers Utagawa Kunisada and Yoshitora made posters depicting the actor Arashi Rikan III as Musashi, while the famous Utagawa Kuniyoshi designed a triptych of the same subject for nontheatrical purposes. Even a series of *kyoga*, a sort of early comic book depicting the actors of the play, was published in 1817.

Variations of the story, including *Ganryu Island: Blossoms Floating Downstream* and *Miyamoto and the Duel at Ganryu Island*, played throughout the Edo and Meiji periods (together, 1603–1912), with the last opening at the Miyakoza theater in Tokyo in 1907. The plays themselves were typically two-dimensional, full of historical inaccuracies, and centered on Musashi as a colorful swordsman who rewarded good and punished evil. Playgoers loved them.

No doubt encouraged by the popularity of these plays, dramatists embellished more than the events of Musashi's life. In the kabuki play *Tale of the White Heron Castle*, still occasionally performed at Himeji Castle, Musashi's skills are extended to being able to fight off the supernatural.

But the kabuki and puppet theater were still plays—dramas that required suspended disbelief, a stage, puppets, and costumed actors. Moreover, most of the theaters that housed these dramas were in the larger urban areas of Japan, and so were accessible only to the people living in or passing through the bigger cities. For the rest of the population, there was a different kind of performance through which Musashi would be known, giving far more breadth to the stories of his life.

PROFESSIONAL STORYTELLERS

While the populace of the large cities like Osaka, Kyoto, and Edo were entertained with dramatizations about Musashi in the kabuki and puppet theaters, people in smaller cities and towns and rural areas had opportunities to see a different style of entertainment in theaters called *engeijo*. These humble theaters were much smaller in size, with stages that could not accommodate the sets for complicated plays or the recessed floors necessary for puppet operators. In keeping with the lower level of sophistication of these audiences, programs might include one or two musicians with a singer or dancer, a comic raconteur (*rakugo* artist), or a professional storyteller (*kodan*) who told elaborate tales of swashbuckling heroes and wrongs brought to right through famous vendettas.

It was through the professional storytellers that Musashi's popular image lived for two and a half centuries: a Musashi who was morally upright, a strong and skillful swordsman, filled with Confucian sentiments of justice and righteousness; but not a Musashi who was particularly influenced by Buddhism, philosophy, or the arts. This was the people's Musashi.

The professional storytellers' tales were also printed and published by the episode in small booklets. In this connection, in April 1887, a "novel" about Musashi written by a Walter Dening was published by Griffith, Farran & Co. of London and Sydney, N.S.W. Entitled *Japan in Days of Yore: The Life of Miyamoto Musashi*, the original was in two parts, hand stitched with folded, uncut pages, and illustrated with woodblock prints. In a footnote, Dening informed the reader that this story of 170 pages (it reads for the most part as a translation) was based on an anonymous work called the *Kokonjitsuroku eiyubidan*, or *Praiseworthy Tales of Authentically Recorded Heroes, Past and Present*. The piece written under this august title seems to be a compilation of professional storytellers' tales in a single presentation, and as such is wonderfully representative of the kabuki, *bunraku*, *kodan*, and even the earlier films that took Musashi as their hero: Musashi as he was known by almost everyone except scholars and swordsmanship specialists until just over fifty years ago. It is, therefore, worth recounting in some detail.

The story begins with the identification of Musashi and his parentage in what will be hallmarks of the work: imagination and "facts" unsupported by historical evidence. Musashi is declared to be Miyamoto Musashi Masaakira, a retainer in the service of Kato Kiyomasa, the lord of Higo, while his father is introduced as none other than Yoshioka Tarozaemon, a retainer of the thirteenth Ashikaga shogun, Yoshiteru. Tarozaemon has been given the name Munisai by the shogun after defeating sixteen famous swordsmen in a match that Yoshiteru had ordered. But the shogunate having fallen, Munisai has moved on to Himeji in Harima, and is making a living by teaching swordsmanship in the town of Shinmi. According to this account, Munisai has two sons: the elder, Seizaburo, a quiet, retiring, and rather sickly man; and Shichinosuke, who is so energetic and bright that, by the age of twelve, he has the bodily strength of an eighteen-year-old and the intelligence of a man of twenty. He is a fighter but not a bully, and is always ready to help the weak.

Eventually, however, Shichinosuke becomes too self-assertive and indifferent to others' rights. Drawn into a confrontation with his disapproving father, he was forced to flee to the village of Nomura, where he takes refuge with his mother's brother, a Buddhist priest.

Shichinosuke stays with his uncle to study and learn discipline. Not much later, however, he happens by the fencing school of Arima Kiheiji Ichiyoken Nobukata and notices that Kiheiji has put up a placard arrogantly proclaiming the superiority of his school. Outraged, Shichinosuke exclaims:[1]

> "What cheek! One would think, to see this notice, that Nobukata was the only fencer in existence. I have heard my father say that the men who have originated styles of fencing are innumerable; and yet this man tries to make out that the style that he has

invented is superior to everything else. It is rightly said that it is peoples' vanity that is the cause of their destruction. I will act in Heaven's stead and punish this man for his presumptuous folly."

There follows a colorful telling of Musashi's first victorious match, and leads to Shichinosuke and his uncle fleeing from Kihei's outraged disciples. During their flight, they are saved by Miyamoto Buzaemon, an old friend of Munisai's and a retainer of Kato Kiyomasa.[2] Buzaemon eventually adopts the boy, giving him the name Miyamoto, and the two travel on to Kumamoto.

The following episode relates the circumstances behind the creation of Musashi's Two-Sword Style. In this rendition, Shichinosuke's father, Munisai, is an expert in Jiken-ryu, a style that used a short sword of fourteen inches, while his adoptive father, Buzaemon, practices the Kurama-ryu, wielding a sword twenty-seven inches in length. In a moral quandary, the youth is torn between his two fathers' styles, when he chances to pass by a festival where a dancing priestess skillfully maneuvers two swords. This is the answer to his problem, allowing him to practice swordsmanship without relinquishing the style of either father, and serendipitously producing an undefeatable style of his own. Later, Shichinosuke explains the style to Buzaemon:

> "Two swords are taken, one in each hand, a long one in the right hand, which corresponds to the male principle (*yo*), and a short one in the left hand, which corresponds to the female principle (*in*). At first, the two swords, like the two principles, remain together, and seem as though they were hesitating how to act: then, they part from each other, the male sword ascending, and thus corresponding to heaven, the female descending, and becoming earth. Then, coming together again in the form of a cross, they produce all manner of results. This crossing of the two is that, like the combining of the two principles, begets

a universe of things. There is no difficulty about changing the positions of the swords a thousand times to suit the ever-varying movements of an opponent—their advance and retreat, their moving up or down is free and unimpeded by any hindrance whatsoever."

While the beginning of this description bears no relation to the contents of *The Book of Five Rings*, the last sentence seems to hint at some acquaintance with the book.

The story now returns to Himeji, where a fencing school has been established by a master of some reputation, Ganryu Sasaki Yoshitaka. Sasaki is here introduced as the son of Sasaki Shotei, a powerful lord in Omi before being defeated by the warlord, Oda Nobunaga.[3] His mother then leaves for the northern provinces and dies when the boy is eleven or twelve, but not before filling his head with the notion that he is better than others, and that he is morally bound to avenge his father's death. He eventually becomes a skillful swordsman and goes on to Kyoto to found a school. Here (and this part of the tale is given some credence) he is discovered by a Kyoto official, Masuda Nagamori, who then recommends him to Toyotomi Hideyoshi. Contrary to Ganryu's high expectations, however, Hideyoshi not only refuses to take him into service, but has him banished from the city of Kyoto for his arrogance.

Ganryu eventually makes his way to Himeji and establishes a sword fighting school. Discovered by Hideyoshi's less prudent nephew, Kinoshita Katsutoshi, he is hired as fencing instructor to the high and mighty. Thus his ego soars.

Munisai, in the meantime, has come under the patronage of the *daimyo*, Mori Terumoto, as a sword instructor, but he is now getting on in years. Taking leave to the hot springs in Arima, he takes along only one servant, Kyusuke. In a convoluted scene, Kyusuke becomes ensnared by Ganryu, who then demands a match with his master,

Munisai. Although the latter tries to demur any number of times, the arrogant Ganryu insists, and in the end an official match is held on the island, Kameshima. Even using treachery, the six-foot Ganryu cannot beat the withered old Munisai, and is eventually humiliated. Thus is created the enmity that turned this tale into a classic vendetta.

Although Ganryu pretends to be truly humbled by his defeat, his thoughts now turn to the destruction of Munisai, which he ultimately accomplishes by a late-night ambush with a gun, estranging him even further from the Way of the warrior. This is the pivotal point of the story; everything that follows leads only to Ganryu Island. Nevertheless, the Edo storytellers had, at this point, just set the hook.

Informed of his father's death, the sickly elder brother, Seizaburo, sends for Shichinosuke to avenge the family. Shichinosuke, still in Kyushu, eventually receives Kato Kiyomasa's permission to start out after Ganryu, but not before a demonstration of his skill—an event that moves the lord to change the hero's name to Musashi, "the storehouse of military knowledge." Musashi starts out on a long journey through the provinces to find Ganryu, going first to Edo, then down the Tokaido highway, and eventually gaining employment with Kinoshita Katsutoshi in Himeji, thinking he might find his man there.

There is an interesting interlude here, only obliquely mentioned by Dening, in which Musashi is possibly bewitched by foxes, and is accused of receiving a stolen sword. For this reason he is put in jail and, too proud to explain the real circumstances of the situation, awaits his fate.[4]

Six years then pass from the time of Munisai's murder, and Sasaki Ganryu decides that it is time to return to Himeji. Informed that Musashi is in jail, he contrives a match with the prisoner, on the condition that the latter be put to death if he loses. The day of the match comes, but in the final moment the apostate Ganryu fires off a *furizue*, a sort of hollow stick containing a ball and chain which are projected out in the manner of a bullet. (Interestingly, Dening notes—no doubt prompted by his storytelling source—that this weapon was invented by Hozoin In'ei, a priest who was an expert with the spear.) Musashi is wounded in the forehead with this dishonorable weapon and declared the loser of the match. Outraged at Sasaki's perfidy, he fights through the constables who have swarmed in to arrest him, leaps over the palisade and, bringing Part I to an end, "as fleet as a deer, fled across the plain, his well trained legs in a very short time bearing him far away out of reach of his numerous foes."

Part II takes the reader through Musashi's numerous adventures on the way to Ganryu Island and is delivered in the same style, with little character development for the hero but plenty of action. This is, of course, exactly what the kabuki, *bunraku*, and storytellers' audiences were expecting, along with the righteous and sometimes tragic underpinnings of the *adauchi*, or vendetta.

Musashi travels on, this time to meet Yoshioka Kenbo (Kenpo). The text here adds even more historical confusion by stating that Kenbo was a former student of Musashi's, but a master of Munisai's style, and that he was an upright, yet licentious, man. Kenbo and Musashi have a match, are mutually impressed, and spend a few happy days together.

Musashi then resumes his travels. He is nearly boiled to death while trapped in a bath by an envious sword instructor, saves a young woman who has been kidnapped by thieves, and subdues and reforms a band of robbers deep in the mountains. Each adventure is related with great flourish and colorful language, and it is easy to imagine the rapt Edo-period audiences listening to these stories in humble venues.

In literature it seems that every swordsman must meet a legendary teacher or two to learn the deepest secrets of the trade, and the *Kokonjitsuroku eiyubidan* is no exception. In the next episode, Musashi makes the acquaintance of an old "priest" who first modestly denies any great knowledge of swordsmanship with a quote that carries a warning:

"Ah, well! The time was when I was fond of fencing, but, as the saying is, 'An inexpert fencer comes in for heavy blows.' This was my experience, and so I gave it up."

After some rude prodding by our hero, however, the old man demonstrates a marvelous skill in swordsmanship, takes Musashi in as a disciple, and teaches him the very heart of his style. When Musashi finally takes his leave and asks his teacher's name, the old priest replies:

My name I cannot reveal to you. All I can tell you is that I am a single sword [Itto] that has buried itself in the mountains.

From this hint, Musashi—and the audience—deduces that the old man is Yagoro Tomokage, or Ito Ittosai (1560–1632),[5] one of the most famous swordsmen of all time, who lived to over ninety years of age.

Through another series of adventures, Musashi makes his way to the isolated house of yet another old man, apparently a retired warrior. By one machination or another, the old man agrees to a bout with Musashi, but confronts him with only a potlid. Musashi is indignant with this approach, but the old man says:

"What stuff! . . . What's the difference whether a spear, sword, halberd, stick or a potlid be used? The principle is the same. If you have any doubt about it, then, see how it acts."

The old man then beats the young swordsman so soundly that he faints. Upon regaining consciousness, Musashi is quick to apologize, stating:

"Though I possess eyes, it was as though I had none . . . for I failed to see that I was in the presence of a superior man."

This scene was one of the most popular in the storytellers' repertoire, and was often illustrated on the handbills advertising *kodan* performances. Musashi is seen coming from behind with his sword raised over his shoulder, ready to strike, while the half-kneeling, long-haired old man turns with the wooden potlid in hand to ward off the blow. In the corner, the contents of a large iron pot boil away against the snowy cold outside.

As it turns out, the old man is none other than Tsukahara Bokuden (1489–1571),[6] another of Japan's most legendary swordsmen, whose death, in fact, predated Musashi's birth by at least thirteen years. The narrator, undaunted by such trivia, tells us that Bokuden was at one time an acquaintance of Munisai's, and is outraged at the circumstances of his death. He now confers upon Musashi the deepest secret of his style, which is not in actual skill with the sword, but in seeing through to the intentions of one's opponent. This, it might be recalled, is one of the basic principles of *The Book of Five Rings*.

Musashi's steps now take him closer and closer to Kyushu and his fateful duel on Ganryu Island. Nevertheless, first he must cross over to the island of Shikoku in his search for his opponent, Ganryu. On the ride across the Sea of Harima, the ferry is endangered by a marauding shark, which Musashi kills after leaping into the water with his sword. This story is likely the source for the wonderful woodblock print by Utagawa Kuniyoshi, *Miyamoto Musashi's Subjugation of the Whale*, in which Musashi, Ahab-like, stands on the back of a huge whale, driving his sword into its back. Fantastic though Musashi's life was, there was something about it that moved storytellers to make it still more fantastic and fanciful.

Sasaki Ganryu meanwhile has also traveled to the west, improved his style by watching and imitating the flight of swallows, and changed his name to Kandayu for fear of being detected by Musashi. He has ingratiated himself with the feudal lord, Kuroda Nagamasa (1568–

1623), who refuses to make him a retainer but allows him to stay in Kokura to teach. Here, for lack of a better plan, a somewhat disgruntled Ganryu settles in to live the life of an instructor of swordsmanship.

By this time, Musashi has returned to the Chugoku area of the main island of Japan and is wending his way toward Kyushu. On a path through the mountains, he meets the famous *jujitsu* teacher, Sekiguchi Yarokuemon (Sekiguchi Jushin, 1598–1670), who apparently perfected his craft by watching a cat fall from a roof and land safely on all fours. He warns Musashi of Kandayu's low character, and informs us that Ganryu is actually about forty years old.

Finally Musashi enters Kokura and decides to stay at an inn that is, serendipitously, run by Munisai's old servant, Kyusuke. Not recognizing Musashi, Kyusuke talks to him about Ganryu and relates the story of Munisai's death and the subsequent suicide of Musashi's elder brother, Seizaburo. At this point, Musashi is at last taken to Ganryu and, after a sequence of harsh words followed by the necessary permissions from their two lords, a match between the two is set.

In this version of the story, we are told that the fight was set to take place on a small island known as Nadashima, and that the date was set for 18 April 1599, some thirteen years before the actual event. The narrator sets the scene:

> The two fencers had spent a decade of years in preparing for this eventful day. Month by month they had each been improving their styles. Musashi had received the benefit of instruction from the two most noted adepts in the art of fencing that the country contained at the time. Ganryu, on the other hand, had been more incessantly engaged in practicing and testing his style at the fencing schools that he had opened than Musashi's wandering life admitted of his doing. The two men hated each other with a deadly hatred, which was intensified by the antipathies of their natures. In the conflict that was about to take place, there were to

be arrayed, on the one side, perfidy, pomposity, cruelty and utter callousness to most of the nobler feelings of human nature; on the other, honesty, humility, benevolence, and a rare mental and moral refinement. But notwithstanding this, the trial was one of skill and not of moral qualities.

The outcome of the match was known by the Edo-period audience and is known by the modern reader as well. After a series of exchanges and an intermission for rest, Ganryu executes his *tsubame-gaeshi*, which here is described as a somersault (this would seem to be indicative of a kabuki or *bunraku* script), and nearly cuts into Musashi's leg. Musashi, however, has employed Bokuden's technique of looking ahead and leaps into the air. The end is near: Ganryu suffers a loss of spirit—"the embryo, as it were, of his defeat"—and Musashi delivers the fatal blows, a left-hand strike to the head followed by a cut across the chest. Musashi then delivers a coup de grâce through Ganryu's throat and finally cuts off his head.[7]

In the final paragraph of Dening's book, he mentions that Musashi wrote good verses, and notes that "some of his paintings are said to be still extant." It is remarkable that a foreigner in Japan in the late 1880s, less than thirty years after the country had been opened to outsiders, had even this much information on Musashi.

No doubt the publication of Dening's book was noted in Japan. And it is not entirely unlikely that a copy of this curious work in English may have found its way into the hands of a young writer by the name of Yoshikawa Eiji, who would, some fifty years later, write the novel through which Musashi is best known today.

THE YOSHIKAWA MUSASHI

On 23 August 1935, the writer Yoshikawa Eiji published the first installment of his new serialized novel, *Miyamoto Musashi*, in the

Asahi newspaper. His story would run for 1,013 episodes to 11 July 1939, and become one of the most successful novels in modern Japanese literature. A perennial seller in Japan, it has been translated into a number of foreign languages and has been the basis for innumerable movies, magazine articles, television series, and, currently, the best-selling comic book series, *Vagabond*. It is through Yoshikawa's novel and the movies that followed its story line that Musashi's image is known throughout the world today. It was also through this book that the common view of Musashi changed radically from what it had been for hundreds of years prior to its appearance—section by anxiously awaited section—in the daily newspaper.

Although editors at the *Asahi* originally argued for a novel based on the traditional *kodan* stories, Yoshikawa was determined to provide his readers with an account that would be far less two-dimensional than that of the professional storytellers. Typical of his other historical novels, Yoshikawa based his work for the most part on the known facts of Musashi's life, then filled in the large gaps with his own imaginative accounts of what could have been. Musashi's encounters with his opponents are portrayed with psychological sensitivity, he suffers through the same problems of love and desire that ensnare us all and, even though primarily a swordsman, he is described as a man who is curious about and accomplished in cultural pursuits. Musashi becomes a "seeker of the Way," whom Hon'ami Koetsu assesses as a man of common talents, but who polishes those talents ceaselessly. In short, Musashi becomes wholly human. The problem for the reader is the tendency to believe that Yoshikawa's Musashi is in fact the historical Musashi. Endlessly entertaining and instructive, it is a story we want to believe is true. At nearly four thousand pages in the original Japanese and abridged to nine hundred and seventy pages in English translation, the story and Musashi have become at least a small part of our lives by the time we reluctantly reach the final paragraphs.

Yoshikawa's *Miyamoto Musashi* begins at the end of the Battle of Sekigahara, with the defeat of the Toyotomi forces and Musashi lying face up in the mud and rain. Although the seventeen-year-old had been brash enough to think that he could make a name for himself in this grisly conflict by simply swinging a sword, Yoshikawa's young warrior departs from the traditional *kodan* and kabuki in the very first few lines by reflecting, "What kind of thing is it . . . this movement of Heaven and Earth? The actions of individual human beings are nothing more than a single leaf in the autumn wind." This sets the tone for the entire four thousand pages: What is the world, and what can a man make of himself in the face of his seeming insignificance? What, really, do we do with our lives?

The ensuing story centers on Musashi's determination to polish whatever talents he has and a continuing but often convoluted expansion of his understanding of how he is to apply those talents to the sword. In this way, while Musashi is the hero of the book, determination and understanding are its twin undercurrents, or Musashi's true two swords, and those attributes are contrasted with the qualities of the characters in the subplots that Yoshikawa weaves into Musashi's tale.

Musashi's boyhood friend, Hon'iden Matahachi, is the archetypical man who passively waits for good fortune to find him. Lazy, impulsive, and without self-discipline, he is the perfect foil for Musashi, and he inevitably ends up disappointed by the poor results of his schemes for quick gain. Along with disappointment, his most outstanding feature is self-pity. With envy, he watches Musashi's character grow and is unable to understand why he himself slides continually downhill.

Love, family, and children are symbolized by Otsu, the woman who follows Musashi throughout the twelve-year span of the novel. At first engaged to the feckless Matahachi, she falls in love with Musashi; and her determination to follow him is exceeded only by Musashi's determination to follow the Way of the Sword. He is not immune to this temptation, however; a major theme of the story is the various ways he deals with his own desire for a normal life and the comforts and distractions it affords.

The Three Obstructions in our lives, according to Buddhism, are Ignorance, Desire, and Hatred. If the first two of these might roughly be embodied in Matahatchi and Otsu, the third is manifested by an old lady whom Yoshikawa portrays as a figure much like the harpy of Greek epics. This is Osugi, the mother of Matahachi, who is so certain that Musashi was the cause of her son's debasement that she will do anything to thwart or even kill him. Her hatred and desire for revenge are frightening, if sometimes comical, and her single-mindedness is on a par with that of Otsu.

Yoshikawa's Musashi attempts to deal with these three obstructions throughout the book. They are the material and companions of everyday life, and Yoshikawa understood that Musashi would have had to contend with them just as we do. It was his further understanding that dealing with such mundane problems was as much a part of working on the Way of the Sword as were Musashi's matches. This is a quantum leap beyond the *kodan* tales and makes Yoshikawa's story more like our own.

———

Another departure Yoshikawa made from the old *kodan* stories of Musashi was on the subject of teachers. The professional storytellers ignored Musashi's statement in *The Book of Five Rings* that he had never "had a teacher . . . in anything at all," and romantically portrayed the young swordsman as meeting and studying under the greatest masters of the time. Yoshikawa, on the other hand, does not give Musashi instructors in swordsmanship, but rather provides him with instructors in life throughout the novel. These instructors, moreover, are perceived as absolutely necessary to the maturity of Musashi's art.

Musashi's first lesson is about the difference between the true aspects of brute strength and courage. This he receives from the Zen master Takuan, who has captured and tied up the young fugitive, and then suspended him from a high branch of an ancient tree. Musashi feels tricked, but not defeated. Takuan replies:

> "In the long run, it doesn't make any difference. You were out-witted and out-talked instead of being outpummelled. When you've lost, you've lost. It would have been crazy of me to try to take you by force. You're too strong physically. It's the same with your so-called courage. Your conduct up till now gives no evidence that it's anything more than animal courage, the kind that has no respect for human values and life. True courage knows fear. It knows how to fear that which should be feared. Honest people value life passionately, they hang on to it like a precious jewel. And they pick the right time and place to surrender it to die with dignity. You were born with physical strength and forti-tude, but you lack both knowledge and wisdom . . . people talk about combining the Way of Learning and the Way of the Samu-rai, but when properly combined, they aren't two—they're one. Only one Way."

> It is this speech that gives the young Musashi the moment to consider his life up to this point, and that provides him with the material for values beyond simply defeating others. It is not the last time in the novel that Takuan will advise Musashi, but it is the hero's first turning point.

The next man who instructs Musashi is Nikkan, the old Nichiren priest from Ozoin temple. Musashi has just defeated the head disciple of the Hozoin spearman-priests, but is still inwardly uneasy, especially after having sensed a frightening aggressiveness from the old priest earlier in the day. Meeting with Nikkan that evening, he at first feels that he is being flattered when the old man tells him that he's too strong. But Nikkan persists with a very simple but fundamental lesson:

> "You're too strong. Your strength is your problem. You must learn to control it, become weaker."

First the foundation of his courage had been attacked by Takuan, and now his strength—one of the central virtues of the swordsman—was being called into question by a doddering old man. Sensing Musashi's doubts, Nikkan invites the swordsman to look into his eyes. Melting before the old man's gaze, Musashi realizes that he has lost to his advisor and that he had better listen for all he is worth. He later learns that the fearsome feeling he had sensed from Nikkan earlier that day was just a shadow of his own aggressiveness.

In a following episode, immediately after defeating Yoshioka Seijuro, Musashi happens upon Hon'ami Koetsu and his mother, Myoshu, enjoying an outing for painting and tea. At first alarmed by the young swordsman's tense aspect, Myoshu quickly warms to him and invites him to her home for a tea ceremony. Watching the elderly woman, now a Buddhist nun, perform the ceremony, Musashi reflects:

> It's the Way, the essence of art. One has to have it to be perfect at anything.

Musashi is invited to participate, but protests he is ignorant of the rules and techniques of the art. Myoshu responds with yet another lesson for Musashi:

> "If you become self-conscious about the proper way to drink, you won't enjoy the tea. When you use a sword, you can't let

your body become too tense. That would break the harmony between the sword and your spirit. Isn't that right?"

Another woman who helps Musashi to a full understanding of the Way is not a Buddhist devotee at all, but the courtesan Yoshino Dayu. Invited to the pleasure quarters by Koetsu, Musashi is introduced to the charms of a geisha house. He participates only minimally, and halfway through the night excuses himself, secretly going off and defeating Yoshioka Denshichiro. Upon his return, he is left with the beautiful courtesan. She invites him to enjoy the evening with her, but he refuses, and she senses his extreme inner tension. In a dramatic moment, Yoshino uses a short sword to split open a lute, and explains the source of the beauty and variety of its tone:

> "To put it in another way, the tonal richness comes from there being a certain freedom of movement, a certain relaxation at the ends of the core. It's the same with people. In life, we must have flexibility. Our spirits must be able to move freely. To be too stiff and rigid is to be brittle and lacking in responsiveness."[8]

Although Musashi is unable to respond to this advice that particular night, it moves him to his very core. As a student of life, Yoshikawa's Musashi takes his instructions from every source possible, from priest or prostitute, without prejudice.

Musashi is instructed by a number of unlikely scenes and objects encountered in his wanderings: the total concentration of a potter, the caustic comments on the samurai's soul by a sword-polisher, the cut stem of a peony sent to the Yoshioka by Yagyu Sekishusai, and even his own plowing of the earth. One of the most dramatic of these is the wordless instruction he receives from the Zen Buddhist priest Gudo. Musashi has been experiencing extreme self-doubt and has been following the priest, imploring him to impart some wisdom, anything to put his mind at ease. Although Gudo has rebuffed him almost violently, taunting him with the Zen phrase that he had "not one thing" to offer,[9] Musashi continues to dog the priest's tracks. Finally, in a moment of exasperation, Gudo takes a stick and traces a circle in the dirt around Musashi. Then, tossing away the stick, he walks away. Musashi is outraged. Is this all he gets for his persistence and dedication? Finally, his anger subsiding, he looks at the circle again.

> The circle—no matter how you looked at it—the circular line was . . . a circle. There was no end, no indentation, no extremity, no wandering. If you expanded this circle out infinitely, it was the universe itself. If you contracted it, it became his own one small point. He himself was a circle, the universe was a circle. They could not be two things. They were one.
> Finally drawing his swords, he checks his shadow within this circle.

> The shadow changed again, but the image of the universe—not by one whit. The two swords were but one. And they were part of the circle.

Yoshikawa read and reread *The Book of Five Rings*, carefully weaving Musashi's principles into the words and actions of Takuan, Nikkan, Myoshu, Yoshino Dayu, Gudo, and the others. In this way he gave us a much more realistic picture of the historical Musashi than the professional storytellers had done.

Or did he? In *The Book of Five Rings*, Musashi informs us that between the ages of thirteen and twenty-eight or twenty-nine he "fought as many as sixty matches," never losing once.

If Musashi had engaged in more than sixty matches during that fifteen-year period, he would have averaged about four bouts a year; and both this total number and the average are far more than the number of bouts Yoshikawa describes in his novel. Moreover, while the conversations with Takuan and the others give a wonderful fictional account of how Musashi came to understand his art, his own words indicate that he began to give serious consideration to those principles only after the age of thirty, after his fight with Sasaki Kojiro. In this respect, at least, the professional storytellers may have been a bit closer to the truth.

Yoshikawa did ample research, however, and the fights he described were for the most part the ones mentioned in the various records of Musashi's deeds. Although the fight with Arima Kihei is given only two sentences, others are covered with a combination of research and imagination. The description of the *dojo* at the Hozoin temple and its background, for example, is well researched; and the reader feels that Yoshikawa may have witnessed a number of such matches himself and experienced the tension and energy involved.

As a serial novelist, Yoshikawa drew out the suspense leading up to the main action scenes as long as possible. Thus, while we are introduced to the Yoshioka clan on page 108 of the English translation, we do not get to the fight with Seijuro until almost two hundred pages later, and the final battle with Genjiro and his eighty or so swordsmen does not occur until well past the middle of the book. With Yoshikawa's delightful combination of action and philosophical assessment of the various players, however, the reader is never disappointed or bored; the historical background and minor characters we meet along the way make the journey every bit as interesting as Musashi's clashes with his various opponents.

The climactic duel with Kojiro is saved for the final five pages of the novel, and this is appropriate, as the first part of the historical Musashi's life also seemed to end on that small island in the Kanmon Straits. As he wrote in the introduction to *The Book of Five Rings*, it was from this point that he began to think back over his life; and it was also from this point that he stopped defining the victory of his bouts as the injury or death of his opponents.

Yoshikawa Eiji took the image of Musashi and changed it radically from the way it had been portrayed for over two hundred years. Within the medium of a serialized newspaper novel, he was able to give the dramatic/fictional Musashi a depth he could not have attained within the time constraints of *kodan*, kabuki, or *bunraku*; he was also able to include Musashi's principles, Zen Buddhist philosophy, Edo-period historical background, and the personalities of Takuan, Hon'ami Koetsu, Yoshino Dayu, and a host of minor characters who may have encircled Musashi during his time. As a historical novel, it only seems to improve with each rereading.

But in *Miyamoto Musashi*, Yoshikawa also created an individual seeking values and "the Way," whose path is marked not only by successes but with failure and doubts; and in that sense, it is more than just a vastly entertaining book, but a spiritually inspiring one as well. Koetsu, it will be recalled, sees Musashi as not much more than a common man, but one who, "understanding his own common nature, is out to polish it unceasingly." With that determination, discipline, and search for higher values, however, Musashi eventually transcends the rough material with which he begins and overcomes even the most formidable of obstacles. In the end, Yoshikawa assesses his victory over Sasaki Kojiro:

> What Kojiro believed in was the sword of technique and strength; what Musashi believed in was the sword of the spirit. That was their only difference.

STILL OTHER IMAGES

As of this writing, Yoshikawa's *Miyamoto Musashi* has never gone out of print, and it is Yoshikawa's Musashi who first comes to the minds of most people in Japan and abroad. But for all the popularity of his novel, Yoshikawa did not hold a copyright on the subject, and a number of other writers tried their hands at recreating Musashi, with differing results.

Shibata Renzaburo, for example, in his *Miyamoto Musashi, Duelist* (1971), presents Musashi as a hard and stern swordsman who bears the guilt of having killed his own mother. In this three-volume work, Shibata describes Musashi making a living for himself during his ascetic wanderings, depicting the economic realities of the *shugyosha*'s life. Interestingly, this author portrays Sasaki Kojiro as the son of a Japanese mother and foreign father, like the hero Shibata is most famous for creating, the nihilistic swordsman Nemuri Kyoshiro.

In yet another *Miyamoto Musashi*, author Tsumoto Akira follows Musashi's sixty bouts, beginning with his fight with Arima Kihei and finishing with his defeat of Sasaki Kojiro. This novel follows Musashi over the length and breadth of Japan as he seeks out and tests himself against men of strength, and in this way fills in a number of the gaps in Yoshikawa's work. Tsumoto's Musashi is depicted as a strong swordsman, but also as a man who sought out the unusual.

Sasazawa Saho's *Miyamoto Musashi* began with the publication of the first volume in 1986, and was brought to completion 5,251 pages later with Volume 8 in 1997. It is the longest of the novels concerning Musashi. This work highlights Musashi's later years, after the fight at Ganryu Island, and follows with some accuracy the extant records of the swordsman's life during this period. Views on the fight with Kojiro not brought out in other novels are explored here, and Sasakawa's novel gives a sense of what Musashi's life must have been like during his final years in Kumamoto.

Another novel about Musashi after Ganryu Island is the single-volume *The Last Days of Miyamoto Musashi* (1959) by Nakanishi Seizo. Seizo writes about the complications that continued for Musashi even after he reached a degree of Zen enlightenment, and his choice of the

Reigan Cave as a place to die. This work is considered a masterpiece for its psychological portrayal of Musashi in his old age.

A number of writers attempted to establish differing views of Musashi. One of these was Mine Ryuichiro, whose *Miyamoto Musashi* (1993), a ten-volume work, portrayed the swordsman as having a very dark side. In this novel, Musashi is self-reliant and confident, yet the victim of a fear and uneasiness he cannot escape. Wavering between these psychological extremes, he continues from bout to bloody bout, driven by a passion that is understood as an almost sexual drive. Although Mine's Musashi is a clouded figure, his fear and uncertainty give him a decidedly more human quality.

Yet another approach to Musashi is found in an interesting newspaper serial novel, *The Two Musashis* (1956–57), written by Gomi Yasusuke for the *Yomiuri Shinbun*. Gomi theorizes that there were actually two Musashis, the Hirata Musashi and the Okamoto Musashi, with very different personalities and styles. Although the book is definitely fiction—Sasaki Kojiro kills both men's teachers, and there are duels within the Yagyu compound and a final match between the two Musashis on top of the volcano, Mount Aso—the theory itself is neither unique nor as far-fetched as it might seem. Records kept during the Edo period were far from infallible, and there has always been speculation that there were two or three swordsmen during that time who took the name Musashi. Also, stories about Musashi seem to illustrate two very different aspects of his personality—hot-blooded intensity and calm self-possession. And last, there are the two different traditions of his birthplace: Sakushu (Mimasaka) and Banshu (Harima).

Finally, although the catalog of books about Musashi is nearly endless, mention should made of the current best-selling comic book by Inoue Takehiko, *Vagabond*. This multivolume series is based on the Yoshikawa Musashi, but with a bit more sex and a lot more gore packed in. Its limited dialogue and narrative are no substitute for Yoshikawa Eiji's work, but there is no denying that it is extraordinarily well drawn—

it received the 2000 Media Arts award for *manga* from the Japanese Ministry of Culture, and the Kodansha award for best *manga*. Lest the reader look with condescension on the concept of comic books in a country with one hundred percent literacy, there are currently over twenty-two million volumes of the series in print. Indeed, *Vagabond* is credited as being influential in introducing Musashi to an entirely new generation. *Manga*, however, has not been the only visual medium involved in this mission.

MUSASHI AT THE MOVIES

In 1954, the director Inagaki Hiroshi introduced *Miyamoto Musashi*, the first of his cinematic trilogy based on the Yoshikawa novel. This movie was soon edited and subtitled for the foreign market, and subsequently won an Academy Award for Best Foreign Film. Suddenly Musashi leapt the borders of Japan and was known not only to a few students of Japanese art or swordsmanship, but to a worldwide movie-going audience that was just developing a taste for things Japanese. In this way, Musashi was introduced to America and Europe in the captivating form of the actor Mifune Toshiro.

Ruggedly handsome, brooding, and full of explosive energy, Mifune was the perfect man for the role. He exemplified everything the overseas audiences could imagine the swordsman to be, and the two subsequent episodes of the trilogy, *Duel at Ichijoji Temple* and *Duel at Ganryu Island*, cemented his identification with the role. With one relatively obscure exception, no other subtitled version of the cinematic Musashi is available even today. Thus, for the non-Japanese audience, Mifune *was* Musashi.

This was not the case for the Japanese audience. Before Inagaki's 1954 work, there had already been at least thirty films about Musashi, and, following the trilogy, there were fourteen or fifteen more. Mifune, as much as he seemed to embody the spirit of Musashi, was only one of many excellent actors who took the role, and was not necessarily considered the best by one and all.

The first "moving picture" about Musashi was entitled *Miyamoto Musashi's Subjugation of the Lustful Old Man*,[10] and was performed by marionettes rather than actors. Produced in 1908, it was based on the professional storytellers' versions of Musashi's life, as were all of the films on Musashi until the late 1930s. The themes of these movies— which after 1908 were acted by people rather than puppets—were often the same, working over various renditions of the swordsman's subjugation of the rake, quelling mountain bandits, or taking revenge on his parents' killer. A number of celebrated actors of the times took Musashi's role, including Onoe Matsunosuke, Kataoka Chiezo and Arashi Kanjuro.

The sea change came in 1940 when Kataoka Chiezo took the role of the Yoshikawa Musashi in a film trilogy, directed by Inagaki Hiroshi. Chiezo had played Musashi before, as had Arashi Kanjuro, but this extended movie took on the proportions of the novel itself in terms of both length and Musashi's character development. Interestingly, Inagaki's direction still owed much to kabuki in the sense that the film's scenes were encapsulated dramatic moments of the story rather than continuous moments of a comprehensible whole. The audience was assumed to be familiar with the novel, and Inagaki's work brought them dramatic renditions of the most interesting and moving scenes of the story. It is still considered a masterpiece, and Chiezo's aristocratic mien gives Musashi an air that contrasts strongly with the earthier characterizations by Mifune and others.

Inagaki, who, like Chiezo, practically made a career of Musashi films, was a master of sword choreography. During the filming of this 1940 trilogy, he often consulted with his friend, Ono Kumao of Kyoto, a seventh-degree black belt in *kendo*. Thus the action scenes were much more realistic in style and rhythm than the usual *chanbara*, or sword-fighting films.

By the 1950s, Musashi's character was beginning to expand again, and, during that time, a number of directors made films that either broadly interpreted Yoshikawa's work or followed other writers altogether. Two examples of this trend were Mizoguchi Kenji's *Miyamoto Musashi*, based on Kikuchi Kan's theory that Musashi was not the strong swordsman people imagined, and Mori Kazuo's *The Coward at Ganryu Island*. In the mid-fifties, the novelist Koyama Katsukiyo wrote *The Young Musashi*, and later *Musashi After That* (6 volumes); both were made into movies showing a different look at Musashi's life, the latter as *The Great Swordsman of the Two-Sword Style*, starring, once again, Kataoka Chiezo. Finally, 1959 saw the release of *The Night Before Ganryu Island*, directed by Osone Tatsuo, in which Musashi becomes almost neurotic in his attempt to break through Kojiro's technique.

New interest was also taken in Sasaki Kojiro, and a number of movies were produced during this same period centering around Musashi's archenemy, portraying him as a sympathetic character. One of these, *Sasaki Kojiro* (1950), another film in three parts directed by Musashi specialist Inagaki Hiroshi, was based on an original work by Murakami Genzo.[11] In this story, Sasaki was portrayed by the handsome kabuki heartthrob Nakamura Jakuemon. Unlike the single-minded, woman-spurning Musashi, he follows his dream of a life of both love affairs and the sword. After a number of sad affairs, he is finally cut down at Ganryu Island, and dies romantically, grasping a white chrysanthemum on a pebbled beach. The high-strung Musashi is played by a young Mifune Toshiro.

One of the most beautifully photographed and choreographed films of this genre is *The Two Musashis* (1960), based on the Gomi Yasusuke novel. The older and more stable Musashi is played by Hasegawa Kazuo, who does not bring much character to the part; but the young saké-drinking, woman-loving Musashi is portrayed with wonderful intensity by Ichikawa Raizo, another actor from a kabuki background, who is most famous for his role as a blind swordsman in the

Daibosatsu Toge series. Katsu Shintaro, who made his career playing another blind swordsman in the Zato Ichi movies, plays a nasty but not exactly riveting Sasaki Kojiro. The very best part of this film is the final showdown between the two Musashis atop the barren and sulphur-fluming Mount Aso. And, in splitting Musashi's character in two, the film itself is possibly the last word in terms of "the other Musashi." Nevertheless, filmmakers did not stop there.

The Actors

Although numerous actors and directors have added their own adaptations and interpretations to the legend of Musashi, three men are especially noted for their portrayals of Musashi. The first, Kataoka Chiezo, is remembered, especially by the older generation, for the almost aristocratic dignity he brought to the role. Indeed, his ability to project a Musashi of innate quiet strength was considered a liability in his portrayal of the young spitfire Takezo suspended from a tree in the temple yard. Temper tantrums did not fit Chiezo's own personality as well as did scenes of controlled confrontation or introspection. The genius of the second actor, Mifune Toshiro, was in manifesting the wildness of Musashi's youth and grimness in the face of battle. Mifune displayed the unyielding aspect of Musashi's personality, and his angst; but critics have commented that he lacked the versatility to bring a broader range of expression to his Musashi.

The actor considered to have given Musashi's character the most realistic development was Nakamura Kinnosuke, also known later as Yorozuya Kinnosuke. His broad portrayal of Musashi was doubtless due in part to his fine acting abilities and his background in kabuki. But it was also due to the five-year span necessary to complete the cinematic version of the Yoshikawa Musashi story. Directed by Uchida Tomu, this five-part epic was produced at the rate of one film per year, beginning in 1961 with *Miyamaoto Musashi*, and continuing with *Duel* at Hannya Pass, Initiation to the Two-Sword Style, Duel at Ichijoji, and Duel at Ganryu Island. Not only did the length of the production allow for a much more complete rendition of Yoshikawa's work, but the duration of the filming provided the time for this excellent actor to mature within the role. After nearly eight hours of cinema, it is little wonder that many Japanese moviegoers now saw Kinnosuke as the definitive Musashi. This is truly one of the most memorable depictions of the other Musashi, and Kinnosuke was ably assisted with outstanding performances by Mikuni Rentaro as Takuan, and a much older Kataoka Chiezo as Musashi's benefactor Nagaoka Sado.

By the late 1960s and early 1970s, film studios in Japan began to lose ground to television, although they continued to produce movies about Musashi. In 1967, Inagaki Hiroshi directed another *Sasaki Kojiro*, this time with Nakadai Tatsuya as Musashi; in 1969, in the "Traditions of the Great Swordsmen of Japan" series, Mikuni Rentaro played a very different Musashi based on author Shiba Ryotaro's original work; and in 1971, Uchida Tomu directed *A Match with Naked Blades*, the story of Musashi's duel with Shishido Baiken, with Nakamura Kinnosuke once again taking the role of Musashi and Mikuni Rentaro as Baiken. The latter was to be Uchida's final film, and was produced posthumously, but Musashi was not laid to rest with this famous director.

MUSASHI ON TELEVISION

The Musashi story is still retold to large audiences via television. In 1957, the first television movie of Musashi appeared on Japanese NTV and starred Yasui Shoji. In subsequent years the role has been played by various actors, including Tanba Tetsuro, Ichikawa Ebizo, and Takahashi Koji. Yorozuya Kinnosuke and Kitaoji Kinya both performed in twelve-hour dramas based on the above-mentioned *Musashi After That*, and so portrayed Musashi at the end of his life as well as his youth.

The commercialization that is part and parcel of television has had

LIFE AFTER DEATH

mixed results. The extended TBS series "Miyamoto Musashi" produced as the New Year's "wide cinema" in 2001, for example, included a theme song with electric guitars and refrains in English, several over-the-top performances by supporting actors, and a sweet-faced Kamikawa Takaya—who seemed to have intensely studied the late Bruce Lee's facial expressions—as Musashi. Nevertheless, it was an action-packed and interesting production of the Yoshikawa Musashi.

In 2003, NHK television offered its own fifty-two–week series on Musashi.[12] Starring kabuki actor Ichikawa Shinnosuke (now Ebizo) in the lead, this presentation generally followed the Yoshikawa novel for the first thirty-eight episodes, but then continued far beyond its climax at Ganryu Island. Each weekly episode was followed by travel information for the various locations connected with Musashi's life, and the entire country geared up for the Musashi pilgrimages that would ensue.

It is difficult to imagine another character from either history or literature who has so captured the imagination of a people. Miyamoto Musashi did not change the politics or shape events in Japanese history. Nor did he write a work that would affect a genre of literature or poems that would become classics. Yet there is something at the heart of his story that has commanded the attention of the Japanese people and others who have heard it. The story as told in any one iteration—any play, movie, novel, or comic book—is never definitive enough. The story of Musashi, even in its paucity of facts, is much too large to fit once and for all in any single package.

Influences on and Parallels to
The Book of Five Rings

Musashi declared that he had never had a teacher in any "Way," and with a reading of *The Book of Five Rings*, it becomes clear that the principles he advocated in his martial art were based in his own practicality and the numerous bouts and battles he had fought throughout his life. But it also seems clear that he was literate and inquisitive, and that one of his fundamental premises was a total rejection of prejudice for or against any particular proposition.

"You should investigate this thoroughly" is repeated more than any other phrase in his book. This is the exhortatory note of Musashi's philosophy and that of the Zen Buddhism he studied so assiduously. Indeed, he quoted no one in *The Book of Five Rings* and wrote on his own authority, but this was no doubt to let his disciples know that none of the book's contents had been taken on faith from former texts or "divine inspirations." This was a book written of flesh and blood, written for the preservation of the same.

It is not unreasonable, however, to assume that Musashi kept his eyes wide open all his life and rejected nothing out of hand. And if he did not have "teachers" along the way, he certainly was not beyond accepting the influences of certain masters of the arts he admired, nor would he have rejected propositions on the martial arts that appeared reasonable to him and proved to be so.

A reading of Musashi's story will quickly show that clear influences on his martial art cannot be documented, but it will be instructive to take a short look at four sources that, if not influential, show a strong parallel in cast of mind.

Sun Tzu

This ancient Chinese classic on the art of war, the *Sun Tzu*, was likely read by every serious literate person in the warrior class in both China and Japan. Musashi, too, would have read this seminal work, and judging from its apparent parallels with *The Book of Five Rings*, not just once or twice. It is not difficult to imagine the solitary swordsman on his long travels throughout Japan, reading and rereading this short but very pithy work, internalizing and working through each phrase and recasting it in the light of his own experiences. Consider the following examples.

We have seen that Musashi's first premise was that the purpose of the martial arts in combat is victory, not the demonstration of beautiful or dazzling techniques, or sincerity through death. Volume 2 of the *Sun Tzu* (II, 19) expresses a similar view:

> Therefore, what is respected in war is victory, not lengthy [campaigns].

Again, while this may seem self-evident, the fact that two of the most well-respected works on combat in the Far East would state the obvious, may indicate that there is a need to keep this core principle constantly in mind.

Musashi also emphasized in both *The Book of Five Rings* and "The

Way of Walking Alone" that his martial art was to be based on experience, not the supernatural as so many others were; and tradition has him walking away from the temptation to pray to Hachiman for victory before one of the fights with the Yoshioka. One was to depend entirely on himself. Concerning this, the author of the *Sun Tzu* wrote, in Volume 11:

> Prohibit the supernatural and avoid its [concomitant] doubts, and you will avoid disasters until the time you die.

The great general Oda Nobunaga (1534–82) showed his understanding of this principle using reverse psychology. When his troops were unnerved by the bad omen of cawing crows just before a battle, Nobunaga flipped a coin declaring that "heads" would mean their victory, "tails" the victory of their opponents. The coin landed "heads" and his encouraged troops went on the victory, never knowing that Nobunaga's piece of currency had no "tails" at all.

The Book of Five Rings also places great emphasis on training and discipline, and while these sentences from the *Sun Tzu* were mentioned in a slightly different context, the phrasing of classical Chinese is so terse and the vocabulary so packed with meaning that one can understand how Musashi might have taken them to fuel his own fires:

> Anciently, those who were good in battle first made themselves undefeatable.

> For this reason, it is a practical law of war not to rely on the enemy's not coming, but to rely on the fact that I am waiting for him; not to rely on his not attacking, but to rely on the fact that I, myself, am unassailable.

In the very first section of the Fire chapter, Musashi discusses the need for a source of light, be it the sun or a fire, either to the rear or to the right, and there is a tradition that he used this tactic in the fight on Ganryu Island, positioning himself so that the sun was in Kojiro's eyes. He further elaborates on gaining a higher elevation than one's opponent, and the advantages of positioning the opponent so that natural obstacles are to his rear so that he might be backed into them (or off them, as in the case of Tzujikaze Tenma). The *Sun Tzu* would have given him much to think about in this regard, including:

In flat territory, make your location an easy one with an elevated area to your right or to your rear. Put death in front of you and life behind.

For the most part, armies prefer taking the high ground, and dislike being at a lower elevation; they value sunny places and despise the dark.

Benefit from the advantages of the land.

We should distance ourselves from these places [of natural obstacles], but have the enemy approach them; and while we face them, the enemy should have them at his rear.

So then, the shape of the land is the fighter's ally.

For this reason it is said, "Knowing the opponent and knowing yourself, your victory will not be in peril; knowing the land and knowing the elements, your victory can be complete."

With these dictums, the fight with the Yoshioka clan at Ichijoji and Musashi's routing of an entire force of men come immediately to mind. This kind of resourcefulness—not just in terms of sword technique but also much broader strategy—must have secured the victory in any number of Musashi's sixty bouts.

Another of Musashi's fundamental principles—fluidity—also finds expression in the *Sun Tzu*. The Chinese strategist predated the beginnings of Zen Buddhism in Japan by about eighteen centuries, so his sentences do not bear the same nuances as those of Takuan, but the idea of not being caught by either circumstances or one's own prejudicial mind is an important theme in his work. Musashi wrote for "the small martial art" as well as the "large," and one can see in the following passages from the *Sun Tzu* how he might have taken this very practical advice for generals and applied it to the solitary martial artist:

Circumstances are the purveyors of benefit; by such create power.

———

Therefore, in battle there are no constant conditions; with water, there is no constant shape.

And, significantly enough:

Therefore, among the Five Elements, none are predominant; among the four seasons, none stay for long; the days are long and then short; the moon waxes, then wanes.

And Musashi must have seen a parallel to his thoughts in "Mountains and Seas" in the Fire chapter, in this next passage:

Therefore, do not repeat what was victorious in one battle, but according to the shape of things, let your [tactics] be infinite.

First arriving late to a match, then arriving early; often fighting with a regular wooden sword, and then arriving with one carved from a boatman's long oar—the opponent was always kept off guard and was constantly left in doubt.

Finally, in a simile that would have appealed to Musashi's sense of never being held to one posture, strike, or tactic:

Therefore, those who are good at practical tactics are likened to a *shuai-jan*. The *shuai-jan* is a snake living in the Ch'ang Mountains. Attack its head, and it will come at you with its tail; attack its tail and it will come at you with its head; attack its center, and both head and tail will come at you.

While Musashi emphasized taking the initiative in combat, and the *shuai-jan* is always reacting, the image of constant flow—of making the necessary change with circumstances—must have impressed him with the similarity as to how he himself had had to react any number of times, especially when confronted with more than one opponent. And again, while Sun Tzu wrote for the general or the commander of large armies, Musashi would have easily been able to make the conversion to a single man holding not one, but two swords: the perfect unstoppable fluidity.

———

Musashi arranged his book in five chapters, each to be read with equal attention, and each one being necessary to the other. The *Sun Tzu* is a possible source for the origin of this structure. The *Sun Tzu* contains, in Volume 5, this interesting three-line passage alluding to the infinite and inexhaustible ways of combat achieved by various permutations of its basic elements. This also supports Musashi's emphasis on keeping an open mind and moving appropriately to any circumstances one may find himself in:

> The number of musical notes do not exceed five, but the changes of these five can never be exhausted in listening to them. The number of primary colors do not exceed five, but the changes of these five can never be exhausted in observing them.
>
> The number of basic flavors do not exceed five, but the changes of these five can never be exhausted in tasting them.

The basic musical notes, colors, and flavors are limited in themselves, but their combinations are innumerable. Musashi found this to be true for his five fundamental stances in particular, and his martial art in general. Could this have been the source for his "five rings"?

Perhaps the most striking similar principle common to Sun Tzu and Musashi is the regular use of psychology. We think immediately of the fights with the Yoshioka clan and Sasaki Kojiro when we read:

> Therefore, the highest form of soldiery is to frustrate the enemy's plans.

Sasaki Kojiro in particular comes to mind with this passage:

> Well then, a man's spirit is sharpest in the morning, but is off guard by the afternoon. Therefore, the man who uses the martial arts well will avoid that sharp spirit and attack the sagging one.

Here we clearly see Kojiro dressed resplendently and sitting on his battle chair in the hot spring sun, waiting for Musashi while losing patience, focus, and spirit with every passing hour.

Throughout *The Book of Five Rings*, Musashi drives home the point that a swordsman of his style must be in control of his opponent at all times. He drives the enemy this way and that, pushes him toward dangerous parts of the surroundings, "twists and contorts" his mind, and constantly pulls out reactions to his own feints. In Volume 6 of the *Sun Tzu* we find:

> Therefore, the man who is good at combat controls others; he is not controlled by them.

This is the underlying premise of both books, whether "controlling" refers to actively controlling the direction of an opponent, or eliciting his movements to better understand his intentions. In "Moving the Shadow," in his Fire chapter, Musashi writes:

> When you cannot see through your opponent's situation in any way, act as though you were going to attack vigorously, and you will see his intentions. When your opponent has taken a stance with his sword behind him or to his side, if you make a sudden movement as if to strike him, his thoughts will be manifested with his sword.

This ploy is also noted a number of times in the *Sun Tzu*:

> Provoke him and so know the principles of his activity or inactivity; manifest some form and so know the ground of his life and death.

> Well then, at first act like an unmarried maiden, and the enemy will open the door for you; then act with the speed of a scared rabbit and he will be unable to resist you.

Other stratagems with parallels to *The Book of Five Rings* include these:

> Therefore, though you are able, make a show that you are not; though ready to deploy, make a show to the opposite; when drawing near, make a show of removal; and when moving away, make a show of drawing near.

———

> Show enticements and invite him in; show confusion and take him.

———

> If he is angry, irritate him; show weakness and he will become arrogant.

———

> Attack where he is unprepared; appear where he is not expecting you.

Sun Tzu declares that "Warfare is the Way of deception." Musashi does not go so far with his words, but constantly discusses the value of disorienting and confusing one's opponent, and using the opponent's mind for his own defeat.

That Musashi would not have read the *Sun Tzu* seems almost unimaginable. What seems probable is that he made it his own, just as he encourages his students to make *The Book of Five Rings* their own. This does not mean imitation or "learning indoors," but to drill and practice with every phrase deeply in mind. In the same way Musashi likely went through his more than sixty bouts ever mindful of the Chinese tactician's short but compact sentences, weeding out what he found to be inappropriate to his own time, place, and circumstances.

Musashi was convinced that the goal of the martial arts was to win, and he must have found great interest in the words of this work written with the same aim some two thousand years before his own time. If he felt, as he wrote in the Earth chapter of *The Book of Five Rings*, that he himself had "no extraordinary skills in the martial arts," from where would his victories have come? The *Sun Tzu* had a key, and it was Musashi's for the turning:

> In this way, the victorious martial [artist] will first win, and later seek to fight; the losing martial [artist] will first fight and later seek to win.

TAKUAN SOHO

In 1631, Musashi visited the northern province of Dewa on the invitation of a Lord Matsudaira Dewa no kami to demonstrate his sword style. This was at precisely the time when the Zen priest Takuan was in exile in Dewa and kept under the watchful eye of a Lord Matsudaira. While a meeting between the swordsman and the priest is not documented, it seems likely that they would have been introduced by their mutual "host," or that they may have renewed their friendship from meeting in former times in Kyoto or elsewhere. If this meeting did take place, they would have had ample time to talk over subjects dear to them such as tea, poetry, Zen, and swordsmanship. At any rate, just a year later, Takuan wrote one of his most famous works, "The Mysterious Record of Immovable Wisdom," a treatise on the application of Zen to the art of the sword, which he sent as a letter to Yagyu Munenori.

Strong similarities in the fundamental assumptions of Takuan and Musashi vis-a-vis the art of combat are difficult to ignore. The following are a few examples.

In the section "Using the Eyes in the Martial Arts" in his Water chapter, Musashi discusses the difference between "seeing" (見), the simple act of looking, and "observation" or "contemplation" (観), the act of looking through. The etymology of the character for seeing (見) is derived from an eyeball on legs, indicating nothing more than the physical activity of the eye. The character for observation or contemplation (*kan*; 観) on the other hand is used by Zen priests in the term *kanshin* (観心), meaning "meditating on the mind," and *kannen* (観念), meaning "meditation" or "deep contemplation." Musashi writes:

> In using the eyes, do so in a large and encompassing way. There is observation and there is seeing. The eye of observation is strong. The eye of seeing is weak. To see the faraway as nearby, and the nearby as faraway is essential to the martial arts. To know your opponent's sword, yet not to see it at all is very important in the martial arts.

Compare this to Takuan in "The Mysterious Record of Immovable Wisdom":

> When facing a single tree, if you look at a single one of its red leaves, you will not see all the others. When the eye is not set on any one leaf, and you face the tree with nothing at all in mind, any number of leaves are visible to the eye without limit. But if a single leaf holds the eye, it will be as if the remaining leaves were not there.
>
> One who has understood this is no different from the Kannon with a thousand arms and a thousand eyes.

Here Takuan neatly ties in his main theme (which is also Musashi's) regarding fluidity of the mind, discussed above, with the function of sight and the mind itself. One must not let the mind be arrested by the act of seeing. If his mind is arrested, he will not only miss the big picture, but give himself away altogether.

Similarly, Musashi notes that the study of many stances only confuses the student, whose understanding of these stances can easily become just so much baggage. With the Stance/No-Stance, the swordsman is left completely free, unarrested by any distracting awareness of how to place his feet, or where to aim his sword. Concerning this, Takuan writes:

> As the beginner knows nothing about either body posture or the positioning of his sword, neither does his mind stop anywhere within him. If a man strikes at him with a sword, he simply meets the attack without anything in mind.
>
> As he studies various things and is taught the diverse ways of how to make a stance, the manner of grasping the sword and where to put his mind, his mind stops in many places. Now if he wants to strike an opponent, he is extraordinarily discomforted.

For the man who has transcended this problem, however:

> While hands, feet and body may move, the mind does not stop any place at all, and one does not know where it is.

Another interesting connection appears in Musashi's section of the Water chapter titled "The Flint and Spark Hit," and in a section of Takuan's work titled "The Function of Flint and Spark." Musashi explains his point in rather short terms:

> The Flint and Stone Hit is executed by striking with great certainty and strength, without raising your sword at all, when your sword is joined with your opponent's. You should put strength into your feet, body and hands, and strike quickly with these three.

Takuan's explanation is almost like a footnote to Musashi's words, expanding them to his own familiar Zen Buddhist theme:

> There is such a thing as the action of flint and spark. No sooner have you struck the stone than the light appears. Since the light appears just as you strike the stone, there is neither interval nor interstice. This also signifies the absence of the interval that would stop the mind.
>
> It would be a mistake to think of this simply as celerity. Rather, it underscores the point that the mind does not stop. When the mind stops it will be grasped by the opponent. On the other hand, if the mind contemplates being fast and goes into quick action, it will be captured by its own contemplation.

Again, Musashi, this time from the Wind chapter:

> Speed in the martial arts is not the True Way. Concerning speed, we say that something is fast or slow depending on whether it misses the rhythm of things.

Finally, there is the correlation between Musashi's emphasis on the discipline of daily training—forging oneself in the morning, tempering oneself at night—and his insistence that the mind of the martial arts must be the everyday mind, and the everyday mind must be the mind of the martial arts. But if the martial art is no different from the everyday mind, what makes it special? And if the everyday mind is no different from the martial art, why train at all? Musashi replies in his Fire chapter:

> Whoever would get to the heart of it, let him do so with conviction, practicing in the morning and training in the evening. After he has polished his techniques and gained independent freedom

of movement, he will naturally gain miraculous powers, and his free and easy strength will be wonderful. This is the spirit wherein; as a warrior, he will put these practices into action.

And in the Water chapter:

Practice what is in this book line by line, engage your opponents and gradually you will grasp the principle of the Way. Keep this unceasingly in mind, but do not be hurried; try your hand from time to time, and learn the heart of each step. The journey of a thousand *ri* proceeds step by step, so think without rushing.

Takuan, in his "Annals of the Sword of Taia," again gives a similar answer:

Do you want to obtain this? Walking, stopping, sitting or lying down, in speaking and remaining quiet, during tea and during rice, you must never neglect exertion, you must quickly set your mind on the goal, and investigate thoroughly, both coming and going. Thus should you look straight into things. As months pile up and years pass by, it should appear like a light appearing on its own in the dark. You will receive wisdom without a teacher and will generate mysterious ability without trying to do so. At just such a time, this does not depart from the ordinary, yet it transcends it.

Musashi declared that he had had no teacher in the martial arts or any of the other arts he practiced; he further advocated investigating every concept in his martial art thoroughly and never departing from the ordinary. The parallels between his views and those of Takuan, however, would seem extraordinary, indeed. Musashi was a mature man by 1631 and would have had the deepest understanding of his art by this time. Takuan was steeped in Zen from many years of study and meditation. Zen and the sword. The sword and Zen. Their conversation must have gone on throughout the night.

Yagyu Munenori

In 1632, a little more than ten years before Musashi finished writing *The Book of Five Rings*, but less than a year after Takuan wrote "The Mysterious Record of Immovable Wisdom," Yagyu Munenori, the sword instructor to the Tokugawa shoguns in Edo, wrote a book entitled *The Life-Giving Sword*. About the same length as Musashi's work, it is sprinkled with quotations from Zen and Confucian masters, and, in a number of places, it paraphrases his friend and correspondent, Takuan. Widely read and well-educated, Munenori, too, had no doubt read the *Sun Tzu* many times, and its influence is just below the surface in a number of sections of his work.

Munenori, one of the most respected swordsmen of his time, also wrote for his students, which as noted, included some of the most powerful men in the country. His father was the legendary Yagyu Sekishusai. His nephew, Yagyu Hyogonosuke Toshiyoshi, was teacher to the Tokugawa shogunate family in Owari (centered in the modern city of Nagoya) at this time. In keeping with his family's long reputation for education, status, and martial pedigree, it was almost Munenori's responsibility to show both a wide range of reading and honored precedent for his style.

There is no evidence that Musashi had read Munenori's book before writing his own, but he would certainly have heard of it, and perhaps heard quotes from one section or another. It should also be kept in mind that Lord Hosokawa Tadatoshi had been an accomplished disciple of the Yagyu school, and then invited Musashi to have a bout with his Yagyu-appointed sparring partner. When the sparring partner was defeated, Tadatoshi himself tried a bout with Musashi, only to get nowhere, and from that time on became a disciple of the Niten Ichi-ryu.

Musashi may well have been loaned a copy of Munenori's book by his admiring disciple Tadatoshi. *The Life-Giving Sword* and other works come readily to mind with lines from *The Book of Five Rings* such as this one from the Earth chapter:

> Now, even in writing this book, I am neither borrowing the ancient words of Buddhism or Confucianism, nor using old examples from the military chronicles or practices.

What Musashi read or didn't read will never be known with certainty—but the similarities and parallels, as well as the differences, give us some hint of the way of the thinking of these accomplished men and give us notice as to how they wished to be remembered.

In explaining how their books should be approached, Musashi and Munenori expressed similar ideas in very different styles. At the beginning of his Water chapter, Musashi writes:

> You will not reach the essence of the martial arts by merely looking at this book. Think that what is written down here was done just for you, and do not consider simply looking at it, familiarizing yourself with it, or trying to imitate it. Rather, you should consider these principles as though they were discovered from your own mind, and continually make great efforts to make them a physical part of yourself.

Here Musashi makes no references to anyone other than himself and the student. The principles contained in the book must be absorbed and assimilated as the student's own. The book is a part of the medium for doing so.

Munenori deemphasizes his book to a greater degree, but does so with reference to yet another book, the ancient Chinese Confucian classic, *The Great Learning* (大学).

The Great Learning is the gate for the beginning scholar. For the most part, when arriving at a house, you first enter through the gate. The gate is the sign that you have approached the house. Passing through this gate, you enter the house and meet the master. Just so, Learning is the gate that approaches the Way. Passing through the gate, you arrive at the Way. But Learning is the gate, not the house. Do not look at the gate and think, "This is the house." The house is within, after passing through the gate. Do not read written works and think, "This is the Way." Written works are like the gate to approach the Way.

It has already been noted how Musashi approached the matter of vision with his division of "seeing" and "observation." The following is Munenori's—again, somewhat similar to Musashi's principle, yet expressed in a slightly more oblique and literary way:

> When your opponent is holding back, you should execute various duplicitous strategies and, while watching what he does, appear as though you are watching him while you're not, and watch while you appear as though you are not. You should not be negligent even for a moment. Rather than looking at one place, watch him while keeping your eyes constantly on the move.
>
> A certain Chinese poem says, "With a stealthy glance, the dragonfly avoids the shrike." "A stealthy glance" means looking furtively. To watch what your opponent does both steadily and furtively, you must move without negligence.

Musashi gives careful attention to rhythm throughout *The Book of Five Rings*, but writes about it extensively in the Earth chapter. He notes especially that all things have their own rhythm, and that the martial artist will ignore them to his peril, for there are rhythms to handling weapons, rhythms of serving one's lord, and even rhythms of success and failure. He writes specifically and clearly, noting toward the end of this section,

> These rhythms are essential to the martial arts. If you are unable to discern the rhythm of resistance to your opponent's rhythm, your martial art will not be correct. In a battle of martial arts, victory is in knowing the rhythms of your various opponents, in using a rhythm your opponent will be unable to grasp, and in developing a rhythm of emptiness (*ku*; 空), rather than one of wisdom.

Munenori begins his section on rhythm specifically, but then seems to get distracted in metaphor:

> When your opponent has grasped his sword and set up a broad rhythm, you should use a short rhythm. If your opponent has a short rhythm, you should use a broad one. You should use an understanding that your opponent and the rhythm should not be in harmony.
>
> A skillful birdcatcher will show a bird his pole, will maneuver the pole from his end in a swaying motion, and then slip up and take the bird. The bird is arrested by the shaking rhythm of the pole; it may flutter its wings again and again, but will be unable to take flight and so will be taken. This is the way in which your opponent and the rhythm should be out of kilter. If the rhythm is off, he will be unable to jump over a ditch, but rather will step right into it.

Musashi makes clear in a number of places that learning too many stances, trying strange and fancy footwork, or concentrating on holding the sword in advantageous ways are all distractions. To prefer one weapon over another, or one stance over another only freezes up the mind and keeps the combatant closed to the true circumstances and possibilities of the situation. His vocabulary is that the mind should be kept "straight," but the meaning, as demonstrated in sections like the one on Stance/No-Stance of the final chapter, is that the mind should abide in Emptiness so that it and the body can go anywhere and do anything. Munenori makes a similar point, but his approach follows that of Takuan:

> To think single-mindedly of winning is sickness. To think single-mindedly of using the martial arts is sickness. To think single-mindedly of demonstrating one's high level of practice is sickness. To think single-mindedly of attacking is sickness, and to think only of waiting is sickness. To think single-mindedly in a calcified way of expelling sickness is also sickness. No matter what it is, in stopping single-mindedly in the mind, it is sickness. All of these different sicknesses are there in your mind, so you should put your mind in order and put them out.

What then follows is a long series of sections on how to "use thought to be free of thought," but the preceding paragraph will give the reader an idea of Munenori's style. Where *The Book of Five Rings* is direct and laconic, *The Life-Giving Sword* seems to wander into philosophical musings, mostly Buddhist in nature. Again, this may indicate a slight difference in motivations behind the books—one to directly instruct the student in the clearest of possible terms; the other to instruct, but also to impress the (Tokugawa) student with literary and religious references, and even a little obfuscation. Or the difference may be simply a matter of style. At any rate, Munenori continues, entering a theme Musashi also touched on with this line from his Water chapter: "Do not let your frame of mind be any different from your everyday mind."

A monk once asked a virtuous priest of long ago, "What is the Way?" The old priest responded by saying, "The everyday mind, that is the Way."

This story has a principle that runs through all Ways. When it is asked, "What sort of thing is the Way," the answer can be "the ordinary mind." This is truly a profound matter. Leaving behind all sickness of the mind and becoming the ordinary mind, one reaches the ground where he can mix with sickness and yet not be sick.

Finally, Munenori seems to have been just as concerned as Musashi that his students might have preferences and prejudices, and might not unfetter their minds to the extent that they would be able to respond to the circumstances of their situations. Both men advised the potential swordsman to keep his eyes wide open to absolutely everything, from the weapons to be used to where his opponent's next strike might be coming from. In questions of strategy, however, Musashi tended to speak from the intuitive point of view, which formed the undercurrent of his martial art, while Munenori took a more didactic Zen Buddhist line of thought. Munenori writes:

The priest Chung Fen said, "Equip yourself with the mind that is the released mind." These words have two levels of meaning. If you release the mind and it stays at its destination, you then bring it back step by step so as not to let it stay where it is. This is the discipline of the first level. This teaches you to strike with the sword and then steadily bring your mind back from the place where your sword has struck.

The deeper level means that in releasing your mind, you let it go where it wants to. "Releasing the mind" means letting it go and having it not stop at all.

And:

One of Manorhata's [an Indian prince who became the twenty-second patriarch of Buddhism] gathas went as follows: "The mind follows the ten thousand circumstances and changes accordingly. It is the changing that is truly difficult to perceive."

In the martial arts, the "ten thousand circumstances" means the numerous activities of one's opponent. The mind changes with each action. For example, if the opponent lifts his sword, the mind changes with that sword. If it swings to the right, the mind changes to the right; if it swings to the left, the mind changes to the left. Thus it is said, "It follows the ten thousand circumstances and changes accordingly."

"This changing is truly difficult to perceive" is the very eye of the martial arts. This should be understood as the mind that leaves no trace, or, as is said, leaving no trace "like the white waves [in Japanese, *shiranami*, which also means 'unknown'] of the moving boat, changing on ahead and never stopping."

"Difficult to perceive" means "vague" and "unseen." This means that the mind does not stop. If your mind stops in one place, you will be defeated in the martial arts.

It is obvious that Munenori borrowed heavily from his friend and mentor Takuan, and that the two of them held a commonality of interests and outlooks with Musashi. That this should be so for three such talented and cultured men should not be surprising, and neither should be their differing and unique styles.

The *Hsinhsinming*

It is quite clear that Musashi made a remarkable career of armed conflict, and that the detritus in his wake must have been devastating. We can assume by what records that exist that most of his opponents were either killed or maimed, and that the lucky ones got off with merely sound humiliation. But it is also clear that he was not a cold-blooded murderer, but a man in pursuit of an art, as many others were during his time, and that the martial arts during this period involved risks that we are little likely to take in modern times.

It is also well known that in Japan the martial arts and the military class have had a long connection with Buddhism, a religion that has as its very first precept the prohibition of killing or causing harm. There were the great number of warrior-priests in Nara during the Heian period (794–1185), the Hojo regents of the Kamakura period (1185–1333) who bolstered themselves against the Mongol invaders with Zen philosophy and meditation, and even among Musashi's opponents one of the most formidable was the spearman-priest at the Hozoin temple.

The Zen sect in particular seems to have been attractive to the warrior class. With its rigorous discipline and uncomplicated methods of concentration, its insistence on the transcendence of the border between life and death, and its emphasis on practice and action rather than intellectual argument, Zen was well suited for warriors who had to put their lives on the line with quick, intuitive decisions. For these men, even some realization of the Zen concepts of *muga*, or No-self, and *munen*, or No-thought, must have helped them live their lives with equanimity.

Although Musashi seems to have begun his life in a Pure Land Buddhist household, and may well have spent time with Hon'ami Koetsu at his mostly Nichiren Buddhist artists' conclave in his Kyoto days, he eventually made a commitment to Zen. This can be understood by his relationship with the Zen priests at the Hosokawa domain in Kumamoto at the end of his life, and most clearly by the subjects of his art such as Bodhidharma and Hotei. As a literate and highly inquisitive man, it is likely that he read through a number of the Zen Buddhist texts, and not just at Kumamoto, but throughout his life. As evidenced by his acquaintance with the concepts of Emptiness and No-thought in *The Book of Five Rings*, he probably had studied such Zen staples as the Heart Sutra, the Diamond Sutra, and the *Mumonkan* long before he arrived in Kyushu.

Another favorite in the Zen library that seems a constant presence in *The Book of Five Rings* is the early Chinese work, the *Hsinhsinming* (信心銘; in Japanese, *Shinjinmei*). This is a long poem of short, easy-to-remember couplets, expounding the basic principles of Zen, and is said to be heavily flavored by Taoist concepts. The monk accredited with its authorship, Seng-ts'an, was the third patriarch of Zen (in Chinese, Ch'an) in China. He is thought to have died around 606 C.E. Just when this work was transmitted to Japan is not known, but it seems to have been widely read by Zen adepts since the thirteenth century.

The reader is by now well acquainted with the principles Musashi emphasized, so perhaps some examples of but a few of the *Hsinhsinming*'s 146 couplets will be sufficient to indicate how the swordsman will have warmed to its philosophy and made it part and parcel of his own.

> To reach the Way is not difficult,
> only avoid picking and choosing.

> If you want to see its manifestation,
> don't live in "order" or "reverse."

> The conflict between correct and incorrect,
> this makes the mind ill.

> With the smallest bit of affirmation or denial,
> the mind is lost in complications.

> Release it and things will be as they are;
> its essence is neither in going nor staying.

If the mind makes no differences,
all things are just as they are.

In the end, ultimately,
things do not reside in ruts or rules.

No residing here, no residing there;
the ten directions before your very eyes.

One thing is exactly everything;
everything is exactly one thing.

If you're able to be like this,
why worry about what is incomplete?

Living and acting without preferences, keeping the mind wide open, applying the same principle to all Ways, and living without regret. The *Hsinhsinming* would have spoken to Musashi and reinforced what he had experienced in the intense affairs of his everyday life. Indeed, it is doubtful that such Zen literature would have "taught" Musashi anything about his art, but instead would have given him an intelligible framework with which to work on the dark and nameless concepts he had already made his own.

A Musashi Filmography

What follows is a chronological listing of cinematic productions concerning Miyamoto Musashi that remain on record. Those produced from 1940 on are generally, if not widely, available today. Each movie's title is given in English and then Japanese, followed by the names of the studio, the director, and, finally, the actors according to their roles. Note that some of these films in foreign release bear titles quite different from the original Japanese titles.

For those movies made before 1924, the names of the directors and actors are lost to history. In fact, much information, like the details of Musashi's life, has been lost. Smaller studios may have produced more obscure movies of which there are no extant records, and even some of the works noted in this list were destroyed in the fire bombing of Tokyo during World War II.

As of this writing, by far the most accessible of the movies available to a non-Japanese audience on home video is the three-part saga by Inagaki Hiroshi known as *Samurai* or *Samurai Trilogy* released from 1954 to 1956, the first of which won an Academy Award for Best Foreign Film. For non-Japanese-speaking film buffs who may want to view some of the non-English releases, familiarity with Yoshikawa

Eiji's novel *Musashi* would go a long way toward following the plots of many if not most of these films.

1908   *Miyamoto Musashi's Subjugation of the Lustful Old Man* (Miyamoto Musashi Hihi Taiji no Ba; 宮本武蔵狒々退治の場) Yoshizawa Shoten (puppets)

1909   *The Legend of Miyamoto's Valor* (Miyamoto Buyu Den; 宮本武勇伝) M. Patei

1911   *The Legend of Miyamoto's Valor* (Miyamoto Buyu Den; 宮本武勇伝) Yokota Shokai

       Miyamoto Musashi (宮本無三四) Yokota Shokai

1914   *Miyamoto Musashi* (宮本武蔵) Nikkatsu Kyoto Director: Makino Shozo Miyamoto Musashi: Onoe Matsunosuke

1915   *Miyamoto Musashi* (宮本武蔵) Tenkatsu Osaka Miyamoto Musashi: Ichikawa Ichijuro

1918   *Miyamoto Musashi* (宮本無三四) Nikkatsu Miyamoto Musashi: Onoe Matsunosuke

1919   *Miyamoto Musashi Den* (宮本武蔵伝) Tenkatsu Kyoto Director: Yoshino Jiro

1921   *Miyamoto Musashi* (宮本武蔵)
Nikkatsu
Miyamoto Musashi: Onoe Matsunosuke

Miyamoto Musashi (宮本武蔵)
Shochiku
Miyamoto Musashi: Sawamura Shirogoro

1924   *Miyamoto Musashi* (宮本無三四)
Nikkatsu Kyoto
Director: Kobayashi Yaroku
Miyamoto Musashi: Onoe Matsunosuke

1927   *The Legend of Miyamoto's Valor* (Miyamoto Buyu Den; 宮本武勇伝)
Toa
Director: Goto Shusei
Miyamoto Musashi: Mitsuoka Ryuzaburo. Sasaki Kojiro:
Segawa Michisaburo

1929   *Miyamoto Musashi* (宮本武蔵)
Chiezo Production
Director: Inoue Kintaro
Miyamoto Musashi: Kataoka Chiezo

1930   *Miyamoto Musashi* (宮本武蔵)
Makino Film Productions
Director: Katsumi Masayoshi
Miyamoto Musashi: Tanizaki Juro. Sasaki Kojiro: Tojo Takeru

1935   *The Legend of the Valor at Sekiguchi* (Sekiguchi
Buyu Den; 関口武勇伝)
Kyokuto

Director: Nishina Kumahiko
Miyamoto Musashi: Shiba Kaisuke

1936 *Miyamoto Mus*ashi (宮本武蔵)
Daito
Director: Otomo Ryuza
Miyamoto Musashi: Mizushima Michitaro. Sasaki Kojiro: Ukita
Shozaburo

Miyamoto Musashi (宮本武蔵)
Kanjuro Production
Director: Takizawa Eisuke
Miyamoto Musashi: Arashi Kanjuro. Otsu: Mori Shizuko.
Matahachi: Sugiyama Shosankyu (BASED ON YOSHIKAWA EIJI'S
MIYAMOTO MUSASHI)

1937 *Miyamoto Musashi*: The Earth Chapter
(Miyamoto Musashi: Chi no maki; 宮本武蔵地の巻)
Nikkatsu
Director: Ozaki Jun
Miyamoto Musashi: Kataoka Chiezo. Otsu: Todoroki Yukiko.
Matahachi: Hara Kensaku (BASED ON YOSHIKAWA EIJI'S MIYAMOTO
MUSASHI)

Miyamoto Musashi: The Wind Chapter
(Miyamoto Musashi: Kaze no maki; 宮本武蔵風の巻)
Jo Studio
Director: Ishibashi Seiichi
Miyamoto Musashi: Kurokawa Yataro. Sasaki Kojiro:
Sawamura Shonosuke. Otsu: Takao Mitsuko. Matahachi:
Kiyokawa Soji
(BASED ON YOSHIKAWA EIJI'S MIYAMOTO MUSASHI)

1938   *Miyamoto Musashi* (宮本武蔵)
Daito
Director: Otomo Ryuzo
Miyamoto Musashi: Matsuyama Sozaburo. Sasaki Kojiro:
Daijoji Hachiro

Miyamoto Musashi (宮本武蔵)
Shinko
Director: Mori Kazuo
Miyamoto Musashi: Otani Hideo

1940   *Miyamoto Musashi:* (1) *The Pioneers* (2) *Gateway to Success* (3) *The One Road of Sword and Mind*
(Miyamoto Musashi: 1. Kusawake no Hitobito, 2. Eitatsu no Mon,
3. Kenshin Ichiro; 宮本武蔵 (1) 草分の人々 (2) 栄達の門 (3) 剣心一路)
Nikkatsu
Director: Inagaki Hiroshi
Miyamoto Musashi: Kataoka Chiezo. Sasaki Kojiro: Tsukigata
Ryunosuke. Otsu: Miyagi Chikako (BASED ON YOSHIKAWA EIJI'S
MIYAMOTO MUSASHI)

1942   *Duel at Hannya Slope* (Kessen Hannyazaka; 決戦般若坂)
Daito
Director: Saeki Kozo
Miyamoto Musashi: Konoe Jushiro. Otsu: Shiroki Sumire
(BASED ON YOSHIKAWA EIJI'S *MIYAMOTO MUSASHI*)
Duel at Ichijoji (Ichijoji Ketto; 一乗寺決闘)
Nikkatsu
Director: Inagaki Hiroshi
Miyamoto Musashi: Kataoka Chiezo. Otsu: Miyagi Chikako.
Yoshioka Seijuro: Asaka Shinpachiro
(BASED ON YOSHIKAWA EIJI'S *MIYAMOTO MUSASHI*)

1943 *Initiation to the Two-Sword Style* (Nito-ryu Kaigan; 二刀流開眼)
Daiei
Director: Ito Daisuke
Miyamoto Musashi: Kataoka Chiezo. Otsu: Soma Chieko
(BASED ON YOSHIKAWA EIJI'S *MIYAMOTO MUSASHI*)

1944 *Miyamoto Musashi* (宮本武蔵)
Shochiku
Director: Mizoguchi Kenji
Miyamoto Musashi: Kawarazaki Chojuro. Otsu:Tanaka Kinuyo
(BASED ON YOSHIKAWA EIJI'S *MIYAMOTO MUSASHI*)

1950– *Sasaki Kojiro* (in three parts) (佐々木小次郎)
51 Morita Production
Director: Inagaki Hiroshi
Miyamoto Musashi: Mifune Toshiro. Sasaki Kojiro: Otani
Tomoemon

1952 *Musashi and Kojiro* (Musashi to Kojiro; 武蔵と小次郎)
Shochiku
Director: Makino Masahiro
Miyamoto Musashi: Tatsumi Ryutaro. Sasaki Kojiro: Shimada
Shogo

Coward at Ganryu Island (Koshinuke Ganryujima; 腰抜け巌流島)
Daiei
Director: Mori Kazuo
Miyamoto Musashi: Morishige Hisaya. Sasaki Kojiro: Oizumi
Akira. Otsu: Sanjo Miki. Nagaoka Sado: Ban Junzaburo

1954 *Samurai I* (a.k.a., *The Legend of Musashi*; *Samurai Trilogy*, part 1)
(*Miyamoto Musashi* ; 宮本武蔵)

Toho

Director: Inagaki Hiroshi

Miyamoto Musashi: Mifune Toshiro. Otsu: Yachigusa Kaoru.

Matahachi: Mikuni Rentaro. Akemi: Okada Mariko

—Academy Award for Best Foreign Film

(BASED ON YOSHIKAWA EIJI'S *MIYAMOTO MUSASHI*)

—*AVAILABLE IN ENGLISH-SUBTITLED VERSION*—

1955   *Samurai II* (a.k.a., *The Duel at Ichijoji Temple; Samurai Trilogy*, part 2)

(Zoku Miyamoto Musashi: Ichijoji Ketto; 続宮本武蔵 一乗寺決闘)

Toho

Director: Inagaki Hiroshi

Miyamoto Musashi: Mifune Toshiro; Sasaki Kojiro: Tsuruta

Koji. Otsu: Yachigusa Kaoru. Matahachi: Sakai Sachio. Shi-

shido Baiken: Mizushima Michitaro (BASED ON YOSHIKAWA EIJI'S

MIYAMOTO MUSASHI)

—*AVAILABLE IN ENGLISH-SUBTITLED VERSION*—

1956   *Samurai III* (a.k.a., *Duel at Ganryu Island; Samurai Trilogy*, part 3)

(Ketto Ganryujima; 決闘巌流島)

Toho

Director: Inagaki Hiroshi

Miyamoto Musashi: Mifune Toshiro. Sasaki Kojiro: Tsuruta Koji.

Nagaoka Sado: Shimura Takashi

(BASED ON YOSHIKAWA EIJI'S *MIYAMOTO MUSASHI*)

—*AVAILABLE IN ENGLISH-SUBTITLED VERSION*—

Summary of the Secret Legend of Moonlight

(Hiden Tsukikage Sho; 秘伝月影抄)

Daiei

Director: Tasaka Katsuhiko

Miyamoto Musashi: Kurokawa Yataro

The Master Swordsman's Two-Sword Style (Kengo Nito-ryu; 剣豪二刀流)
Toei
Director: Matsuda Sadaji
Miyamoto Musashi: Kataoka Chiezo. Sasaki Kojiro: Azuma
Chiyonosuke

1957   *Sasaki Kojiro* (Part 1) (佐々木小次郎・前編)
Toei
Director: Saeki Kiyoshi
Miyamoto Musashi: Kataoka Chiezo. Sasaki Kojiro: Azuma
Chiyonosuke
Sasaki Kojiro (part 2)   (佐々木小次郎・後編)
Toei
Director: Saeki Kiyoshi
Miyamoto Musashi: Kataoka Chiezo. Sasaki Kojiro: Azuma
Chiyonosuke

1959   *The Night Before Ganryu Island* (Ganryujima Zen'ya; 巌流島前夜)
Shochiku
Director: Osone Tatsuo
Miyamoto Musashi: Mori Miki. Sasaki Kojiro: Kitagami Yataro

1960   *The Two Musashis* (Futari no Musashi; 二人の武蔵)
Daiei
Director: Watanabe Kunio
Hirata Musashi: Hasegawa Kazuo. Okamoto Musashi: Ichi-
kawa Raizo. Sasaki Kojiro: Katsu Shintaro

1961   *Miyamoto Musashi* (a.k.a., *Zen and Sword*, part 1) (宮本武蔵)
Toei
Director: Uchida Tomu
Miyamoto Musashi: Nakamura Kinnosuke. Otsu: Irie Wakaba.

Matahachi: Kimura Isao (BASED ON YOSHIKAWA EIJI'S *MIYAMOTO MUSASHI*)

1962 *Duel at Hannya Pass* (a.k.a., *Zen and Sword*, part 2)
(Hannyazaka no Ketto; 般若坂の決斗)
Toei
Director: Uchida Tomu
Miyamoto Musashi: Nakamura Kinnosuke. Otsu: Irie Wakaba.
Takuan: Mikuni Rentaro (BASED ON YOSHIKAWA EIJI'S *MIYAMOTO MUSASHI*)

1963 *Initiation to the Two-Sword Style* (a.k.a., *Zen and Sword*, part 3)
(Nito-ryu Kaigan; 二刀流開眼)
Toei
Director: Uchida Tomu
Miyamoto Musashi: Nakamura Kinnosuke. Sasaki Kojiro:
Takakura Ken. Otsu: Irie Wakaba. Akemi: Oka Satomi
(BASED ON YOSHIKAWA EIJI'S *MIYAMOTO MUSASHI*)

1964 *Miyamoto Musashi: Duel at Ichijoji* (a.k.a., *Zen and Sword*, part 4)
(Ichijoji no Ketto; 一乗寺の決斗)
Toei
Director: Uchida Tomu
Miyamoto Musashi: Nakamura Kinnosuke. Sasaki Kojiro:
Takakura Ken. Otsu: Irie Wakaba. Yoshioka Seijuro: Ebara
Shinjiro. Yoshioka Denshichiro: Hira Mikijiro. Osugi: Akagi
Harue & Naniwa Chieko
(BASED ON YOSHIKAWA EIJI'S *MIYAMOTO MUSASHI*)

1965 *Duel at Ganryu Island* (a.k.a., *Zen and Sword*, part 5)
(Ganryujima no Ketto; 巌流島の決斗)
Toei

Director: Uchida Tomu
Miyamoto Musashi: Nakamura Kinnosuke. Sasaki Kijiro: Takakura Ken. Otsu: Irie Wakaba. Nagaoka Sado: Kataoka Chiezo. Yagyu Tajima no kami: Tamura Takahiro (BASED ON YOSHIKAWA EIJI'S *MIYAMOTO MUSASHI*)

1967 *Sasaki Kojiro* (佐々木小次郎)
Toho
Director: Inagaki Hiroshi
Miyamoto Musashi: Nakadai Tatsuya. Sasaki Kojiro: Onoe Kikunosuke

1971 *Swords of Death* (Shinken Shobu; 真剣勝負)
Toho
Director: Uchida Tomu
Miyamoto Musashi: Nakamura Kinnosuke. Shishido Baiken: Mikuni Rentaro. Shishido's wife: Okiyama Hideko
(BASED ON YOSHIKAWA EIJI'S *MIYAMOTO MUSASHI*)
—*AVAILABLE IN ENGLISH-SUBTITLED VERSION*—

1973 *Miyamoto Musashi* (宮本武蔵)
Shochiku
Director: Kato Tai
Miyamoto Musashi: Takahashi Hideki. Sasaki Kojiro: Tamiya Jiro. Otsu: Matsuzaka Keiko. Matahachi: Franky Sakai. Takuan: Ryu Chishu
(BASED ON YOSHIKAWA EIJI'S *MIYAMOTO MUSASHI*)

NOTES

Prologue

1. The other battleship was the Yamato, the ancient name for Japan. These twin ships and the ideals that they represented gave hope to the country toward the end of the war, and it seems fair to imagine that these names were chosen because the spirit of one was considered identical to the spirit of the other.

CHAPTER
──────
ONE

The Way of the Sword: Banshu to Ganryu Island

1. *Gaki daisho*: leader of a children's gang or group of kids. *Gaki* means "hungry ghost," the inhabitants of the second-lowest of the six realms in Buddhist belief. They have distended stomachs and pinhole-sized throats, and can never get enough to eat. Japanese people still affectionately call children "*gaki.*" *Daisho* (*Taisho*) means general.

2. There are a number of differing versions of the *shugyosha*'s seven austerities. One of these versions, the *Bukyo shigen*, written during the Edo period (1603–1868), lists them as follows:

    —Bear up under days of cold and heat, withstand exposure to wind and rain, and walk mountain roads and difficult paths.

241

—Do not sleep under a roof; consider it fundamental to sleep out in the open.

—Be patient with hunger and cold. Carry no money or food provisions.

—If there is a battle at one's destination, participate and achieve meritorious deeds. Be direct in combat; avoid acting like a thief.

—Go alone to places frightening to the common run of men: places where evil spirits congregate or where there are bewitching foxes and poisonous snakes.

—Become a criminal on purpose, be put in jail and extricate yourself by your own wisdom.

—Consider your own position to be lower than that of farmers and make your living by helping in the paddies and fields.

These would seem to be a little too pat and organized, not unlike the rules for a haiku poet thought to have been written by Basho during the same period. Many *shugyosha*, however, likely went through these experiences of necessity.

3. The *Sayo gunshi* story also departs from tradition by stating that Musashi was living as a guest of the Tazumi family at this time and took upon himself the task of "punishing" Kihei. The fight, according to this record, lasted only a moment, Musashi finishing Kihei off with one quick stroke of a sword.

4. Some accounts have Bennosuke leaving Hirafuku immediately and starting his own travels as a *shugyosha*.

5. Although Musashi himself claims in *The Book of Five Rings* to have been born in Harima, there are a number of locations that officially declare themselves to be Musashi's birthplace. The village of Miyamoto, Sanomo-mura in the old province of Mimasaka (now in Ohara-machi, Aida-gun, Okayama Prefecture) claims that Omasa, his father's first wife, was Musashi's true mother and that Musashi was born there. Indeed, the *Miyamoto-mura kojicho*, a copied edition of a longer village record compiled in 1689, states that a Miyamoto Muni and his son Musashi lived in a house in Miyamoto sometime between 1575 and 1596. According to another theory, however, Musashi's real mother was Yoshiko and Musashi's birthplace was the village of Hirafuku, in Sayo-gun, in the old province of Harima (now Hyogo Prefecture). Yet another location, the village Miyamoto, Iho-gun, in Harima (currently Taishi-mura in Hyogo

Prefecture) claims Musashi as its own, on the basis of statements to that effect in the *Harima no kagami*, written in 1762. And there are others.

6. There are a number of questions about Musashi's father, who is variously called Muni, Munisai, and Muninosuke. Some writers consider these individuals to have been separate people—variously his adoptive father, his uncle, or his teacher. Another theory has his real father as a Tahara Jinbei Iesada. Muni's family name was Hirata, and he is thought to have been aged thirty-one at the time of Musashi's birth. His grave marker, however, which still exists today in Okayama Prefecture, states his death to have been in 1580, or four years before Musashi was born. This would clearly have made it a little difficult for him to have fathered Musashi. On a more reasonable note, the *Hiratake keito* states that Muni died in 1590 at the age of sixty-three, or six years after Musashi was born. The problem in this case is that, counting backward, Muni would have been born in 1528, but this same *Hiratake keito* dates Muni's father's death to 1503 and his mother's to 1505. What is more, the theory that names Tahara Iesada as Musashi's father dates Musashi's birth to 10 February 1573. The reader can see the problem, which is probably better left to other disciplines.

7. Just as the *shugyosha*'s required austerities are defined, there is also a formal list of the possessions that he is permitted.

    —CLOTHING: a padded cotton garment, underwear, an undersash, a bleached cotton shirt, a three-foot-long hand towel, a dyed headband, a cord (for drying things as necessary)
    —FIRE-MAKING MATERIAL: flint and steel, tinder, small kindling
    —EATING UTENSILS: a straw wrapper (for rice or other leftovers), a bamboo canteen
    —MISCELLANEOUS: a travel pass, paper, a portable brush-and-ink set, medicine, scissors, straw sandals, hempen cord, wattled hat

    All *shugyosha* would have carried most of these items. The list is very similar to the possessions carried by traveling priests. The difference is that priests would not, in addition to these articles, have been carrying a set of swords.

8. Scholars have hypothesized that the six were probably: the attack on Fushimi Castle just prior to the Sekigahara campaign; the attack on Gifu Castle, also in

the year 1600; the Battle of Sekigahara; the Winter Campaign at Osaka Castle in 1614; the Summer Campaign of the same castle in 1615; and the Shimabara Rebellion of 1637–38.

9. There is a theory that Musashi was with his father Munisai for the action against Otomo Yoshimune, an ally of the Western forces, at Ishigakihara in Beppu (Bungo Province in Kyushu). If this is true, then Musashi fought in the campaign of Sekigahara on the side of the Eastern forces under the Kuroda clan.

10. *Koku*: A measurement of rice equalling 5.119 U.S. bushels. This was the unit in which the stipends for samurai ware paid, and also defined the allowances of income for the various *daimyo*.

11. The Rendaiji Moor is still called by that name today, although it has changed considerably since Musashi's time. Now mostly a residential area, the once extensive temple compound has been reduced to only a few buildings. According to one of the residential priests, Musashi fought his bout with Seijuro near the Jizodo, a temple that has now disappeared altogether. Interestingly, off to the side of the remaining temple are row after row of extremely weathered stone buddhas. These were unearthed recently during road construction and are considered to be about four hundred years old.

12. The Ichijoji temple was no longer extant even during Musashi's time, but a pine said to be the second or third generation of the one under which the fight occurred still stands at a crossroads within a residential area. This was where the junction of the old and new roads to Omi Province was during Musashi's time, and the place still has the flavor of traditional rural Japan. Just up the road is the Hachidai Shrine, where Musashi famously did not pray to the gods and where today a section of the trunk of the old pine is preserved in a glass case. Farther up the mountain is Tanuki-dani ("Racoon Dog Valley"), and a waterfall—now close to a large temple—under which Musashi is said to have meditated often for self-discipline. The waterfall, now just a trickle, falls into a narrow grotto spanned by a huge straw rope. Within the grotto itself is a moss-covered statue of Fudo Myo-o, behind which is a sword cut from stone. Huge cryptomeria and junipers border the two hundred stone steps up to the waterfall, and other than the smoke of incense and the call of birds, there is only the quiet of the mountain.

13. Much has been made of Matashichiro's age, and he has often been depicted as a young boy just seven years old. But while he is considered to have been young, theories range from seven to seventeen to a young man in his early twenties. It is thought most probable that he was a teenager at the time of this fight, and it must be remembered that he had more or less been raised in the *dojo* of the famous Yoshioka clan. It should be remembered too that Musashi fought his first bout at the age of thirteen.

14. There are a number of other stories concerning Musashi's fights with the Yoshioka clan. According to the admittedly one-sided *Yoshioka-den*, published in 1684, Musashi was a retainer of Matsudaira Tadanao in Echizen and matches were arranged with the Yoshioka clan in order to establish Musashi's style, called the Muteki-ryu, in which he effectively used two swords. The match originated from Tadanao's desire to see combat between two respected swordsmen and was arranged by the Kyoto Shoshidai (magistrate), Itakura Katsushige. In this story, the bout with Seijuro was tense, with neither man giving way, but in the end Musashi was struck on the forehead, blood was drawn, and the match was declared over. When the judges ruled the match a draw, Seijuro was enraged and demanded a rematch, but Musashi declared himself happy with the decision. The *Yoshioka-den* further declares that on the day of Musashi's match with Denshichiro, he did not show up at all, and the story was circulated that Denshichiro had been victorious without having to leave his seat. And in this version, Musashi's opponents may not have been Seijuro and Denshichiro at all, but the Yoshioka brothers, Genzaemon Naotsuna and Mataichi Naoshige.

In the records of the *Koro sawa*, the story goes that Musashi and Seijuro were to meet at the Seven Pines of Kitano in Kyoto and that Musashi made Seijuro wait by arriving late. In this version, Seijuro used a wooden sword while Musashi used one made of bamboo, and the match was considered to have been a draw. Both received blows from the other: Seijuro on the left side of his head, and Musashi above his left brow. The *Honcho bugei shoden* also notes that the match with Seijuro ended in a draw.

Other versions of the story abound. One states that when Musashi and Seijuro fought, they both received blows on the head from one another's swords; but that Seijuro's headband was done in the White Hand Style, which, because of its color, clearly showed a quick flow of blood. Musashi, whose headband was colored persimmon, showed no blood at all. Yet another story relates that the instant Seijuro cut through Musashi's headband, Musashi cut through

Seijuro's *hakama*. The final statement, however, may well be that Musashi's style is still alive and well today, while nothing remains of the once powerful and influential Yoshioka style.

Yet the clan seems not to have disappeared as quickly as is reported in the *Nitenki*. According to a document of the times, the *Shunpu seijiroku* for 1614, a "Yoshioka Kenpo" caused a disturbance during a Noh performance at the Imperial Castle on June 21, and was struck down and killed by Itakura Katsushige's retainer, Ota Chubei. This unseemly event has been recorded in other documents as having occurred in 1602, 1611, and 1613; and would indicate a clan falling further into degradation.

Nevertheless, perhaps they struggled on. According to the record known as the *Mukashi banashi*, written by Chikamatsu Shigenori, about lord Tokugawa Yoshimichi, the fourth-generation lord of the Owari clan, Yoshimichi studied the Yoshioka style and received its book of traditions from a Yoshioka Kahei in the mid-Edo period.

What seems clear, however, is that after the fights with Musashi, the Yoshioka clan slid from a state of prominence and power in the world of swordsmanship back to the role of makers of dye-goods. The stains on their hands were now once again the colors of indigo and tea rather than blood-red.

15. The Hozoin style was later carried to Kokura by Takada Matabei, a man who had learned the art from In'ei's greatest disciple, Nakamura Naomasa, and who was considered to have been the reincarnation of In'ei. Mataemon was later to have a match with Musashi, during which Musashi used a short wooden sword similar to the one that so frustrated the priest from the Ozoin.

    The Hozoin itself was abandoned during the Meiji period's (1868–1912) anti-Buddhist movement. The ground where it was located, where the priests worked so hard at forging their skills, is now a corner of the Nara National Museum. The spear technique created by In'ei and improved by Inshun, however, survived and is still taught today.

16. According to the *Nitenki*, Gonnosuke's initial match with Musashi occurred in Edo, but the *Kaijo monogatari*, written in 1666, states that it occurred when Musashi was residing in Akashi in the province of Harima.

17. Tsujikaze's fall was probably about eighteen feet—no short distance.

18. Karl F. Friday, *Legacies of the Sword*, 89.

19. A number of controversies surround the fight at Ganryu Island, one of which is Kojiro's age on 13 April 1612. It is often suggested that he was eighteen at this time, but there are some problems with that conclusion. The *Nitenki*, for example, is the source that records Kojiro to have been "employed as a sparring partner and disciple of Toda Seigen." Now this Seigen, according to the *Honcho bugei shoden*, was ordered in 1560 by the lord of Mino, Saito Yoshitatsu, to have a match with the sword instructor, Umezu, a match which he won. Thus, supposing that Kojiro was a disciple and at least fifteen years old at this time, he would then have been close to seventy at the time of the fight with Musashi on Ganryu Island. Further, Seigen's younger brother, Kagemasa, who was beaten by Kojiro, died in 1593 at the age of seventy. This means that if Kojiro had been eighteen at the time of the fight on Funa Island, Kagemasa would have died before Kojiro was born. There are other theories on Kojiro's age at the time, but the responsible suggestion, it seems, is that he was likely about the same age as Musashi. This was a match condoned by the Hosokawa clan, after all; and Tadatoshi would not likely have pitted a septuagenarian against a man in his prime, no matter how talented Kojiro might have been.

Seigen himself was an excellent practitioner of the Chujo style who, during the time that he employed Kojiro as a sparring partner, developed an excellent method of using a long sword and is said to have actually initiated the Ganryu style. According to the *Gekken sodan*, written by Minamoto Tokushu, a sword instructor in the Bizen Okayama fief:

> In this style there is something called "One Mind, One Sword." This is taking a stance in a way that you might make a strike straight to the opponent's forehead. Advancing straight ahead, you eye the tip of the opponent's nose, and then suddenly strike at the forehead. . . . [But] as you strike, you bend forward, coming up from below to the place you would have struck from above.

Another tradition differing from the *Nitenki* account concerns not the material, but the actual number of Musashi's weapons. The commonly held story is that Musashi used only one wooden sword in his duel with Kojiro. The *Gekken sodan*, however, states the following:

> At the time he was to meet this person, Ganryu, he asked the boatman for an oar and carved out two swords. Ganryu fought the match with a real sword, but in the end Musashi won by striking and killing Ganryu.

Again, in the *Nitenki* and the Kokura Hibun it is stated that Musashi had asked for the duel at Funa Island (Funashima), but in the *Busho kanjoki* of 1716, there is this account:

> The famous master of the Niten style, Miyamoto Musashi, had become a retainer of the lord of Higo Kumamoto, Hosokawa Etchu no kami Tadatoshi; and when he came to Kyushu from Kyoto, the swordsman, Ganryu, communicated to him that he would like to have a match and would be waiting for him at Funa Island. Funa Island is in the offing out of Shimonseki in the province of Nagato.

The greatest controversy concerning this fight, however, finds its source in the *Numata keki*, the records of the Numata clan, senior vassals to the Higo Kumamoto fief. In this version, the fight between the two men brought on a great swelling of pride among their respective disciples about the question of whose martial art was superior. Although spectators had been banned, Musashi's disciples ignored the edict, secretly crossed over to the island, and when the fallen Kojiro began to recover, rushed over and beat him to death. When Kojiro's disciples learned of this, the account goes, they were determined that Musashi must now die and they crossed over to Funa Island to take revenge. Musashi then sought help from Numata Nobumoto, the castle warden at nearby Moji, and later became a retainer to the Numata clan in the gunnery squad.

It is difficult to understand how this story has had any credence at all. Funa Island is small enough today to walk the circumference in less than fifteen minutes, and through soil buildup and reclamation, it is thought to now be about five times the size it was at the beginning of the seventeenth century. The tiny pine-covered mound toward the northern edge of the island could barely have hidden anyone from the official witnesses, and the remaining land is flat enough to have been used until recently for farming (there are two natural springs on the island). It should also be noted that this version is not recorded in the official Hosokawa family records.

If the differing versions of Kojiro's age, the number of swords Musashi used, and the source of the duels request are matters of hearsay that change over time, the account in *Numata keki* is, on the contrary, a complete fabrication.

As a final note on this episode, it should be mentioned that in Musashi's later years, during his time in Kumamoto, he was asked about the kind of sword he used against Kojiro. Selecting a piece of wood, he quickly and expertly carved out a replica that is a treasure still owned by the Matsui (Nagaoka) family today. It has a blade of just over four feet in length, is studded with two shorn-off nails, and is carved, toward the tip, with an indentation about the size and shape of a gingko nut. This "sword" has been whittled to six edges, becomes thicker from handle to tip, and manifests a surprising grace in its lines that belies its extraordinary weight. It gives the impression of having been fashioned by a man very familiar with a carving knife.

By most accounts, Kojiro had never met Musashi until that late morning on Funa Island. But by the time he saw the scruffy swordsman over six feet tall with this large wooden sword, it was too late.

CHAPTER

TWO

The Way of the Sword and the Way of the Brush: Osaka to Kokura

1. There are various theories as to which side Musashi joined during the destruction of the Toyotomi at Osaka Castle, and a number of scholars believe that he joined the forces inside the castle. As proof, they cite the Kokura Hibun:

    > Whether at the time of the insurrection of the Taiko Toyotomi's favorite retainer, Ishida Jibunosuke, or at the time of Lord Hideyori's rebellion at Osaka in Settsu, Musashi's valor and great fame could not be overstated, even if the oceans had mouths or the valleys had tongues.

    This, however, appears to substantiate only that he fought at both Sekigahara and Osaka. It is interesting to note, however, that had he fought inside the castle, he would have found himself in rather close quarters with the remnants of the Yoshioka clan, who demonstrated its bad run of luck once again by taking up the Toyotomi cause.

2. According to the records of the Akashi town officials in 1618, "Miyamoto Musashi, a retainer of Ogasawara Ukondayu, delineated the town." It was also noted that he knew very precisely how to arrange the samurai quarters beyond the inner moat and the town beyond the outer moat. Musashi was an expert in conflict, and did not confine his thoughts to conflicts of one-on-one encounters. Nor did he stop at the problems of armies on the battlefield.

3. There is some evidence here that, after the sixty bouts of his youth, the climactic fight at Ganryu Island and the horribly bloody fighting at Osaka, Musashi began to see his life in a different light—that he began to distance himself

249

from simple carnage and to see his own art in terms of an altogether broader sense of Art. Further, his fight with Sasaki Kojiro had involved the prestigious and artistic Hosokawa clan and an entire system—boats, lodging, official permission, and observers—rather than simply an unobserved bout with another *shugyosha* on the road; and it is likely that he was now aware of himself as having the possibility of taking a place in history. It is also likely that his contemplation of all these events stimulated a deeper interest in Buddhism in general and Zen in particular. Musashi had by this time met a number of priests and generals who manifested the effects of their Zen practice, and he implicitly understood that this practice could have the same effect on his own life. Thus, on the one hand his life was coming into clearer focus, and on the other he was finding other mediums to express that focus. The Ogasawara family was clever enough to see this in Musashi, and to commission him to extend his art from the martial into the aesthetic area of garden design.

4. The word "samurai" comes from the classical Japanese verb *saburau* (侍う), meaning "to serve." Although Musashi "served" both the Ogasawara and Honda, it was in a limited capacity, and one that did not tie him down to a lifelong commitment. In this sense, Musashi was a warrior and an artist, but not particularly a samurai.

5. Gunbei is said to have been pushed into this fight by Honda Masatomo, brother to Tadamasa, and an avid swordsman.

6. Purple Robe Affair: In 1627, the government cancelled the emperor's prerogative to appoint priests to the highest ecclesiastical positions, taking that right for itself. This came to a near crisis in 1629 when the emperor Go-Mizunoo abdicated in protest of this insult. Takuan also let his opposition to this governmental move be known, and was temporarily banished to Dewa for his efforts. Purple robes were worn only by the very highest ranking abbots

7. "The Mysterious Record of Immovable Wisdom" is included in Takuan Soho, *The Unfettered Mind* (Boston: Shambhala Publications, 2012).

8. Fudo Myo-o is a manifestation of the central cosmic Buddha Vairocana. His angry countenance is there to scare off the enemies of Buddhism: greed, hate

and ignorance. In his right hand he holds a sword to cut through our ignorance, in his left a rope to tie up our passions.

9.   According to the *Sekisui zatsuwa*, Mikinosuke was a descendent of Nakagawa Shimanosuke, a family retainer and shogunate administrator of the *fudai daimyo* (hereditary vassal to the Tokugawa shogunate) Mizuno Katsunari; he may have been related to Musashi through his father. He was said to have been an expert in the two-sword style, and received a stipend of seven hundred *koku*. According to one story, before Mikinosuke was employed by the Honda clan, Musashi had already been hired as Tadatoki's martial arts instructor. When he resigned, he recommended Mikinosuke, who is said to have done very well in fulfilling this position. This would indicate how much he had learned from his adoptive father.

10.   The genealogy of Iori's grandson states that Iori was, in fact, the second son of Musashi's eldest brother, Tahara Jinbei Hisamitsu, and therefore Musashi's nephew. According to this document, he was born 21 October 1612 in the village of Yoneda in Harima. Thus, the story of the boy with the mudfish may be a fictionalized account giving additional color to Musashi's already colorful story. The account, however, is found in the *Nitenki*.

11.   Another theory has it that Yoshinao dismissed Musashi after the bout because of the thorough beating the latter gave to the Tokugawa retainer. The high officials observing the match considered this a breach of etiquette on Musashi's part, and it was determined that Musashi's services would not be needed, particularly given Yoshinao's observation that "Musashi's appearance is somewhat strange and his character eccentric."

   Others in Nagoya were not of the same mind, however, and Musashi's popularity soared. Students lined up at his door, and he remained in Nagoya for three years. The following are two of the poems he wrote at this time:

   After exhausting both
        Principle and Reason;
   The ancient "Not One Thing"
        That knows not
        The bright moonlight.

   The "ancient 'Not One Thing'," (*mu ichimotsu*; 無一物) is a reference to the Sixth Patriarch's stanza, "Fundamentally, not one thing exists" (*honrai mu ichimotsu*; 本来無一物), the defining phrase for Zen Buddhism from the T'ang Dynasty onward. This is the Void or Emptiness, about the inexpressible understanding of which Musashi would attempt to write further in *The Book of Five Rings*. This poem suggests that he had already found this transcendent quality to be the foundation of his own style.

> Thoughtlessly
> > I approached
> Human habitation;
> > Having visited the mountain depths
> > For so long.

This would seem to have been written just before he left Nagoya, or at least to indicate readiness to depart. Was it disappointment in his students, or with the Tokugawa family members in Nagoya? Or was Musashi just ready to be traveling again, and to plunge back into the full force of the natural settings he loved so much?

12. In 1601, Yagyu Muneyoshi (Sekishusai) sent a collection of his own poetry concerning the martial arts to his friend, Konparu Shichiro, the head of the Konparu style of Noh, on the occasion of the latter's seventieth birthday. Titled *Sekishusai's One Hundred Poems on the Martial Arts*, these poems express not only Sekishusai's concerns about the martial arts but also his very real humility and sense of blending the martial with the literary. The following are a few poems from that collection. (It should be noted that the "stone boat" of the third and fourth of these poems is a pun on the name Sekishusai.)

> Having no particular skill
> > for passing through this world,
> I reluctantly entrust myself
> > to one sole refuge:
> > the martial arts.

> A good thing
> > to entrust oneself
> To a refuge!
> > But the martial arts are useless
> > in discord and in strife.

> Though you may be victorious
> > in the martial arts,
> They are but a stone boat
> > that will not cross
> > the melancholy sea of life.

> The martial arts may be
> > an unfloatable
> Stone Boat.
> > But I'm unable to discard
> > My weakness for this Way.

13. Another book, the *Gekijo yoroku*, took the same story of Musashi's connection with Kumoi from the *Dobo goen*, but stated that the man who visited her was the "second-generation Musashi," by whom he may have meant Iori.

14. There is yet another story about Musashi and the women in his life. In the summer of 1604, Musashi stayed at the Enkoji temple of Takino in Harima, and the chief priest of the temple, his younger brother Tada Hanzaburo, and a local samurai, Ochiai Chuemon, became his disciples. Tada Hanzaburo was three years Musashi's senior, and Ochiai Chuemon was a year younger. The *daimyo* of the area had prepared a *dojo* in the temple grounds, and Musashi was the instructor there. Musashi had written the *The Mirror of the Way of War* and was at the point of giving it to Hanzaburo and Chuemon.

During this time, Musashi had a love affair with the priest's oldest daughter. The two pledged themselves to one another, and the following year promised to become man and wife. In the end, however, Musashi could not settle down, and left to roam the country while perfecting his art. It is also conjectured that the girl's father and uncle had misgivings about her relationship with a man of doubtful origins, and made her break off relations with Musashi.

CHAPTER
THREE

The Way of the Brush: Kumamoto

1. A bare-bones road map for these family connections might be as follows:

2. It is also said that Musashi was drawn to the Hosokawa clan by the great efforts of Nagaoka Okinaga, who had previously facilitated the match with Sasaki Kojiro; and by the Kumamoto-fief warrior, Sawamura Daigaku. According to the records of the Terao clan, which continued Musashi's style:

253

At the time he was going about the provinces, he came here and stayed thanks to his intimate friend, Sawamura Daigaku.

Thus, there may have been a number of people who hoped that Musashi would move to Kumamoto.

3. The Kokura Hibun is still standing outside of Kokura at nearly the highest point on Mount Tamuke. It is about twenty feet high and so weathered that the Chinese characters are for the most part illegible. Off to its left is a much smaller modern monument to Sasaki Kojiro. The Inland Sea is just barely visible through the pines that cover the mountain ridge.

4. The full list of headings for *The Thirty-five Articles of the Martial Arts* is as follows:

—Calling this the Way of Two Heavens, One Style
—The Diagnosis of the Way of the Martial Arts
—The Method of Handling the Sword
—The Positions of the Body
—Movements of the Feet
—Use of the Eye
—Distance between Opponents
—Frame of Mind
—Knowing the Three Grades of the Martial Arts
—Itokane
—The Way of the Long Sword
—Striking and Hitting
—The Three Initiatives
—Crossing the Ford
—Exchanging the Body and the Sword
—Two Feet
—Stepping on the Sword
—Controlling the Shadow
—Moving the Light
—Releasing the Bowstring
—The Lesson of the Small Comb
—Knowing the Space of Rhythm
—Pushing Down the Pillow
—Knowing Conditions
—Becoming the Opponent

—The Remaining Mind and the Mind Released

—Striking the Connection

—Applying Lacquer and Glue

—The Body of the Autumn Monkey

—Comparing Stature

—The Lesson of the Door

—The Lesson of the General and the Soldiers

—Stance/No-Stance

—The Body of a Rock

—Knowing the Moment

—Ten Thousand Principles/One Void

It is interesting to note that there is another work ascribed to Musashi that may have preceded *The Thirty-five Articles*. The story goes that Musashi wrote a short "book" in 1604 at the age of twenty-three, while living in Edo. The work was called *The Mirror of the Way of War* and was an outline of the style that he had created, called the Perfect Enlightenment Style. Proof of this is said to be a certificate (*inka*), still extant, awarded to a certain Ochiai Chuemon that contains the phrase *Enmei Ichiryu no Heiho* (Martial Art of the Single Style of Perfect Clarity). The book was supposedly given to Ochiai the year before the presentation of this certificate.

The first edition of *The Mirror* contained only eighteen articles, but this was later amended to thirty-five. And while many consider it to be a forgery, it does bear similarities to *The Thirty-five Articles* and *The Book of Five Rings*, especially in its emphasis on taking the initiative, and it may have been Musashi's prototype for the latter two works.

5. It should be noted that at Tadatoshi's death, seventeen of his retainers committed *junshi*, or ritual suicide to accompany their lord, and the entire famous Abe clan followed him in death. Although *junshi* was later prohibited by the Tokugawa shogunate and many of the ruling clans, it was still permitted at this time. An outsider like Musashi, however, would never have been granted the same privileges as retainers who had been with the clan for generations, and he would never have even hoped for such privileges.

6. Can we know the depth of the painter's spiritual attainment by observing his work? In the Emptiness chapter of *The Book of Five Rings*, Musashi wrote that "Knowing the existent, you know the nonexistent. This, exactly, is Emptiness."

7. Watanabe Kazan, a warrior-painter renowned for his portraits, found this painting in a shop window of an antique store and was so impressed that he made the rounds of his friends in order to raise enough money to purchase it. It is perhaps Musashi's most striking painting, and it so moved Kazan that he felt he was looking directly into the spirit of Bushido itself. Is Musashi the shrike, or is the shrike Musashi?

8. This twenty-page essay is included in Takuan Soho, *The Unfettered Mind*.

9. Art critics have seen the quality of No-Mind (*mushin*) in Musashi's cormorant, contrasting it to the conscious and planning mind (*ushin*) of mankind. But there is also a hint of sadness in this bird's expression, a sense later brought to poetry by the haiku poet Basho:

> At first quite charming,   *Omoshirote*
>   but in the end, sad: *yagate kanashiki*
> the cormorant boats.   *ubune kana.*

10. Ch'uang T'zu, 180.

11. Musashi's refusal to favor any weapon over another was further reinforced by Ch'uang T'zu's lines that preceded the Chinese writer's famous words on the owl:

> From the point of view of function, if we regard a thing as useful because there is a certain usefulness to it, then among all the ten thousand things there are none that are not useful. If we regard a thing as useless because there is a certain uselessness to it, then among the ten thousand things there are none that are not useless.

We immediately understand why Musashi reached for a piece of firewood in his match with Muso Gonnosuke, a master of the five-foot staff.

12. It has been suggested that this painting was based on the famous tale of the noble geese in the *Jakata Tales*, a collection of stories about the Buddha in former incarnations. According to this story, before his incarnation as Gautama, the Enlightened One, the Buddha took birth as a virtuous king of the geese living on a lake in India. A local human monarch, hearing of the wonders of this bird, was determined to capture him for his own. Creating a lake even more

beautiful and attractive than the one where the geese lived, the monarch hired a skillful fowler to set traps that would ensnare them. The curiosity of the flock was enough for them to migrate to the beautiful new lake, but the king of the geese alighted first in order to test for safety. Caught in one of the traps, he let out a pitiful cry and sent the rest of the flock into flight. Only one goose, the king's loyal commander-in-chief, remained pleading with the fowler to take him in place of the king. The fowler, though a hardened hunter, was not made of wood or stone and, feeling great pity, released the goose to freedom. But now the fowler's fate was in jeopardy, and so the two geese volunteered to go freely to the monarch, even though it might mean ending up as the main dish on the dinner table. When the birds were brought before the monarch and the story brought to full light, he was so impressed with the selflessness, loyalty, and courage displayed by the geese that he dismissed them with kind and honorable words. Both monarch and fowler were said to have become saintly men themselves, and the king of the geese and his commander-in-chief were later reincarnated as the Buddha and his closest disciple, Ananda.

These screens—with their depiction of selflessness, loyalty, and courage—were no doubt displayed in a place of honor, affording contemplation and reflection to all those who saw them.

13. This painting gives the impression of a mountainlike Daruma, immovable and steady with solid concentration and a stonelike will. A number of writers have pointed out that this particular Daruma brings to mind Musashi's symbol of a certain mentality in swordsmanship: the body of a rocky crag. In *The Thirty-five Articles of the Martial Arts*, Musashi states: "The body of a rocky crag does not move, its mind is strong and expansive."

Nevertheless, although the first impression of this Daruma is its solidity, in the mouth and eyes there is something else. Could it be warmth or an internal ease? Or could it be the "great doubt" spoken of in Zen? Musashi leaves it to the viewer to come to his own conclusion.

14. Although the Chinese word *pi-kuan* (壁観) has been interpreted a number of ways over the centuries, it is popularly understood as "wall contemplation," in reference to Daruma's nine years of sitting meditation in a cave near the Shaolin Temple. The various sects of Zen have put this legendary action to various degrees of practice. When Dogen (1200–53) brought the Soto sect to Japan from China, he said, in what is probably the most radical declaration on *zazen* meditation ever made, that it is not just the means to the Buddha's state

of mind, but that it is that state of mind, itself. All sects, however, employ the practice liberally, much to the discomfort of beginning students.

Musashi himself was quite experienced with *zazen*, and meditated the last several years of his life at the Reigan Cave outside Kumamoto. He was so familiar with the subject that there can be little doubt that the parallels between his experience and that of the founder of the Zen sect would not have escaped him. The painting he has executed is within the tradition of the "Wall-Facing Daruma" in that it shows the upper body of the patriarch viewed either from the side or diagonally. As the story of Daruma at the wall was meant to transmit the core teaching of Zen Buddhism, paintings of this type are considered to be the best symbols of that teaching.

15. Musashi's triptych, with floating ducks on either side of Daruma, is said to be without precedent. Certainly, it seems that the painter was happy to have included the animals he had observed along the rivers in the Kumamoto area or in his peregrinations through the provinces of Japan, indicating his affection for nature's other inhabitants. Despite being flanked by these animals, the cast of his eyes gives the central figure of Daruma a sense of loneliness that Musashi himself must have felt many times in his life.

16. It seems certain that Musashi saw either Liang K'ai's painting or Yusho's or both, but even a quick look at the three renditions shows that Musashi's rendering of Hotei is radically different from those of the other two artists. Musashi's Hotei is intense, concentrated, alert, and intelligent, while the Hotei of Yusho and Liang K'ai seem almost to be transported to simple and childlike wonderment. Musashi's Hotei is clearly aware of the consequences of the cocks' action, while the Hotei of the other two seem totally oblivious of the matters of life and death. Both reactions are, perhaps, valid Zen Buddhist views, but Musashi's Hotei seems to have been at the borderline between the two realms.

17. The inscription over the napping figure of Hotei reads:

> Tossing aside body and mind, forgetting one's self-nature,
> For the moment propping up both hands, taking a light afternoon nap;
> His bag on his staff, he's utterly negligent,
> Dreams filled with the Heavenly Palace, when called he won't be surprised.

The first half of the first line is a recounting of Dogen's famous dictum that Zen is the dropping off of both body and mind; the second half of this line perhaps alludes to his saying in his essay, *Genjo koan*, that "to study Buddhism is to study the self. To study the self is to forget the self." The second half of the third line is no doubt based on the Chinese understanding that Zen is "eating when hungry, sleeping when sleepy." Finally, Hotei's dreams are of the palace in the Tsushita Heaven, so he'll have time to nap before he's called.

Again, Musashi seems to have been attracted to birds, and especially the kingfisher, whose concentrated gaze here is immediately familiar. He watches the golden scales of the fish in the pond with the same No-Mind with which the swordsman would have watched his opponents, and will drop just as quickly on his prey.

18. An enigmatic painting to say the least, as the eccentric Hotei is sometimes depicted as napping or even possibly sleeping one off. As the incarnation of the Bodhisattva Maitreya, the Buddha of the Future, however, there is another dimension to his yawn. Buddhist lore has it that this bodhisattva currently lives in the Tsushita Heaven, and will come into the world for its salvation 5,670,000,000 years after the Buddha Shakyamuni's passing (about 2,500 years ago). Thus, he has a long time to wait and may be permitted a yawn from time to time.

19. Although Hotei was the subject of many unorthodox paintings in both China and Japan, Musashi's painting of him riding an ox seems to be unique. Musashi seems to have been thinking of the *Ten Oxherding Pictures*, a series of twelfth-century paintings by the Chinese Buddhist master, Kuo-an Shih-yuan, allegorically depicting the monk's progress in the realization of his true nature. The sixth painting depicts the oxherd astride the bull, and is accompanied by the comment (translated by Paul Reps),

    Astride the bull, I observe the clouds above.
    Onward I go, no matter who may wish to call me back.

    This is an appropriate quote for the once-wandering Musashi, who was now paying so much of his attention to meditation. Tellingly, the tenth of Kuo-an's twelve paintings does not include an ox at all, but instead shows the oxherd talking with—Hotei! The verse (also translated by Paul Reps) reads:

    Barefoot and naked of breast, I mingle with the people of the world. My clothes are ragged and dust-laden, and I am ever blissful. I use no magic to extend my life; Now, before me, the dead trees come alive.

This could also be Musashi toward the end of his life, perhaps without the "ragged and dust-laden clothes," but walking and mingling with the people of Kumamoto, free from his former cares.

20. This statue has taken on a smoky gray color over the centuries, and manifests an explosive energy rising to just below its surface. It seems to be the very substance of determination. One theory has it that Musashi carved this piece during his self-imposed isolation after Tadatoshi's death, either as an offering to Fudo in thanks for his own immovable mind or as a meditation to gain such.

21. For clarity's sake, a portion of the previous quote by Takuan has been repeated here.

CHAPTER
FOUR

The Way of Life and Death: Reigan Cave

1. One theory has it that Musashi was too sick to finish the final chapter of *The Book of Five Rings*, and that it was left to his disciples to arrange it as well as they could. Both the chronology of Musashi's last days and the chapter itself would seem to argue against this. If the language is sparse and difficult to follow compared to the rest of the text, consider the subject itself. Zen Buddhism (and Buddhism in general) has always contended that the Void is beyond any ability of language to describe, and yet Buddhists have been writing about it for millennia. The reader must understand that his words are a guide to be meditated upon, that they are directed toward the intuition rather than the intellect. This, again, is the failure of language, not of the writer or his disciples.

2. *Enso*: A circle, or symbol of the Absolute reality.

3. Shingon meditation was not unknown to the swordsmen of Musashi's time. Recall that both Yoshioka Seijuro and members of the Yagyu clan had disciplined themselves in these practices.

4. The principles covered in *The Book of Five Rings* have also been viewed as a glimpse into the more than sixty bouts Musashi fought in the first thirty years of his life. Though he chose not to write about them in historical detail, he did write about them in terms of what he had learned. In this sense, *The Book of Five Rings* can be read as something more than a book of strategy.

5. Musashi's motives for writing *The Book of Five Rings* have been questioned by almost everyone who has written about him, and there are more than a few theories. It would seem that his most immediate motive was his sense of the fatal disease that would soon take his life, and thus the knowledge that he had little time left in the world to leave a written legacy. The question that writers have often asked, however, is to whom this legacy was addressed.

The cynical but not uncommon explanation is that, despite his disease, Musashi still hoped to the very end to be awarded some sort of official position in keeping with his talents and accomplishments, thus validating his life in the manner that was most accepted in the society of his time. This theory is part and parcel of the idea that what Musashi had wanted all his life was just such a position, and that his greatest effort toward this desire and the most disheartening rebuff for him was his fight with Sasaki Kojiro on Ganryu Island, the motive of which was actually to get Sasaki's job as sword master to the Hosokawa.

If there was ever a warrior to carry himself in a manner that would least likely bring him such a position, however, it was Musashi. The samurai employed in official positions by the great *daimyo* were always expected to be properly dressed and groomed as both a discipline and as representatives of their fiefs. Their clothes were clean and neat, and the hair on their foreheads was cut back in the familiar style seen in period pieces in Japanese cinema. A hundred years after Musashi, Yamamoto Tsunetomo, writer of *Hagakure*, informs us that it was even a practice of the samurai to apply a little rouge to their cheeks in order to give the appearance that they were healthy and looking properly ready to die for their lords.

Musashi, on the other hand, was widely reported never to have bathed, never to have washed his hair, and, in general, never to have carried himself as any bureaucratically-positioned official would have in his lord's attendance or anywhere else. If he had felt rebuffed after his defeat of Sasaki Kojiro and had wanted to change his position badly enough, he had over twenty years to make a personal adjustment—which he quite clearly did not.

Nor did Musashi's life as an artist and sculptor appear to be in harmony with a settled position. His mind would have demanded a wider margin to his life, not the cramped and conformist life in a hierarchy. He seems, above all, to have been a free spirit, and one who knew the consequences of his actions from early on.

Finally, although *The Book of Five Rings* includes instructions for those who would command great armies, it fundamentally deals with the problems of the martial arts as a discipline of the mind during combat. This means that it is intended for those in armed conflict, regardless of circumstances, and not necessarily for those who are in service to one lord or another. The emphasis of this book is on the warrior, or *bushi* (武士), literally the man stopping the enemy with a spear, not the samurai (侍), whose very nomenclature is derived from the word "to serve." Thus, the theory that *The Book of Five Rings* was written not to keep his students from making mistakes in combat but in desperation for an official position appears to disregard the man's life, work, and the book itself.

6. A *ri* is a traditional measure of distance equaling 2.44 miles.

7. Musashi's declaration of not having used the "old words and phrases of the Confucianists or Buddhists," both here and in *The Book of Five Rings*, may have been a gentle stab at Yagyu Munenori, whose book on the martial arts, *The Life-Giving Sword*, was peppered with quotes from Zen Buddhist books and sages.

8. Two different theories exist concerning the name of the cave. One is that it was named for the spirit of Ganryu Sasaki Kojiro, hence 霊巌洞 (literally, "Spirit Gan Cave"). The other theory is that the cave already had this name long before Musashi's time. At any rate, the site had been used as a place for mental training since the Heian period (794–1185).

9. "The Way of Walking Alone" has been criticized by various writers as being no more than shallow articles of common sense scribbled down by a dying man. Musashi, as has been noted, has not been without his detractors, both while he was alive and after his death; and he might have answered this criticism with the following short story from the Chinese Zen work, the *Tao rin yulu*:

> Po Chu-i [a great Tang-period poet who would have been about eighty years old at this time] asked the Buddhist Master Tao-lin, "What is the great meaning of the Buddhist teachings?" The Master said, "Do no evil, but do what is good." Po replied, "Even a three-year-old child understands that!" The Master then said, "Although a three-year-old child is able to say this, even an eighty-year-old man is unable to do it." Po bowed and departed.

"The Way of Walking Alone" was not written to be a list of common sense suggestions on living well, but was rather the final notes on Musashi's intense life, and not to be taken lightly. Its emphasis on repressing one's own desires, not being jealous of others, not taking a liking to "things" like utensils, antiques, and unnecessary property showed that Musashi, not unlike Zen priests, considered such to be distractions and illusions. Furthermore, the conscious inclusion of these items may indicate that he himself was not immune to these distractions, and this would seem to make him all the more human. Certainly by 1645, with the world at peace and the economy prospering, material goods and their concomitant emotions of greed and jealousy were becoming the obstacle then that they are today to a life dedicated to anything other than contented consumption. This was not Musashi's Way.

Finally, it may be mentioned that a large bronze plaque containing "The Way of Walking Alone" stands a few yards to the left of Musashi's grave at the Eastern Burial Mound.

10. There are two official burial sites for Musashi in Kumamoto today: the Eastern Burial Mound, which is situated in the suburbs and is considered to contain his remains; and the Western Burial Mound, which is closer to the center of the city and may simply be a marker to the great man. But there are uncertainties with the Eastern Burial Mound as well: some say that Musashi's body was eventually dug up and cremated, and that his ashes were then re-interred at the site; others say that his ashes were spread elsewhere. Still others declare that his body was not buried there at all, but was taken by his disciples to a secret grave still unknown to anyone.

APPENDIX
1

Life After Death

1. Compare his comment to Musashi's expressed antipathy in *The Book of Five Rings* toward schools of swordsmanship that made exaggerated claims.

2. It is interesting to note that Musashi has been incorrectly identified as a retainer to Kato Kiyomasa even into modern times, no doubt through the influence of *kodan*. Kiyomasa was lord of Kumamoto until his death in 1611, but there are no reliable records tying Musashi to Kumamoto at this time.

3. The reference here is to Rokkaku Yoshikata (1521–98), a member of the Sasaki Clan in Omi. He was indeed an important man in Omi and had his

own school of the martial arts, the Sasaki-ryu. In 1559, he shaved his head and took the name Jotei. Toward the end of his life, he seems to have wandered from province to province. There is no mention in historical dictionaries of his having been Sasaki Kojiro's father.

4. Recall, however, that being thrown in jail and escaping by one's own wits was considered to be one of the disciplinary practices of a *shugyosha*.

5. Again, there is no historical record of Musashi's ever having met Ittosai.

6. Tsukahara Bokuden was the progenitor of the Shinto-ryu, receiving his instructions from a god in a dream after ensconcing himself in the Kashima Shrine for a thousand days. He was an instructor to the thirteenth and fourteenth Ashikaga shoguns, and also taught the prestigious Kitabatake and Takeda clans. Tradition has it that he traveled around the country with an entourage of over eighty men, fought at least nineteen duels with naked blades, participated in thirty-seven battles, and killed over 212 opponents, never once being defeated.

7. Perhaps this coup de grâce allowed him to do in fiction what a number of commentators thought he should have done in reality.

8. The lessons that the characters Myoshu and Yoshino Tayu are giving here are in fact taken directly from *The Book of Five Rings*.

9. "Not One Thing." Recall Musashi's poem written while residing in Nagoya.

10. Alternative translations for "lustful old man" include "dissolute person," "rake," and "satyr." The movie has since been lost, so we are in the dark as to whom or what Musashi subjugated here.

11. The small monument dedicated to Kojiro close by the Kokura Hibun is inscribed with a poem written by Murakami Genzo.

12. The NHK Taiga Drama on the Yoshikawa Musashi ran throughout 2003. It drew an enormous viewing audience all year and resulted in an explosion of sales of Musashi-related books and of tourism to Musashi-related sites.

GLOSSARY

adauchi (仇討): A vendetta, usually between two clans or families. A popular subject of Edo Period (1603–1868) drama.

Akamatsu clan: Ancient warrior clan in the Harima area that came to an end in 1441. Musashi's progenitors through his mother Yoshiko.

Akiyama: Swordsman from Tajima. Killed in a match with the sixteen-year-old Musashi.

Arima Kihei: Swordsman of the Shinto-ryu. Killed in a match with the thirteen-year-old Musashi.

Arima Shinto-ryu. See *Shinto-ryu*.

Ashikaga shogunate (1336–1573): Founded by the general Ashikaga Takauji (1305–58), and ruled Japan from the Muromachi district in Kyoto. Known both for high cultural achievements, such as the development of Noh, and for its devastating civil wars.

Battle of Sekigahara. See *Sekigahara*.

Bennosuke: Musashi's given name until his late teens.

Bessho clan: Junior line of the Akamatsu clan.

Book of Five Rings, The (*Gorin no sho*; 五輪書): The book on swordsmanship that Musashi wrote toward the end of his life. Much of the undercurrent of the book is based on Musashi's understanding of Zen Buddhism and the importance of the psychological approach in this art. Considered to be the most accomplished book on swordsmanship in Japanese history.

bunraku (文楽): The puppet theater developed during the Edo period (1603–1868). The puppets are about one-half to two-thirds life size, and are manipulated by handlers who wear gauzy black robes and hoods, and who, by agreement with the audience, are "not seen." Hand drums and a shamisen make up the music, while the puppets are given voice by chanters, who also recite the narrative.

chanbara (ちゃんばら): Cinema and television dramas usually depicting fictional events during the Edo period (1603–1868), including much action and sword-play. Perhaps equivalent to American Westerns.

chudan. See *jodan*.

Chujo-ryu (中条流): Swordsmanship style established during the Kamakura period (1185–1333) by Chujo Hyogonosuke. It is considered the ancestor of a number of different styles.

daimyo (大名): The lords of territories who were allotted an annual income of ten thousand *koku* of rice or more, they were for the most part military rulers from the warrior class. The size of their estates varied widely: for example, Yagyu Munenori held title to an estate which raised a revenue of 10,000 *koku*, while the Hosokawa territory raised 540,000.

Daruma (Sanskrit, Bodhidharma): Said to be born as prince in either south India or Persia, he became the twenty-eighth patriarch of Buddhism and is considered to be the first patriarch of Zen. He brought Zen to China about 520 C.E. A favorite subject of Zen painters.

Dening, Walter: Wrote the first "novel" about Musashi, published in 1887. Entitled *Japan in Days of Yore: The Life of Miyamoto Musashi*, it was based on the tales of the professional Japanese storytellers. See Appendix 1.

dojo (道場): Literally, "place of the Way." Once a place for meditation in Buddhist temples, or a separate hall for the same purpose in temple compounds, then a training hall for the martial arts. A Zen and tea saying has it that "The straight-forward mind, this is the *dojo*." *Jikishin kore dojo*.

Dorinbo: Musashi's maternal uncle, a priest residing at the Shoren-in temple near Hirafuku. Tutored and looked after Musashi in his early years.

Edo: Before the arrival of Tokugawa Ieyasu, a small fishing village far to the north-east of Kyoto. With Ieyasu, it became the capital of the Tokugawa shogunate. It is now called Tokyo, the current capital of Japan.

Edo period: (*Edo jidai*; 江戸時代).The period of the Tokugawa shogunate, from 1603 to 1868.

engei-jo (演芸場): Theaters, usually smaller venues than those for kabuki or *bunraku*, used for public entertainment. Usually set up for dancers, musicians, comic raconteurs, or professional storytellers.

Enmei-ryu (円明流): Perfect Enlightenment Style. A swordsmanship style Musashi developed around 1604 while he was in Edo, it was probably a precursor to the Niten Ichi-ryu.

enso (円相): The circle. In Zen Buddhism, the symbol indicating the perfect fundamental enlightenment that every person has, whether he is aware of it or not. Often found on the memorial markers of priests or enlightened persons who have passed away.

Fudo Myo-o: The "Immovable Brightness King." Manifestation of the Vairocana Buddha, much associated with Musashi and swordsmanship in general. His fierce expression is meant to scare off the enemies of Buddhism: greed, hate, and ignorance.

Fugai Ekun: Eccentric Zen painter, contemporary of Musashi.

gaki daisho: "Commander-in-chief of ruffians and troublemakers." Phrase used to describe Musashi as a child.

Gan-ryu (巌流): The swordsmanship style developed by Sasaki Kojiro, Musashi's greatest rival. He is said to have been a student and sparring partner of Toda Seigen of the Chujo-ryu, but may have in fact studied under Seigen's disciple, Kanemaki Jisai.

Ganryu Sasaki Kojiro. See *Sasaki Kojiro*.

Ganryujima (巌流島): Ganryu Island. *Jima* (*shima*) means "island." The island where Musashi fought his famous duel with Sasaki Kojiro. Also known as Funa Island (Funashima) and Mukai Island (Mukaijima).

gedan. See *jodan*.

Gion Toji: Legendary swordsman said to have been an influence on the Yoshioka school.

go (碁): A board game originally from China, played on a grid of 19 by 19 lines with black and white stones. The object of the game is to capture as much territory on the grid as possible, surrounding the opponent's stones without having one's own stones surrounded. Games can go on for extraordinary lengths of time. Favored by Chinese and Japanese military men since ancient times.

hachimaki (鉢巻): A small towel or strip of cloth folded neatly and tied around the forehead. Originally used to stop perspiration from getting into one's eyes, it now connotes determination. Used by laborers, soldiers in battle, students during exam periods, men carrying heavy sacred objects during festivals, and sometimes even pregnant women during labor.

hakama (袴): Traditional wide, almost skirtlike, pants worn by both men and women during different periods in Japanese history. Today worn almost exclusively by men for official, often religiously linked ceremonies. Often worn during official bouts or matches for some of the martial arts.

haori (羽織): A traditional jacket made of heavy material (plaited cotton or hemp). It has wide sleeves into which small personal items may be placed, and is worn over other clothing.

harakiri (腹切): Ritual suicide by plunging a sword into one's belly. Also called *seppuku* (切腹). The form of this ritual changed over the centuries. *See* also *junshi*.

Heart Sutra, The (*Hannya Shingyo*; 般若心経): Shortest of Mahayana Buddhism's Wisdom Sutras. Said to distill transcendental wisdom of emptiness down to a few hundred Chinese characters, it is chanted every day by millions of Buddhists, both priests and laymen.

Hirata Munisai (Muni): Musashi's father. An expert at the *jitte* and other weapons. Served the Shinmen clan and took its name, as did Musashi.

Hon'ami Koetsu: 1558–1637. A sword polisher, potter, calligrapher, and garden designer. Was at the center of the Kyoto Renaissance.

Honda clan: Warrior clan established at Himeji during Musashi's time. The family is said to have employed Musashi to design the castle town there and seems to have held him in great esteem.

Honshu (本州): The largest of the four main islands of Japan. The mainland of the country.

Hosokawa Tadatoshi: 1586–1641. Lord of the Hosokawa domain in Kumamoto,

Kyushu. Son of Hosokawa Tadaoki (Sansai). A keen swordsman and disciple of Musashi.

Hozoin (宝蔵院): The Buddhist temple in Nara where the monk In'ei developed a style of combat with the spear. It was here that Musashi defeated the spearman-priest Ozoin with only a short wooden sword.

iai-do (居合道): A martial art based on techniques for drawing the sword, cutting down visualized opponents, and then calmly returning the sword to its scabbard.

Inagaki Hiroshi: Japanese filmmaker who specialized in movies on Musashi. His three-part treatment of Musashi 1954–56 starring Mifune Toshiro was very well received in both Japan and the West. See Appendix 1.

Inshun: The priest who reestablished the Hozoin spear style after Kakuzenbo Hozoin In'ei's demise. Studied under the priest/practitioner Ozoin.

Itto-ryu (一刀流): A style of swordsmanship founded by Ito Ittosai (1560–1653), who first studied with Kanemaki Jisai of the Chujo-ryu, and then went out on his own. The style emphasizes training to deal with unexpected attacks, insisting, as author and *kendo* instructor Kiyota Minoru has phrased it, that the practitioner be able to act with "an instantaneous union of intuition and action." Ittosai passed his mantle on to Ono Tadaaki, who became an official instructor of swordsmanship to the shogun along with Yagyu Munenori.

jitte (十手): Also pronounced *jutte*. Refers to a small metal rod about 1 ½ feet long, with a sort of crooked thumb just above the handle. Used to disarm an opponent by catching the blade of his sword between the rod and the metal thumb of the instrument, and then wrenching the sword away. Often used by minor officials and policemen during the Edo period (1603–1868).

jodan, chudan, gedan (上段, 中段, 下段): Stances taken with the sword aimed at the opponent's head, chest, and feet or legs, respectively.

joruri. See *bunraku.*

jujitsu (柔術): Also *jujutsu.* A martial art of grappling or combat using only the hands and feet. Anciently called *yawara*, it was transformed into the modern martial art and sport of judo by Kano Jigoro early in the twentieth century.

junshi (殉死): Ritual suicide committed on the death of one's lord, in order to accompany him into the next world. Although a traditional and honorable custom, it was outlawed by many *daimyo* during the first years of the Edo period (1603–1868), and by the central government in 1683. See also *harakiri*.

jutte. See *jitte*.

kabuki (歌舞伎): A form of drama created by a dancer named Okuni in 1603. Originally a somewhat "lowbrow" form of entertainment, it became extremely popular and developed into one of the great Japanese dramatic genres. It is full of action and bombast, compared to the restrained and elegant Noh.

Kage-ryu (陰流): A style of swordsmanship. Considered by many to have been founded by Aisu Ikosai, who based his techniques on natural elements (waves, the wind, and mountains) and the movements of animals. Author and *kendo* instructor Kiyota Minoru states that although these factors may display an emphasis on "rhythmic and synchronized motion," they may also indicate that Ikosai was developing a "swordsmanship of totemism with the intent to incorporate the power of natural phenomena" into his art. Ikosai was from Iga, and his style is considered to be the ancestor of the Western schools of swordsmanship.

Kaiho Yusho: An older contemporary of Musashi. At first a well-known spear practitioner, and then a famous painter. His painting of Hotei and the fighting cocks is said to have influenced Musashi, but this is unsubstantiated.

Kakuzenbo Hozoin In'ei: Buddhist priest and innovator of a spear style made famous at his temple, the Hozoin.

Kamiizumi Ise no kami Hidetsuna (or Nobutsuna): 1508–77. Master swordsman of the sixteenth century. Easily defeated Yagyu Sekishusai, and then became his instructor.

kana (仮名): The syllabary of Japanese orthography. Divided into two styles: the more fluid *hiragana* and the more angular *katakana*.

Kansai (関西): Generally considered to be the region around Kyoto, Osaka, Kobe, and, in broader terms, also includes areas farther to the west. Contrasted with Kanto, the area around Tokyo (Edo, during Musashi's time).

Kanto. See *Kansai*.

Kashima Shinto-ryu. See *Shinto-ryu*.

katana (刀): The Japanese sword. A curved blade with a single edge, and generally held with two hands. It changed in length and the way it was worn as styles and circumstances in combat changed over the centuries. Known as the "samurai sword" in the West. See also *tachi* and *wakizashi*.

Kataoka Chiezo:1903–83. An actor and producer who starred in many early films on Musashi.

Kato Kiyomasa (1562–1611): One of the fiercest of the general/*daimyo* allied to the Toyotomi clan. After the death of Toyotomi Hideyoshi, he sided with Tokugawa Ieyasu, and fought with the Eastern army at Sekigahara. He was appointed *daimyo* of Kumamoto, and rebuilt the castle there to a massive size.

Katori Shinto-ryu. See *Shinto-ryu*.

Kiichi Hogen: Legendary twelfth-century swordsman. The Yoshioka swordsmen are said to have studied in his line.

kodan (講談): Professional storytelling, usually performed at smaller venues. Popular from early on, but especially so from the Edo period (1603–1868) to just after World War II.

Koetsu. See *Hon'ami Koetsu*.

koku (石): 5.119 U.S. bushels. This was the unit of measure for rice, and was the standard both for the grants given to the various *daimyo* and lords and for the samurai who served them.

Kokura Hibun: A stone monument dedicated to Musashi outside the city of Kokura on Mount Tamuke, erected by his adopted son Iori in 1654. It is about twenty feet tall, and is inscribed with the story of Musashi's life written in a style of classical Chinese.

Kumoi: A courtesan in Edo with whom Musashi is said to have had an extended intimate relationship while he was in his mid-fifties.

Kuroda clan: Warrior clan in Fukuoka, northern Kyushu. Was first allied with the Toyotomi but changed its allegiance to the Tokugawa and fought for them at the Battle of Sekigahara.

kusarigama (鎖鎌): A weapon consisting of a chain attached to the handle of a sickle. The chain is swung to ensnare and neutralize either the sword of the opponent or the opponent himself, while the sickle is used to finish him off.

Kyoto (京都): The political and cultural capital of Japan between the eighth and twelfth centuries. It remained the cultural capital even after the center of political power moved elsewhere.

Kyushu (九州): Third largest of the four main islands of Japan, to the southwest of Honshu. Separated from the latter island by the Kanmon Straits.

Life-Giving Sword, The (*Heiho kadensho*; 兵法家伝書; title translates literally as, The Book of Clan Traditions on the Martial Arts): Book on the Yagyu Shinkage-ryu school of swordsmanship written by Yagyu Munenori in about 1632. It includes both technical advice and related psychology and philosophy based on Zen Buddhism.

Matsudaira Izumo no kami Naomasa: *Daimyo* of Matsue Castle in Izumo (Shimane). Had an instructional bout with Musashi in 1638.

Mifune Toshiro: Actor famous for (among many other roles) his portrayal of Musashi under the directorship of Inagaki Hiroshi. See Appendix 1.

Mirror of the Way of War, The (*Heidokyo* or *Heido no kagami*; 兵道鏡): Short book said to be written by Musashi in 1604 when he was in Edo. It may have been an outline for the style he was developing at that time, the Enmei-ryu, or Perfect Enlightenment Style. The first edition of the book contained eighteen articles, which were later expanded to thirty-five.

Miyake Gunbei: Skillful swordsman of the Togun-ryu and a retainer of Honda Tadamasa. Defeated by Musashi in Himeji in 1621, he later became a disciple of the Niten Ichi-ryu.

Miyamoto Iori: Musashi's second adopted son. Met Musashi in 1624 and was later employed by Ogasawara Tadazane. Eventually rose to the position of chief retainer to the Ogasawara. Died in 1678.

Miyamoto Mikinosuke: Musashi's first adopted son. Said to have been a pack horse driver when first encountered by Musashi in 1619. Employed as a page by Honda Tadatoki, he committed ritual suicide upon his master's death in 1626.

Murakami Genzo: Writer famous for his portrayal of the rivalry between Musashi and Sasaki Kojiro in the serial novel *Sasaki Kojiro* (1949–50). A film of the same title was produced in 1950, starring Mifune Toshiro as Musashi. See Appendix 1.

Muso Gonnosuke: Master of staff technique, defeated by Musashi in Edo in 1608.

Muto-ryu (無刀流): The No-Sword style. Style created by Kamiizumi Ise no kami Nobutsuna and perfected by Yagyu Sekishusai and his son Yagyu Munenori. With his own bare hands joined in a prayerlike lock, the practitioner arrests his opponent's stroke just before its execution, by grasping either the hilt or blade of his opponent's sword.

Nagaoka Sado no kami Okinaga: Retainer to the Hosokawa clan, and student of Musashi's father Munisai. Helped Musashi obtain permission for a match with Sasaki Kojiro.

Nagaoka Yoriyuki: Adopted son of Nagaoka Sado Okinaga. One of Musashi's close disciples. Helped care for Musashi during the swordsman's final illness.

Nakamura (Yorozuya) Kinnosuke: Actor originally from a Kabuki family, famous for his portrayal of Musashi in a five-part film directed by Uchida Tomu.

Nen-ryu (念流): Style of swordsmanship founded by the priest Nen'ami Jion in 1368. Currently emphasizes breathing, shouting (*kiai*) and footwork techniques. Jion began his practice as a young boy, and at the age of ten was instructed at Mount Kurama by a mysterious character who subsequently disappeared. He later studied the Chujo-ryu and wandered the country, finally becoming a Zen priest.

Niten Ichi-ryu (二天一流): The Two-Sword Style. The combat style of using two swords, developed by Miyamoto Musashi. Musashi's practice of swordsmanship is clearly described in *The Book of Five Rings*. See also Enmei-ryu.

Nitenki: A compilation of stories about Musashi and his disciples published in 1755 through the research of Toyoda Matashiro and his son and grandson.

No-Sword style or technique. See *Muto-ryu*.

Noh (能): a stately and restrained drama developed in the fourteenth and fifteenth centuries. The chanting, dancing, and playing of musical instruments in the genre were highly respected, especially by the warrior class. Men from *daimyo* to swordsmen like Musashi studied one form or another of this art.

Obuchi Genko: Older Buddhist priest at the Taishoji temple in Kumamoto. Likely instructed Musashi in Buddhist philosophy.

Ogasawara Tadazane: Lord of Akashi who then moved to Kokura in Kyushu. Employed Musashi's adopted son Iori, and later gave Musashi the status of guest, from 1634 through 1640.

Ogin: Musashi's older sister.

Okuni: Said to be the creator of kabuki theater. Performed on the banks of the Kamo River in Kyoto in about 1603.

Omasa: Hirata Munisai's first wife. Said by some to be Musashi's real mother.

Osedo Hayashi: Yagyu stylist defeated by Musashi in Edo in 1610.

Ozoin: The priest/spearman of the Hozoin style defeated by Musashi in Nara at the Hozoin temple in 1604.

Praiseworthy Tales of Authentically Recorded Heroes, Past and Present (*Kokonjitsuroku eiyubidan*; 古今実録英雄美談): Apparently a compilation of professional story-tellers' tales, used as the basis of Walter Dening's novel on Musashi published in 1887 (see Appendix 1). Very likely typical of the stories told about Musashi from the time of his death on into the early twentieth century.

Reigan Cave (霊巌洞): The cave on Mount Gandono outside the city of Kumamoto where Musashi practiced sitting meditation, began *The Book of Five Rings*, and where he hoped to die. The Chinese characters for the name of the cave, can be taken to mean "the cave of Gan's [Sasaki Kojiro's] spirit," but the name may pre-date Kojiro's demise.

ronin (浪人): Warriors and samurai who no longer served a *daimyo* or lord. A man may have found himself in this state for a number of reasons; anything from his lord being defeated in battle or dispossessed of his fief to simple dismissal by a lord whom a samurai had displeased. See also *shugyosha*.

ryu (流): A style of the martial arts. Thus, the Toda-ryu is the Toda style; the Shinkage-ryu becomes the Shinkage style and so on.

Sasaki Kojiro: "The Demon of the Western Provinces." Master swordsman of the Ganryu style defeated and killed by Musashi on Ganryu Island in 1612. Perhaps Musashi's most famous adversary.

satori (悟): Buddhist term for enlightenment.

Sekigahara (関ケ原): The field in Mino Province (now Gifu Prefecture) where, on 20 October 1600, the decisive battle was fought between the Toyotomi forces (the Western army) and the Tokugawa forces (the Eastern army). Although the number of troops on each side were initially almost equal, the advantage tipped to the Eastern forces when some generals of the Western army defected to the Tokugawa. This marked the beginning of a new era in Japan, the Tokugawa or Edo period (1603–1868). The Tokugawa shogunate, formally established in 1603, ruled for nearly 260 years.

Seppuku. See *harakiri*.

Shikoku (四国): The smallest of the four main islands of Japan. Situated opposite Honshu and, with it, contains the Inland Sea.

Shindo Muso-ryu (神道無想流 or 真道夢想流): A style of fighting created by Muso Gonnosuke, a contemporary of Musashi, that uses the staff against a sword. It was revealed to Gonnosuke in a dream after he had prayed and meditated.

Shinkage-ryu (新陰流): The "New Kage-ryu" of swordsmanship founded by Kami-izumi Ise no kami Nobutsuna. Improved under Yagyu Sekishusai and his son Munenori, whence it became known as the Yagyu Shinkage-ryu. Nobutsuna had his students practice with *fukuro shinai*—swords made of thin bamboo cuttings, split in several places, tied together, and covered with a leather sheath. This allowed his practitioners to have "real matches" without the danger of injury.

Shinmen (新免) clan: The clan in Mimasaka to which Musashi was related through his father's first marriage. Musashi's father, originally named Hirata Munisai, was actually given permission by that clan to take its name because of his long service to the family as a warrior and martial arts instructor.

Shinto-ryu (新当流): An Eastern style of swordsmanship founded by the legendary Tsukahara Bokuden (1489–1571). Various substyles are the Katori Shinto-ryu (香取新当流), the Kashima Shinto-ryu (鹿島新当流) and the Arima Shinto-ryu (有馬新当流). The Shinto-ryu is known for its *ichi no tachi*, or "One Cut," and emphasizes single-mindedness and striking at points on the body not protected by armor or thick bones. In this style—which is based on battlefield conditions—each opponent should be felled by a single strike.

Shioda Hamanosuke: Accomplished practitioner of the staff and of take-down techniques and a retainer of the Hosokawa clan. Defeated by Musashi in 1640. He became Musashi's disciple and Musashi incorporated Hamanosuke's techniques into his own style.

Shishido: Master of the sickle and chain. Defeated and killed by Musashi in Iga Province in 1607.

shugyosha (修業者 or 修行者): A swordsman in training who traveled the country, making his own way without money or steady employment. Exposed to heat and cold, he suffered various hardships as he disciplined himself in his art. Not a few died or were maimed in matches with other *shugyosha*, as they tested their own strength and technique. See also *ronin*.

Shunzan: Young Zen Buddhist priest in Kumamoto with whom Musashi sat in Zen meditation.

shuriken (手裏剣): Weapons thrown by hand. They had varying shapes: some were shaped like knives with blades on both ends, others like stars with four or five points.

suibokuga (水墨画): Monochromatic paintings, executed with various shades of India ink wash on silk or Japanese paper.

Sun Tzu: The fifth- or sixth-century B.C.E. Chinese author of the book by the same name, often given the English title *The Art of War*. This book is the first and most respected Chinese work on strategical and tactical doctrines of war, and was read by generals and warriors in both China and Japan. It emphasizes the idea that victory in combat is based on deception and flexibility.

tachi (太刀): A Japanese sword worn hung from a belt with the sharp edge facing up. The length varied, but it was generally longer than the *katana*, and with a more dramatic curve.

tairo (大老): The five highest ranking ministers, usually *daimyo* of great status. As he lay dying, Toyotomi Hideyoshi selected the *tairo* to act as regents until his young son was old enough to rule. One of these was Tokugawa Ieyasu, who betrayed this trust very quickly after Hideyoshi passed away. This eventually led to the Battle of Sekigahara and the establishment of the Tokugawa shogunate.

Taisha-ryu (タイ捨流): A style of swordsmanship founded by Marume Kurandono-suke in the latter part of the sixteenth century. There are a number of ways of writing Taisha, but the *sha* is generally written with the Chinese character for "throw away" or "abandon," and this is taken to mean the throwing away of fear or doubt. Part of this school's training consisted of cutting down, with abandon, one straw-wrapped pole after another, thus ridding the practitioner of hesitation. This style was popular in Kyushu during Musashi's time.

Takada Mataemon: Skilled practitioner of the Hozoin style of spear technique. Defeated by Musashi in a match arranged by Ogasawara Tadazane in Kokura in 1634.

Takuan Soho: 1573–1645. Zen priest famous for his calligraphy, poetry, and other writings, and for the invention of the *takuan* pickle. Wrote *The Unfettered Mind*, a treatise on the relationship between swordsmanship and Zen.

Terao Kumanosuke Nobuyuki: Terao Katsunobu's younger brother and one of Musashi's favorite disciples. He received *The Thirty-five Articles on the Martial Arts* upon Musashi's death.

Terao Magonojo Katsunobu: Musashi's favorite disciple and the recipient of *The Book of Five Rings* upon Musashi's death.

Thirty-five Articles of the Martial Arts, The (*Heiho Sanjugokajo*; 兵法三十五カ条): The summation of the Niten Ichi-ryu that Musashi wrote for Hosokawa Tadatoshi. Now considered to be the prototype for *The Book of Five Rings*.

Toda Seigen: Master swordsman of the sixteenth century who specialized in the short sword. Said to have been the teacher of Sasaki Kojiro.

Toda-ryu (戸田流, 富田流). A style of swordsmanship founded by Toda Seigen and his younger brother, Kagemasa. Seigen disciplined himself in using shorter and shorter swords, and was said to have employed Sasaki Kojiro—who used a long sword—as his sparring partner. Seigen based this style on the Chujo-ryu, and emphasized timing and the distance ("interval") between opponents. He hoped to develop a No-Sword style, but was afflicted by failing eyesight in his later years.

Tokugawa Ieyasu: 1542–1616. Final unifier of Japan. Took control of the country after the death of Toyotomi Hideyoshi, and established the Tokugawa shogunate.

Tokugawa shogunate (1603–1868): Founded by the *daimyo* Tokugawa Ieyasu (1542–1616), and ruled Japan from Edo (Tokyo). The last and longest of the shogunates, remarkable for its relatively lasting governmental stability.

Tomita-ryu. See *Toda-ryu*.

Tori-ryu (当理流): The swordsmanship style developed by Musashi's father, Shinmen Munisai. It teaches the use of the sword, armor, and the *jitte*.

Toyotomi Hideyoshi: 1542–98. One of the unifiers of Japan in the sixteenth century. Rose from peasant status to the very high rank of *taiko*, and as such was the supreme ruler of the country.

tsubame-gaeshi (燕返し): Technique used by Sasaki Kojiro, and possibly developed by Toda Seigen. Its method is not clear, but it seems that the practitioner would bring his sword down from a *jodan* position and, before the stroke reached its nadir, swing the weapon back up, cutting the opponent from beneath. Said to be named after a similar motion in the flight of the swallow.

Tsujikaze Tenma: Strong swordsman defeated by Musashi in Edo in 1610. As he attacked Musashi, he fell from the veranda, hit his back, and died.

Tsukahara Bokuden: 1489–1571. Master swordsman of the sixteenth century.

tsumeru (詰める): The ability to pull one's strike with the sword, just before or just at contact.

Two-Sword Style: See *Niten Ichi-ryu*.

Ujii Yashiro: Hosokawa Tadatoshi's instructor of the Yagyu style of swordsmanship. Had a secret demonstration bout with Musashi for Tadatoshi in 1640. The results were to be kept secret, but, afterward, Tadatoshi abandoned the Yagyu style and began to study Niten Ichi-ryu.

Ukita Hideie: 1573–1655. *Daimyo* in Bizen. Defeated with the Toyotomi troops at Sekigahara. Musashi is thought to have fought under his command at that battle.

Unfettered Mind, The (*Fudochishinmyoroku*; 不動智神妙録): Book relating Zen to the art of swordsmanship, written by the priest Takuan around 1832 for Yagyu Munenori.

wakizashi (脇差): The shorter companion sword to the *katana* worn only by members of the warrior class.

"Way of Walking Alone, The" (*Dokko-do* or *Dokko no michi*; 独行道): A short manuscript expounding the heart of Musashi's philosophy. Written on 12 May 1645, just a week before Musashi passed away, it consists of twenty-one short maxims.

Wisdom Sutras. Said to distill transcendental wisdom of Emptiness down to a few hundred Chinese characters, it is chanted everyday by millions of Buddhists, both priests and laymen.

Yagyu Hyogonosuke Toshiyoshi: 1577–1650. Grandson of Yagyu Sekishusai. Established the Owari branch of the Yagyu Shinkage-ryu, instructing the Tokugawa line in swordsmanship at Nagoya Castle. Met Musashi in Owari in 1628.

Yagyu Munenori: 1571–1646. Son of Yagyu Sekishusai. Established the Edo school of the Yagyu Shinkage-ryu. Was the official sword instructor to three consecutive Tokugawa shoguns, and wrote the famous sword manual, *The Life-Giving Sword*.

Yagyu Muneyoshi Sekishusai: 1529–1606. Already a famous swordsman, he studied under the legendary Kamiizumi Ise no Kami Hidetsuna and established the Yagyu Shinkage-ryu.

Yorozuya Kinnosuke. See *Nakamura Kinnosuke*.

Yoshikawa Eiji: 1892–1962. Wrote the highly popular serial novel *Miyamoto Musashi* (serialized from 1935 through 1939 in the *Asahi* newspaper), interpreting Musashi as a "seeker of the Way." His novel has heavily influenced cinematic and television treatments of Musashi. The novel remains in print to this day.

Yoshiko: Hirata Munisai's second wife, and most likely Musashi's mother.

Yoshioka Denshichiro: Younger brother and successor to Yoshioka Seijuro. Was defeated and killed by Musashi in a match outside Kyoto temple in 1604.

Yoshioka Kenpo (Naomoto): A textile dyer in Kyoto who originated the Yoshioka style of swordsmanship. He became sword instructor to the twelfth Ashikaga shogun Yoshiharu, establishing a generational teacher-student relationship between the Yoshioka family and the Ashikaga clan.

Yoshioka Matashichiro: Nephew to Yoshioka Seijuro and titular head of the Yoshioka school after the death of Denshichiro. Killed in Musashi's "battle" with the Yoshioka disciples near the Spreading Pine at Ichijoji in 1604.

Yoshioka Seijuro: Master swordsman and head of the Yoshioka family and school during Musashi's time. He was defeated and maimed by Musashi in a match at the Rendai Moor in 1604, and afterward became a priest.

BIBLIOGRAPHY

Works in English

Awakawa, Yasuichi. *Zen Painting*. Tokyo: Kodansha International Ltd., 1970.

Ch'uang T'zu. *The Complete Works of Ch'uang T'zu*. Translated by Burton Watson. New York: Columbia University Press, 1968.

Compton, Dr. Walter A., et al. *Nippon-to: Art Swords of Japan*. Tokyo: Japan Society, Inc., 1976.

Dening, Walter. *Japan in Days of Yore: The Life of Miyamoto Musashi*. London: Griffith, Farran, & Co., 1887. Reprint, London: Fine Books Ltd., 1976.

Fischer, Felice. *The Arts of Hon'ami Koetsu, Japanese Renaissance Master*. Philadelphia: Philadelphia Museum of Art, 2000.

Friday, Karl F., with Humitake Seki. *Legacies of the Sword: The Kashima-Shinryu and Samurai Martial Culture*. Honolulu: University of Hawaii Press, 1997.

Hakeda, Yoshito. *Kukai: Major Works*. New York: Columbia University Press, 1972.

Kiyota, Minoru. *The Shambhala Guide to Kendo: Its Philosophy, History and Spiritual Dimension*. Boston: Shambhala, 2002.

Kapp, Leon, Hiroko Kapp, and Yoshihara Yoshindo. *The Craft of the Japanese Sword*. Tokyo: Kodansha International Ltd., 1987.

Leach, Bernard. *Kenzan and His Tradition*. New York: Transatlantic Arts, 1967.

Lowry, Dave. *Bokken: The Art of the Japanese Sword*. Santa Clarita, California: Ohara Publications, 1986.

Lubarsky, Jared. *Noble Heritage: Five Centuries of Portraits from the Hosokawa Family*. Washington, D.C.: Smithsonian Institution, 1992.

Miyamoto Musashi. *The Book of Five Rings*. Translated by William Scott Wilson. Boston: Shambhala Publications, 2012.

Nagayama, Kokan. *The Connoisseur's Book of Japanese Swords*. Tokyo: Kodansha International Ltd., 1997.

Nitobe, Inazo. *Bushido: The Soul of Japan*. Tokyo: Kodansha International Ltd., 2002.

Reps, Paul. *Zen Flesh, Zen Bones*. Rutland, Charles E. Tuttle, 1967.

Richie, Donald. *A Hundred Years of Japanese Film*. Tokyo: Kodansha International Ltd., 2002.

Sansom, George. *A History of Japan, 1615–1867*. Stanford: Stanford University Press, 1963.

Skoss, Diane, ed. *Koryu Bujutsu: Classical Warrior Traditions of Japan*. Berkeley Heights, New Jersey: Koryu Books, 1997.

Sonobe, Koichiro. *A Field Guide to the Birds of Japan*. Tokyo: Kodansha International Ltd., 1982.

Sugawara, Makoto. *Lives of the Master Swordsmen*. Tokyo: The East Publications, 1985.

Takuan Soho. *The Unfettered Mind: Writings from a Zen Master to a Master Swordsman*. Translated by William Scott Wilson. Boston: Shambhala Publications, 2012.

Tanaka, Fumon. *Samurai Fighting Arts: The Spirit and Practice*. Tokyo: Kodansha International Ltd., 2003.

Toganoo, Shozui Makoto. "The Symbol-System of Shingon Buddhism." In *Mikkyo Bunka*, Vol. 102, March 1973, 61–84.

Wilson, William Scott. *Ideals of the Samurai: Writings of Japanese Warriors*. Burbank, California: Ohara Publications, Inc., 1982.

Yagyu, Munenori. *The Life-Giving Sword: Secret Teachings from the House of the Shogun*. Translated by William Scott Wilson. Boston: Shambhala Publications, 2012.

Yamamoto, Tsunetomo. *Hagakure*. Translated by William Scott Wilson. Boston: Shambhala Publications, 2012.

Yamasaki, Taiko. *Shingon: Japanese Esoteric Buddhism*. Fresno, California: Shingon Buddhist International Institute, 1988.

Yoshikawa, Eiji. *Musashi*. Translated by Charles S. Terry. Tokyo: Kodansha International Ltd., 1981.

Yoshimura, Akira. *Battleship Musashi: The Making and Sinking of the World's Biggest Battleship*. Tokyo: Kodansha International Ltd., 1991.

Yumoto, John M. *The Samurai Sword: A Handbook*. Tokyo: Charles E. Tuttle, 1958.

Works in Japanese

Dogen. *Shobogenzo*. Vol. 1. Tokyo: Iwanami Shoten, 1990.

Domon, Fuyuji. *Miyamoto Musashi no Jinseikun*. Tokyo: PHP, 2000.

Futamaru, Nobuaki, ed. *Rekishi Gunzo shirizu*. Vol. 63, *Miyamoto Musashi*. Tokyo: Gakken, 2000.

Ichikawa, Kakuji. *Miyamoto Musashi: Niten Ichi-ryu no ken to Gorin no sho*. Tokyo: Tsuchiya Shoten, 1985.

Inoue, Takehiko. *Bagabondo*. 20 vols. Tokyo: Kodansha, 1999–2004.

Isami, Tomoyuki. *Yume-oi no ken*. Kumamoto: Mogura Shobo, 2002.

Kaku, Kozo. *Miyamoto Musashi jiten*. Tokyo: Tokyo-do Shuppan, 2001.

Kawaguchi, Hisao. *Wakanroeishu*. Tokyo: Kodansha, 1982.

Kawamura, Akira. *Miyamoto Musashi: Monogatari to shiseki o tazunete*. Tokyo: Seibido Shuppan, 1998.

Kubo, Michio. *Miyamoto Musashi to wa nanimono datta no ka*. Tokyo: Shinchosha, 1998.

Maruoka, Muneo, ed. *Miyamoto Musashi meihin shusei*. Tokyo: Kodansha, 1984.

Miyamoto Musashi. *Gorin no sho*. Annotated by Nakamura Naokatsu. Tokyo: Kodansha, 1970.

—*Gorin no sho*. Annotated by Watanabe Ichiro. Tokyo: Iwanami Shoten, 1985.

—*Gorin no sho*. Translated into modern Japanese by Kamata Shigeo. Tokyo: Kodansha, 1986.

Naramoto, Tatsuya. *Bushido no keifu*. Tokyo: Chuokoronsha, 1973.

Nishio, Minoru. *Hojoki tsurezuregusa*. Tokyo: Iwanami Shoten, 1975.

Okouchi, Shoji. *Gorin no sho*. Tokyo: Kyoikusha, 1992.

Ozaki, Nobuo. *Kojiki shinsaku*. Tokyo: Kato Chudokan, 1959.

Sagara, Toru, ed. *Koyogunkan, Gorin no sho, Hagakure*. Tokyo: Chikuma Shobo, 1972.

Terayama, Tanchu. *Miyamoto Musashi no ken to bi*. Tokyo: Seishun Shuppansha, 2002.

Tobe, Shinjuro. *Zusetsu: Miyamoto Musashi*. Tokyo: Kawade Shobo Shinsha. 2001.

Watatani, Kiyoshi and Yamada Tadashi, eds. *Bugei ryuha daijiten*. Tokyo: Tokyo Kopii Shuppanbu, 1978.

Yabushita, Hideki. *Miyamoto Musashi densetsu*. Tokyo: Hochosha, 2001.

Yagyu, Munenori. *Heiho kadensho*. Annotated by Watanabe Ichiro. Tokyo: Iwanami Shoten, 1985.

Yamamoto Tsunetomo. *Hagakure*. Edited by Kurihara Arano. Kumamoto: Seicho-sha,1975.

Yoshida, Yutaka, ed. *Budo hidensho*. Tokyo: Tokuma Shoten, 1938.

Yoshida, Yutaki. *Buke no kakun*. Tokyo: Tokuma Shoten, 1973.

Yoshikawa, Eiji. *Miyamoto Musashi*. 8 vols. Tokyo: Kodansha, 1940.

Works in English and Chinese

Blyth, R. H. *Zen and Zen Classics*. Vol. 1, *General Introduction: From the Upanishads to Huineng*. Tokyo: Hokuseido Press, 1960.
—*Zen and Zen Classics*. Vol. 4, *Mumonkan*. Tokyo: Hokuseido Press, 1966.

Giles, Lionel. *Sun Tzu on the Art of War*. London: Luzac & Co., 1910.

Red Pine. *The Zen Teaching of Bodhidharma*. San Francisco: North Point Press, 1989.

ALSO AVAILABLE FROM
SHAMBHALA PUBLICATIONS

The Book of Five Rings, by Miyamoto Musashi

Along with *The Art of War* by Sun Tzu, *The Book of Five Rings* is widely considered to be one of the greatest masterpieces on the subtle arts of confrontation and victory to have ever emerged from Asia. Composed in 1643 by the legendary swordsman Miyamoto Musashi, *The Book of Five Rings* analyzes the process of struggle that underlies every level of human interaction and reveals the way to mastery over conflict. For Musashi, the way of the martial arts was not purely one of technical prowess, but first and foremost a mastery of the mind—and it is this path to mastery that shines at the core of Musashi's teaching. William Scott Wilson's landmark translation includes Musashi's rarely published "The Way of Walking Alone," an insightful introduction to Musashi's historical context, and notes on ambiguities in the text.

Cultivating Ch'i: A Samurai Physician's Teachings on the Way of Health,
by Kaibara Ekiken

This acclaimed medical text from eighteenth-century Japan known as the *Yojokun* ("Lessons on Nurturing Life") offers holistic health advice for living and long and satisfying life. Drawing from Chinese medical classics and the great philosophical traditions of East Asia, Kaibara Ekiken explains the essential principles of *ch'i* (vital cosmic energy) and *jen* (human-heartedness), and gives counsel on a wide variety of topics on medicine and healthy living for all ages, such as: diet, physical fitness, sex, mental health, and emotional well-being.

Hagakure: The Book of the Samurai, by Yamamoto Tsunetomo

Originally a secret text, *Hagakure* reveals the author's view that bushido, the Way of the Samurai, is fundamentally the Way of death, a selfless approach to life that embraces death with courage and honor. Yet, the Way of death is also seen as a subtle concept resonant with the Zen idea of the death of the ego. William Scott Wilson's all-new introduction gives the historical and philosophical background for the deeper, metaphorical reading of this samurai classic.

The Life-Giving Sword: Secret Teachings from the House of the Shogun, by Yagyu Munenori

Yagyu Munenori, the renowned seventeenth-century swordsman, presents essential teachings on Zen and the way of the sword. In *The Life-Giving Sword*, Munenori explores the art of No-Sword—the way to overcome opponents not with techniques of violence and cunning, but by means of spiritual preparedness and mental freedom. Through the art of No-Sword, Munenori teaches the way to win by giving life, rather than taking it.

Master of the Three Ways: Reflections of a Chinese Sage on Living a Satisfying Life, by Hung Ying-ming

Both witty and profound, *Master of the Three Ways* presents the teachings of seventeenth-century Chinese sage Hung Ying-ming on the essence of human nature and the way to live a simple yet satisfying life. Drawing on the wisdom of the "Three Ways"—Taoism, Confucianism, and Zen Buddhism—Hung Ying-ming shows an approach to everyday life that is artistic and poetic, delighting in the simple elegance and beauty of the ordinary.

Tao Te Ching: An All-New Translation, by Lao Tzu

The *Tao Te Ching* is the quintessential text of Taoism, emphasizing simplicity, spontaneity, tranquility, and non-action. William Scott Wilson renders Lao Tzu's words in a brand new light, taking into account both the ancient text and the even older Great Seal script that was used during Lao Tzu's time. The result is a fresh and nuanced translation that stands out sharply from the many others available both for its beauty and its accuracy. The text is accompanied by Chinese ink paintings and illuminating commentaries on Taoist influence on the martial arts and Zen.

The Unfettered Mind: Writings from a Zen Master to a Master Swordsman,
by Takuan Sōhō

In Japan, sword and spirit have always been closely associated—but it was during the Tokugawa shogunate that swordsmanship became infused with the spirit of Zen. *The Unfettered Mind* is a book of advice on swordsmanship and the cultivation of right mind and intention, written by the incomparable Zen master Takuan Sōhō, for the samurai Yagyu Munenori, Miyamoto Musashi's great rival. Takuan was a brilliant renaissance man, who was an advisor to samurai and shoguns, and *The Unfettered Mind* has been essential reading for generations of Zen students and martial artists.